The Restless Anthropologist

The Restless Anthropologist

NEW FIELDSITES, NEW VISIONS

Edited by Alma Gottlieb

The University of Chicago Press   CHICAGO & LONDON

Alma Gottlieb has conducted long-term fieldwork with the Beng in Côte d'Ivoire and more recently with diasporic Cape Verdeans. She is the author or editor of, among other works, *The Afterlife Is Where We Come From: The Culture of Infancy in West Africa*; *A World of Babies: Imagined Childcare Guides for Seven Societies* (with Judy DeLoache); *Blood Magic: The Anthropology of Menstruation* (with Thomas Buckley); and (with Philip Graham) *Parallel Worlds: An Anthropologist and a Writer Encounter Africa* and *Braided Worlds*. She teaches anthropology, gender and women's studies, and African studies at the University of Illinois at Urbana-Champaign.

The University of Chicago Press, Chicago 60637
The University of Chicago Press, Ltd., London
© 2012 by Alma Gottlieb
All rights reserved. Published 2012.
Printed in the United States of America

21 20 19 18 17 16 15 14 13 12   1 2 3 4 5

ISBN-13: 978-0-226-30489-2 (cloth)
ISBN-13: 978-0-226-30490-8 (paper)
ISBN-10: 0-226-30489-2 (cloth)
ISBN-10: 0-226-30490-6 (paper)

Library of Congress Cataloging-in-Publication Data

Gottlieb, Alma.
  The restless anthropologist : new fieldsites, new visions / edited by Alma Gottlieb.
    p.   cm.
  Includes bibliographical references and index.
  ISBN-13: 978-0-226-30489-2 (hardcover : alkaline paper)
  ISBN-13: 978-0-226-30490-8 (paperback : alkaline paper)
  ISBN-10: 0-226-30489-2 (hardcover : alkaline paper)
  ISBN-10: 0-226-30490-6 (paperback : alkaline paper)
    1. Anthropologists—Attitudes. 2. Anthropology—Fieldwork. I. Title.
  GN20.G68 2012
  301—dc23

                                                        2011034665

♾ This paper meets the requirements of ANSI/NISO Z39.48-1992 (Permanence of Paper).

Should I stay or should I go now?
If I go there will be trouble
And if I stay it will be double
So you gotta let me know
Should I stay or should I go?

THE CLASH

[Fieldwork is] the central ritual of the tribe [of anthropologists].

GEORGE STOCKING

CONTENTS

The Challenges—and Pleasures— of Switching Fieldsites

Alma Gottlieb

I always assumed that, as with spouses, cultural anthropologists chose their fieldsites for life. Boas and the Kwakiutl . . . Malinowski and the Trobriands . . . Fortes and the Tallensi . . . Geertz and the Balinese. . . . These classic professional pairings are seared into our disciplinary consciousness, our own James-Joyce-in-Dublin couplings of person and place.

Of course, as with marriages, one sometimes hears of separations. Even Malinowski's work with the Trobrianders followed (brief) engagements with two other Melanesian groups (the Motu and Mailu), and Geertz, after his famous stint in Indonesia, pulled up stakes to start all over again in Morocco. Nevertheless, the ideal, I somehow accepted for years, is for anthropologists to remain monogamously partnered with their first field community forever. This stubbornly persistent scenario I have come to think of as the *One Scholar/One Fieldsite* model—a corollary of the "my village" or "my tribe" mentality to which at least some long-term fieldworkers still feel wedded.[1]

When I last carried out fieldwork in a small Beng village in the rain forest in Côte d'Ivoire in summer 1993, I began having doubts about the One Scholar/One Fieldsite model. But I struggled for over a decade to identify a

---

1. In recent years, scholars have launched critiques of this trope from a variety of perspectives (e.g., Brown 1981; Fluehr-Lobban 1994, 2000; Gladney 2003; Gupta 1995), yet it retains staying power for many anthropologists; for an eloquent defense of the deep intellectual and emotional satisfactions that can come from a lifelong engagement with a single place, see Vogt (1995).

new research project in a new geocultural space (see chapter 4). In reflecting on the obstacles—both internal and external—to making such a change, I encountered few published discussions of the pros and cons of sticking with a first fieldsite versus choosing a new one.

Given the current interpretive turn in cultural anthropology, which has inspired many to reflect critically on the discipline (from fieldwork and writing practices to the politics of both academic and nonacademic workplaces), it is all the more striking that we have not yet addressed the career trajectory issues that face us as we move through our own personal and professional life cycles. Although some anthropologists have begun analyzing aging as a culturally shaped experience when it comes to other people's lives (e.g., Cohen 1998; McConatha and Stoller 2006; Newman 2003), and more recently some have addressed "middle age and other cultural fictions" (Shweder 1998; cf. Brandes 1985), we have not yet applied this developing perspective to ourselves.

Frustrated by the relative disciplinary silence that greeted me as I asked myself (perhaps, unconsciously), "Should I stay or should I go?"—and goading myself to confront my own doubts and hesitations—I organized a conference session with that question as its title. Seeking inspirational role models, I recruited colleagues who had made significant changes in fieldsite—thoughtful scholars with much to say about their decisions, and strong writing skills to articulate their decision-making processes. Whether moving from North Dakota to North Sumatra (Edward Bruner), or from the Pacific island of Vanatinai to the Pacific coastline of California (Maria Lepowsky), our authors have all found professional inspiration in new geocultural spaces, and have harnessed their analytic insights to reflect on the issues they confronted in so doing. This book represents an expansion of the conversations we began during that meeting.

*

By no means do cultural anthropologists have a monopoly on midcareer research shifts. Yet the fieldwork-based methods that distinguish our research from that of many other academic disciplines present particular challenges. Locating projects in a new area often requires learning one or more new languages precisely at a time when many anthropologists find themselves ensconced in increasingly challenging family relationships (especially, caring for children, aging parents, or both) as well as greater disciplinary obligations (especially, administrative responsibilities both on and off one's own campus). While midcareer scholars who choose new historical eras to explore, or authors to read, or galaxies to study, surely face challenges, the necessity of becoming competent in a new language in midlife is daunting in particular ways.[2] Even when new fieldsites do not require learning a new language, the immersion that characterizes fieldwork for cultural anthropologists—our vaunted "participant observation"—renders the nature of the change unique in the academic disciplines. As Virginia Dominguez points out in chapter 1, the "emotionally engulfing choice of fieldsite that marks the life of an anthropologist" produces a deep feeling of regret when one leaves—a regret that is probably not experienced by scholars in other disciplines. The uniqueness of our disciplinary challenges suggests the need for special attention to be paid to our career trajectories. The essays assembled in this volume constitute a first step in that direction.

While the primary audience for this collection is thus anthropologists themselves, we also hope that our career narratives will provide food for thought for scholars in other disciplines. There is nothing like being confronted with alien practices to shine a bright light on one's own. Contemplating the challenges and rewards that face midcareer cultural anthropologists in conducting research in new fieldsites may inspire scholars in other disciplines to consider the challenges and rewards of switching research projects in their own disciplines across a long career.

*

Because of complications associated with family and work, midcareer anthropologists often face a difficult choice: either select new fieldsites or end their fieldworking days altogether. The latter course eventually carries significant career penalties. Although a few renowned scholars have forged illustrious careers with no long-term fieldwork beyond an early project (Claude Lévi-Strauss, Rodney Needham, and Thomas Beidelman leap to mind), it is more likely that an academic career will stagnate or founder when an anthropologist cannot, or will not, continue an active fieldworking career.

2. When US-based scholars in other disciplines embark on research in another country, they typically collaborate with English-speaking colleagues; learning a new language is then, we might say, an elective. The trend toward communicating in English with one another is increasingly relevant for scholars from non-anglophone countries as well.

The reasons to resist a return to a first site vary. For many scholars working, especially, in the global south, conditions of structural violence—poverty, famine, civil war—often lead to worsening local circumstances that put a return out of the question. Such grim realities lay behind my own decision not to return to Côte d'Ivoire after my last field stint in 1993 (see chapter 4).[3] In such places, a fieldworker's own identity markers (religion, political orientation, first language, "racial" classification) may also conspire to make a return to a previous fieldsite more difficult.

More locally, institutional pressures from the academy may discourage scholars from returning to former research spaces. These pressures often take the form of financial constraints. For example, scholars cannot always obtain grant support to return to the same place year after year. Such returns require new projects, or at least increasingly exciting perspectives on old projects. Some scholars simply lack the time (and intellectual space) to write this sort of cutting-edge grant proposal.

Beyond such pragmatic factors, theoretical considerations may prevent us from returning to a previous research area. While it may be painful to admit, some anthropologists eventually lose interest in the issues posed by a first fieldsite, or conclude that they have nothing more to say about the place. For example, Paul Stoller acknowledges that after visiting his field community in Niger just about annually over the course of some twenty years, he could have kept going—writing on (barely) new topics—but eventually he recognized that he had nothing new to say, that his heart was no longer in it (personal communication). (Linda Seligmann and I acknowledge similar feelings in chapters 6 and 4, respectively.)

In more dramatic cases, exceptional scholars have switched disciplines to pursue radically new intellectual agendas. The celebrated Gregory Bateson—whose research sites moved from Melanesian and Balinese villages in the 1930s to cybernetics and psychiatric labs in the 1950s to porpoise waters in the 1960s—remains an inspiration to many. Yet few have the institutional or psychological foundations to forge such radically new career paths.

Ironically, the academy (which claims to promote free and creative in-

---

3. Regional instability has even forced some young scholars to change research plans while still in graduate school. For example, JoAnn D'Alisera and Michelle Johnson were compelled to switch fieldsites to diasporic locales when their original West African field communities (Sierra Leone and Guinea-Bissau, respectively) became mired in civil war (see D'Alisera 2004, Johnson 2006). Other countries presenting more significant challenges than even an intrepid fieldworker can abide include, as of this writing, Iran, Iraq, Afghanistan, Pakistan, the Palestinian territories, Burma, Cuba, Sudan, and Somalia.

quiry) can dissuade anthropologists from striking out to a new space. For anthropology departments, hiring preferences often target a specific regional slot. In such cases, department chairs and deans expect a colleague to continue teaching classes on that region, attracting and training graduate students interested in pursuing research in that region, and participating in (and sometimes organizing) campus conferences and lecture series concerning that region (Herzfeld 2009b:xii–xiii). In effect, our long-term commitment to a particular place constitutes a kind of social and intellectual capital. The thought of relinquishing that symbolic capital can seem like squandering the "investment" we have made over the course of years, or even decades.

Indeed, in cultural anthropology, our years of ever-deepening expertise in an area—its history, daily practices, deep cultural assumptions, and especially its language(s)—are a just source of pride, an achievement we exhibit as a prime distinction between us and survey researchers and other quantitatively oriented colleagues (Foster et al. 1979; Fowler and Hardesty 1994; Kemper and Royce 2002). With the exponentially expanding knowledge base about the world's remotest corners now insistently and continually announcing itself online, how likely is it that we might develop, in a new place, the deep level of regional and linguistic expertise that we worked so hard to develop earlier? I can think of few midcareer Western scholars who possess the audacity (not to mention brainpower) to study new languages as difficult as Thai and Mandarin Chinese, or Arabic, as Michael Herzfeld and Virginia Dominguez (respectively) have done. Yet if we cannot pass for "area experts," with the linguistic prowess such a title implies, what legitimacy do we wield in analyzing a new area? With these concerns no doubt front and center, it is not surprising that a good number of anthropologists do not consider retraining, convinced that they could never achieve enough depth to become expert in new fieldsites. More pragmatically, for those lucky enough to be hired on a tenure track, abandoning the job description of the hire is rarely an option before tenure—and if it is pursued, the results may prove disastrous (see Bruner's account in chapter 7); once achieving tenure, routine sets in and institutional expectations reify.

The ever-increasing demands of the academy for teaching, research, and service produce further demands on our time that may make it less likely for us to strike out into new research territories. The academy can push (or seduce) us into bureaucratic regimens that claim our hours—and our imaginations. Yet creative solutions can be found by the lifelong scholar; for example, in chapter 2 of this volume, Gustavo Ribeiro writes:

As the decades pass, my growing involvement in the politics and management of academia and of anthropology has coincided with a lack of time to do ethnographic fieldwork. But that does not mean my research curiosity has diminished. In reality, it has kept on growing. . . . Maybe I will not be able to do the related ethnographies myself—maybe I will be able to convince Brazilian graduate students to do the fieldwork. In this case, I will keep my passion for ethnography alive through their eyes.

In other cases, careers founder when anthropologists find themselves unable either to return to an earlier fieldsite or to strike out to a new one.

The structure of hiring in the academy—with positions in cultural anthropology typically privileging expertise in a single region of the world—echoes the hypercompetitive world of national grants, which likewise rewards longstanding regional expertise. Even if we want to challenge ourselves beyond our prior regional expertise, how many grants exist that support scholars to retrain for a new world area, let alone a new language? Quite the opposite: most granting agencies expect regional and linguistic expertise on the part of the applicant—the more so the older and presumably more distinguished in that world area we become. I recall with sadness the case of one of my advisors in graduate school. A brilliant and well-respected scholar, he decided in midcareer to retrain in another world area. After spending a few years reading extensively in the ethnography of that region, he submitted funding proposals to begin a new fieldwork project there. His proposals were all rejected—because, he learned, he didn't have the career profile of an area specialist in that region. Sensing our revered mentor's palpable discouragement, his other students and I learned an early, and scary, lesson: Changing field areas is professionally risky; it is much safer (for an academic career) to keep returning to the same world region.

Applied anthropologists who work as consultants outside the academy may also feel reluctant to explore new field areas, and for the same reason: doing so entails a risk of being perceived by potential employers as lacking sufficient, long-term regional expertise, and therefore not being hired. For other scholars unlucky enough to remain on underpaid, overworked, short-term teaching contracts, having the time to develop grant proposals for a new fieldsite is even less likely.

Implied in this discussion is the existence of institutional area studies programs. Such programs have varied both by country and by historical era, but, details notwithstanding, whatever is academically acceptable vis-à vis area studies programs frequently shapes our career options in ways we may not entirely recognize.[4]

Individuals' biographies fill in the gaps between these macro-level structural concerns, as personal issues further constrict our options. As adult relationships deepen, we may become increasingly reluctant to leave the "significant others" in our lives—children, spouses/life partners, aging parents—for lengthy periods; conversely, life partners and children themselves may refuse to disrupt their own increasingly busy lives to accompany an adventurous anthropologist to a new fieldsite. Sudden divorces or new partnerings may further make long-term travel to new spaces emotionally untenable.

Medical conditions may further complicate or prevent travel. Even absent specific conditions, our aging bodies, combined with increasingly complex family and professional entanglements, may discourage us from taking the sort of health and safety risks we may have nonchalantly accepted earlier in our careers. And psychological pressures further inhibit us. Leaving the comforts of a scholarly home for the uncharted waters of a new fieldsite surely carries anxieties in midlife for all but the terminally intrepid.

*

Despite the serious obstacles I have outlined, and despite the normative disciplinary agenda of conducting long-term fieldwork in a single fieldsite, many cultural anthropologists, even from Boas's day, *have* managed to change fieldsites. Although the pragmatic challenges of travel, and of gaining access to information, may have made fieldsite switches more daunting in earlier eras than they are now, those impediments may have been counterbalanced by the far smaller quantity of knowledge necessary to "master" a new place. One need look no farther than that fearless world traveler, Margaret Mead, to find an illustrious exemplar. In this volume, Linda Seligmann outlines several models of earlier fieldsite shifts, from Kroeber and Lowie in the United States to Evans-Pritchard and other key figures in the British tradition (chapter 6).

4. In the United States, for example, the second half of the twentieth century saw the social sciences wedded to an area studies paradigm for reasons relative not only to intellectual but also to political and, indeed, military factors (Guyer 2004; Ludden 2000; Mintz 1998; Nugent 2008a, 2008b). Elsewhere, specific area studies traditions of anthropology have developed ensconced in their own local politics. For example, "In an earlier colonial period, Dutch [anthropologists] were committed to Indonesian studies and British [anthropologists] to African studies" (Edward Bruner, personal communication).

What is it that propelled—and continues to propel—scholars to venture beyond their original research area to a new site (or multiple new sites), even in the face of formidable challenges? Here, I explore a variety of factors, ranging from structural to personal, that emerge from the narratives in this collection.

At the intellectual level, theoretical questions may drive the choice of a new fieldsite. In these pages, Gustavo Ribeiro illustrates how his research moves have been largely theory-driven (chapter 2). After working with Brazilian workers recalling their memories of constructing their nation's new capital, Brasília, Ribeiro realized that the theoretical issues he had plumbed in his oral history research had incited his curiosity to explore how similar issues might play themselves out in a contemporary setting:

> I [had] posited that the form of production I had chronicled in Brasília was typical of large-scale construction projects carried out in isolated areas. I suggested that it would, in effect, be possible to test this claim by comparing the construction of Brasília with the construction of a major hydroelectric dam, Tucuruí, that the development-oriented military government was building in the Amazon jungle. My theoretical intuition was that the form of production . . . had recurrent structural characteristics and was linked to the expansion of capitalism. . . . In other words, I was following a theoretical question and I needed to check its viability in another setting.

Beyond such theoretically driven agendas, institutional opportunities may push anthropologists toward new research sites. In the United States, for example, large universities and small liberal arts colleges alike are increasingly "internationalizing" in many ways, one of which is to encourage their faculty to lead students in "study abroad" programs. Leading such a program may well inspire an anthropologist to develop a new research project in the destination country. Such a shift may be especially attractive in teaching-oriented colleges, where the reward structure for faculty is typically tied to pedagogical payoffs. In these and other ways, many second projects nowadays engage with broad institutional structures, and are more likely to have been conceived as part of larger interdisciplinary projects than are first projects (Marcus 1998c).

Another critical factor concerns the scheduling of new research projects. Like real estate agents who tell us that choosing the right house is all about three factors—location, location, location—we might say that choosing a new fieldsite is about three factors—timing, timing, timing.

When do we allow ourselves the luxury of switching fieldsites? For academically employed anthropologists, having tenure certainly decreases the risks; conversely, not having tenure increases them. Although many scholars nowadays deplore the inflation of tenure standards to extraordinarily high levels, tenure was never easy to achieve. In this volume, Ed Bruner reveals that he was denied tenure at Yale in 1960 precisely because he had switched fieldsites after being hired and was unable to publish enough about either site to satisfy his tenure committee (chapter 7). Conversely, Michael Herzfeld acknowledges that his fieldwork move from Italy to Thailand entailed relatively little risk, insofar as he was already a full professor at Harvard and knew that he could fall back on his previous research in Greece and Italy if the Thai adventure failed (chapter 5).

Timing also includes serendipity: anthropologists who change fieldsites may take advantage of new opportunities unexpectedly thrown their way. When Bruner switched from working with Native North Americans to working in Indonesia, he did so largely because he found extraordinary opportunities for Southeast Asian studies at his new Yale campus. The very act of moving from one campus to another may itself propel soul-searching that results in a new fieldwork agenda. Michael Herzfeld speculates, for example, that when he accepted a new teaching position, "something in that change of location [from Indiana to Massachusetts] may have added to the desire to change field location as well."

No matter the individual motives and constraints, it seems undeniable that increasing numbers of cultural anthropologists now venture to a new area in midcareer—or earlier.[5] No doubt, this trend derives at least in part from the declining importance of area studies–oriented training programs. In the United States, these programs had their heyday from the 1960s through the 1990s (Martin 1996). Nowadays, although Title VI funding through the US Department of Education continues to support such programs in US universities, the area studies paradigm that rose to prominence in the US and some other Western countries in the mid-twentieth century has in other ways waned (Shami and Anativia 2007). This waning is reflected in the changing

---

5. I make this claim based on my observations of the discipline over the nearly four decades since I presented my first paper at a professional anthropology conference in 1974. I am not aware of any comprehensive study of the profession that documents this trend in any statistically reliable way, although I suspect that such a study may well be commissioned sooner rather than later.

priorities and internal administrative structures of many other funding agencies, both governmental and private.[6] To the extent that scholars shape new research projects with funding priorities in mind, such administrative shifts may contribute to a greater willingness on the part of more scholars to contemplate second projects in areas beyond those of their first projects.

Behind both these shifts looms the changing nature of the world itself, with our tectonic trend toward globalized everything. When I first conducted fieldwork in a small village in the West African rain forest in 1979, I chuckled at the sight of a child who had never heard of Muhammad Ali wearing a T-shirt with the boxer's image printed on it; now, I wouldn't chuckle, and the boy might well know much of Ali's biography. Objects now travel, images now travel, and people now travel, all at dizzying paces. Greater ease in moving from one point of the globe to the other—both logistically and intellectually—doubtless inspires increasing numbers of anthropologists to contemplate switching fieldsites.

Keeping in mind the effects that globalizing flows now produce, George Marcus has observed that cultural anthropologists' "second projects are often conceived in terms of transcultural or transnational spaces" (1998d:251n4), rather than in single areas, as they once were. In effect, our globalizing world increasingly demands multisited ethnographies, as our research communities themselves cross borders—fleeing political or economic or bodily abuses, following mobile kinship networks, searching for their own expanding opportunities (e.g., Amit 2000; Dresch, James, and Parkin 2000; Faubion and Marcus 2009; Gupta and Ferguson 1997; Ortner 1997; Rasmussen 2003; Stoller 1997).[7] My current project working with diasporic Cape Verdeans, for example, is taking me well beyond Lisbon, where I began my research: already I have conducted interviews and participant observation with Cape Verdeans

6. Within the US Social Science Research Council, for example, the previous area studies committees that determined all doctoral student funding were replaced in the 1990s by a single committee that privileges comparative and global perspectives over single-area projects. More generally, as Virginia Dominguez points out, "support for area programs has given way to funding for issues of social justice and research with policy implications" (personal communication).

7. I use the term "multisited ethnography" in its more commonly understood sense, to refer to a single ethnographic project with a group of people whose networks take them to two or more cultural spaces; others scholars may have in mind the pursuit of the same theoretical project or long-term conceptual question in different cultural spaces, with unrelated communities (something close to what Ribeiro reports on in this volume); I am grateful to Linda Seligmann (personal communication) for pushing me to account for these dual meanings.

in Providence, Boston, and Paris, as well as Praia and Mindelo; I could easily follow my consultants across Europe (to London, Amsterdam, Rome, and Gibraltar, for starters), thence to Latin America (Buenos Aires, much of Brazil) and elsewhere in the United States (New York, New Jersey, Connecticut, Florida, California), back to Africa (especially Morocco, Guinea-Bissau, São Tomé and Principe, Angola, and Mozambique), and even (following the old Portuguese empire) to Goa, on the west coast of India. While Cape Verdeans probably represent an extreme end of the diasporic spectrum in their passion for international travel, many other groups are now expanding their geographic reach to one extent or another, whether by preference or in response to force, and we anthropologists feel increasingly willing to follow them in their treks.[8] If some scholars worry that our disciplinary distinctiveness risks erosion from peripatetic projects that border on journalistic superficiality, others struggle to craft means to retain the "cultural intimacy" that marks our ethnographic approach to research (e.g., Herzfeld [1997] 2004).

As graduate students take proliferating global flows into account, multisited studies become increasingly common even as first projects. When young scholars design initial projects as multisited, it is ever more likely that they will continue to design multisited projects through the length of their careers. In short, to the extent that the One Scholar/One Fieldsite model remains relevant at the discursive level, a significant gap now distances our classic image of "the field" from the reality that more and more scholars are straying from that model. Our disciplinary stereotype of the single-fieldsite–based career model has ceded the territory to more dynamic models.

In addition to such scholarly issues, more personal factors often drive our midcareer decisions, determining when we leave a first fieldsite, and whether and where we choose a new one. If anthropologists have been slow to acknowledge the importance of emotion in the lives of the communities we study, we have been even slower to acknowledge the role of emotion in our own life decisions (but see Hovland 2007; Kleinman and Copp 1993). Yet some scholars—perhaps most—put emotionally salient relationships front and center in choosing new fieldsites. In this collection, most contributors signal the importance of a variety of emotional entanglements that shaped their later fieldwork decisions. These include relations with life partners, as discussed by Virginia Dominguez (chapter 1) and myself (chapter 4); with

8. Like all trends, this one is not absolute. In the current volume, two contributors have chosen more classic, place-based projects in midcareer: Lepowsky, working with native peoples of Los Angeles, and Herzfeld, working with Italians in Rome and Thais in Bangkok.

children, as discussed by Linda Seligmann (chapter 6) and myself; with parents, as discussed by Maria Lepowsky (chapter 3); and with lifelong friends, as discussed by Michael Herzfeld (chapter 5). It is notable that all of the female contributors—and none of the men—forefronted conjugal or kinship obligations as determinative in fieldsite choice. If our small sample is representative, the "kin-work" that so frequently devolves to women in Western societies may be as relevant to the career choices that female anthropologists make as it is (normatively) to the career choices of other women (Burton and Stack 1993). Male anthropologists may well make fieldwork choices oriented around kin ties too, but may be less inclined to explore that point in print.

Many scholars—perhaps most—choose new fieldsites closer to home, and often (though not always) for the sake of personal life factors. In this collection, the essays by Lepowsky, Seligmann, and Paul Stoller (afterword) elegantly explore a range of reasons for moving from international to domestic fieldsites. Other scholars—probably far fewer—choose fieldsites that are more exotic and even farther from home than their first research area— whether geographically, culturally, or linguistically—to allow for midcareer adventure. The essays here by Dominguez, Herzfeld, and Edward Bruner (chapter 7) offer dramatic examples of what I call "explorer mentalities"—the tendency to seek out especially challenging new geocultural spaces. Significantly, all three of these scholars have worked in more than two fieldsites; and all three either have no children or embarked on these midcareer adventures after their children had grown up and left home. Between these two extremes lies a spectrum of reasons for exploring new fieldsites neither close to home nor more exotically challenging than the first fieldsite, as chronicled by Gustavo Ribeiro (chapter 2) and myself.

Even when a fieldsite move occurs within a single region, its impact on the scholar probably varies. Virginia Dominguez has pointed out that because some version of Spanish is spoken across so much of Latin America, for example, fieldsite changes within that region may be less dramatic than are moves within Europe, Africa, or Asia, where a scholar might have to learn a radically new language despite remaining on the same continent. For anthropologists who pursue new projects with diasporic populations, the possibility that they may need to master two or more languages presents an even more daunting challenge.

If *fieldwork at home* versus *fieldwork abroad* offered the operative choice of previous generations, that distinction itself has become ever more problematic, with all manner of local and life circumstances now complicating that seemingly easy duality (e.g., D'Alisera 1999; Hastrup 1993; Jacobs-

Huey 2002; Myerhoff 1980:1–39; Plese 2005; Rasmussen 2003). When an anthropologist marries a "native" while "in the field," then later returns to visit her in-laws, for example, is she "doing fieldwork" (D'Amico-Samuels [1991] 1997)? What is a "native anthropologist," anyway? Is shared gender, or sexual orientation, enough to brand one a "native" (Alcalde 2007; Kirsch 1999; Lewin 1993; Zavella 1996)? What about shared country of origin when complicated by differences in migration status (Narayan 1993), class and education levels (Rosas 2012), or religiosity (Littman and Myerhoff 1986)? These are just a few of the many factors that can make it impossible to categorize a particular anthropologist as "native" or not (see Robertson 2002). Moreover, as members of even distant research communities now read our work, it becomes harder to hide behind the assumption, once taken for granted, that fieldwork in distant places remains distant (Adler and Adler 1993; Brettell 1996; Feld 1987). *Collaborating as partners* with members of a community, rather than *studying them as subjects*, produces another kind of continuing engagement that blurs the home/away distinction at a more theoretical level (Killough 2009; Lassiter 2005; Smith 1999; and cf. Gershon 2009 for fields beyond anthropology).

On yet another level, our biographies offer their own challenges to the home/away divide, as we ourselves reflect the tangle of religious, ethnic, linguistic, class, and other identities that characterize twenty-first-century lives. Thinking about her research move back to the US state in which she spent most of her childhood, for example, Lepowsky writes that her "life and fieldwork in twenty-first-century Los Angeles and its hinterlands" have become "hopelessly intermingled":

> In the process of attempting to understand the cultural histories of Los Angeles's indigenous inhabitants, I've come to see that indigenous Southern Californians and I routinely cross borders of personal identity and cultural practice, including the borders of ethnographic research and political action. We are each doing different yet interwoven kinds of anthropologies at home.

Here, the issue of "fieldsite overlap" becomes salient. In leaving one fieldsite in body, does one entirely leave the place in spirit? For some fieldworkers, such a thought is inconceivable—as Dominguez discusses in this collection, chronicling her long-term relationship to Israel. Then too, an author might return at length to an earlier fieldsite in spirit, to revisit the experience and write about it in hindsight (Gottlieb and Graham 2012; Lepowsky, in press). In any case, one might say that for all anthropologists beginning research in a new fieldsite, the scholars we have become have been shaped by our prior field experiences. As Bruner points out, "Geertz was still an Indonesianist when he went to Morocco," although Bruner further suggests that the notion of what "counts" as a switch in fieldsites has probably varied by historical era (personal communication).

At this moment, a range of new fieldwork strategies is already remaking our understanding of fieldwork. Conducting ethnography by cell phone was a first step (Sunderland 1999)— although new technologies of communication do not always make communication easier. In my recent project in Lisbon, for example, I found that I hesitated longer than I might previously have done in making first contacts with new consultants precisely because of cell phones: calling a stranger meant opening a conversation without eye contact and body language—all in a new language in which I was still faltering. Other anthropologists (more fluent in the local language), by contrast, have discovered the pleasures of ethnography by cell phone (Johnson n.d.).

Even more than cell phones, the advent of online ethnography dramatically destabilizes the very distinction between fieldwork "away" and fieldwork "at home." In effect, we can now travel to a faraway field while remaining in our home study—or wherever else we bring a laptop and find an Internet connection (Boelstorff 2008; Carter 2004; Kuntsman 2004; Markham 1998; Pleše 2005). Recently, I "met" over Facebook the now-adult daughter of a long-ago consultant in Côte d'Ivoire, and we have begun a conversation in this virtual space. Many other anthropologists now use social-networking sites and other virtual spaces to continue conversations that began in three-dimensional encounters. What is added to the ethnographic experience—and what gets lost—in such online (and often public) encounters remains to be charted (Herzfeld 2009a).

We might summarize the changes enumerated above with a statement that Seligmann writes in this volume:

Once they do field research, anthropologists realize that they do not simply enter, leave, or return to it but rather engage it as part of their ongoing lives in a range of locations that constitute both a part of field research itself and a part of the lives of their interlocutors. Hence nowadays, "shifting fieldsites" entails not only the sort of dramatic shifts that a previous generation of anthropologists experienced, but also more mundane and subtle ones, such that shifts themselves are not wholly alien to the normative practice either of the discipline or of anthropologists' daily lives. . . . Eventually, the discourse itself may change.

*

In short, we anthropologists are just beginning to take stock of all the intellectual and biographical issues that fieldsite selection continually throws our way as fieldworking scholars. When scholars switch fieldsites—whether once or frequently; whether to a place farther from home (wherever "home" is, and whatever it means), just around the corner, or online; whether to a single new site or to a collection of new, interlinked sites—a multitude of questions arise that the contributors to this volume think bear reflecting on. In soliciting essays for this book, I asked colleagues to consider a range of issues that constitute a common, critical, yet entirely undertheorized challenge in our fieldwork-oriented discipline; we think it is time that we address that challenge.

The chapters that follow take these questions as starting points to discuss the ways in which our earlier and later projects have compared with each other on both scholarly and personal levels. We discuss our motivations to conduct fieldwork in a second fieldsite—and in some cases, in multiple fieldsites. We consider the pleasures as well as the frustrations we have faced once there, and the issues and implications our experiences may hold for the discipline. And we reflect on the biographical events and institutional structures alike that—for better or worse—have contributed to our decisions to inaugurate a new project. In short, we look at the human dimension to the anthropological ritual of fieldwork by focusing on the choice of second (and later) fieldsites as a human decision—one that is limned by structures of experience, structures of the workforce, our own embeddedness in structures of kinship and marriage, and, lest we forget that most personal but often neglected of all factors, structures of feeling.

In exploring our fieldwork stories, we aim to avoid the solipsistic autobiographical-account-for the-sake-of-autobiographical-account that we all, no doubt, find tiresome. At the same time, I feel confident that neglecting the human factor in any discipline—but especially in anthropology, which focuses so insistently on the human—risks neglecting a critical component of our professional engagement in "the field"—that is, both the field of anthropology, and the field of our research site. As Maria Lepowsky observes in chapter 3, "Strands of personal and intellectual biography are woven more visibly into ethnographic research projects than they are those of other disciplines." Attending to the decisions we make—can make, must make—as scholars means attending to the contours of the field, speaking to the knowledge we aim to produce, and expanding the boundaries of that knowledge.

It can be lonely making the switch to a new fieldsite without anyone to confide in. We may even feel a sense of shame in changing research areas, as if we have somehow failed in our commitment to a place—a commitment that, after all, serves to distinguish us in good part from our sister discipline, sociology. In articulating the issues involved in second (and subsequent) field projects and offering successful examples of such career moves, the contributors to this collection hope to provide food for thought for younger scholars still ensconced in their first fieldsites. At the same time, we aim to inspire and bolster colleagues who face their own mid- and late-career issues. At a more theoretical level, we hope to destigmatize the project of a new fieldsite—to challenge the unrealistic One Scholar/One Fieldsite model that still dominates much of our disciplinary discourse.

The scholars represented here have taken many kinds of risks. Initially, they took intellectual, emotional, social, and sometimes political risks in moving from one field region to another—sometimes across oceans and languages. In writing their chapters, they have taken yet another kind of risk. It is one thing to pull up stakes, surrender the hard-won status of expert (a challenge Maria Lepowsky, Linda Seligmann, and I explicitly address), and do all one can, lacking the luxury of years of full-time graduate training, to become an "emergency expert." It is another thing to acknowledge publicly, in print, all the doubts and costs involved in such a decision. These anxieties may explain why the issues we raise have not previously found their way into scholarly writings. Switching fieldsites can indeed be painful. Nevertheless, the authors of this volume have found profound scholarly pleasures in their new fieldsites, and they are persuaded of the importance of chronicling their experience for the benefit of colleagues and students.

Seligmann takes the point further: "As difficult as shifting fieldsites might be for the anthropologist," she writes, "it is often healthy for the discipline itself. And it may be healthy for the anthropologist as well." Gustavo Ribeiro agrees: "Switching fieldsites," he writes, "is a way of keeping your anthropological awareness sharp." The intellectually restless anthropologist, we might say, is the inquiring anthropologist—the scholar who pushes herself to question old truths, old habits, old systems of common sense (Geertz [1975] 1983). Indeed, discussing the project behind this collection, Fredrik Barth has wisely commented:

> Doing new fieldwork reminds us of how to be naïve, as we compel ourselves to ask new questions in new fieldsites. One might even say that insofar as doing new fieldwork is intrinsic to the anthropological mission, it is what makes us anthropologists. (Personal communication, Barth to Edward Bruner)

In that sense, the chapters that follow all explore how their authors have re-made themselves each time they have undertaken a new field study. And in reinventing ourselves, we each, in our own, modest way, contribute to the re-invention of the discipline.

ACKNOWLEDGMENTS

I presented an earlier version of this chapter at the annual meeting of the American Anthropological Association in Washington, DC, in November 2007. The session, "Should I Stay or Should I Go? The Challenges—and Pleasures—of Switching Field Sites," was sponsored by the Society for Humanistic Anthropology and was greeted by questions and comments from an especially lively and engaged audience. Following the conference, the session participants—Edward Bruner, Maria Lapowsky, Linda J. Seligmann, Paul Stoller, and myself—continued the conversation online; Virginia Dominguez, Michael Herzfeld, and Gustavo Lins Ribeiro later joined the book venture. Ed Bruner, Philip Graham, Maria Lepowsky, and Linda Seligmann offered me especially helpful comments on an earlier draft of this introduction, while Michael Herzfeld generously took time from his own fieldwork travels to share extensive comments, both conceptual and editorial. I thank all these interlocutors for the generous gift of their time and thoughts, and beg their indulgence if I have not done all of those comments justice. Expert copyediting by Joel Score helped put the finishing touches on the complete book manuscript, and Angela Glaros expertly compiled the index. Finally, at a time when academic publishers are suffering the same marketplace pressures that have compelled other businesses to retreat, constrict, or go under, I remain indebted to my longtime editor extraordinaire, the near-legendary David Brent, for encouraging me to develop our conference session into a book from the moment I approached him with the idea.

ONE

Unexpected Ties:
Insight, Love, Exhaustion

Virginia R. Dominguez

Alma Gottlieb has a vision, a hunch that those of us who have done long-term anthropological fieldwork in more than one country or region of the world are unusual, and may have a role to play in becoming less unusual. Alma's enthusiasm is infectious. I also trust her sense that there is something here worth exploring. But I want to open with an admission. I went into this project not at all sure that there would be much to say about my having worked in very different parts of the world over the course of an anthropological career. I had grown up moving from country to country—six of them by the time I was eighteen—and added another three as an adult.[1] Many anthropologists I know in the United States had far fewer border crossings in their childhoods and find mine somewhat exotic. But like many others who have grown up with

---

1. I was born in Cuba and completed third grade in Havana, though both before my birth and during my early childhood, my extended family spent much time in the United States on vacations and family visits or for schooling, especially between 1900 (well before my birth) and 1960. My parents, their siblings, and most of their friends had been partly educated in the US; on my father's side, even my grandmother and her siblings had. Crossing national borders was a way of life even in my young childhood. After we left Cuba altogether in July 1960 and my father began to work for US corporations, "promoting US business abroad," we moved often. I completed fourth and fifth grades in New York, sixth grade in San Juan, Puerto Rico, seventh and eighth grades in Bergen County, New Jersey, and all of high school in Montevideo, Uruguay. I lived with my parents in Guadalajara, Mexico, between graduation from high school at the age of sixteen and my return to the United States in the fall of 1969 to start college at Yale. Then my parents moved to Beirut, Lebanon; I joined them there the summer I was eighteen, and on shorter trips later. As an adult, I have also lived in Surinam, Israel, and Hungary.

extensive border-crossing experiences, I find moving around a fairly standard way to live one's life and pursue one's career. So initially, the thought of writing a full-length essay on my own scholarly experience, entailing fieldwork in the United States, Surinam, and Israel since the early 1970s, did not seem all that intellectually interesting. I remember thinking that something might "come out" if someone interviewed me and I interviewed them, but that we'd end up with a conversation that ranged far wider than Alma's original focus. I should have trusted Alma more. When I sat down to see if I had anything to say, I apparently did—and what "came out" partly surprised me.

Instead of writing a chronology of my field experiences or comparing them, I found myself charting an emotional landscape—I wrote about intensity and attachment, leaving *and* returning, exhaustion and survival, and even about dancing the unconventional tango. I always knew I had intellectual reasons for starting serious fieldwork in the Middle East after years of concentrating on the Afro-European societies of the Western hemisphere. Over the years, I had also noted the intensity of my connection to people in Israel and the life I led when I was there (my non-Jewishness notwithstanding). But in chronicling my field life, I found myself connecting the two sites and thinking about reasons for leaving the first and taking a break, pulling back, staying away, returning, and allowing every nerve cell in my body to feel it all and think it all. This essay is about fieldwork, then, but it is also about inexplicable ties that have much to teach.

*

I began to write this piece in early June 2008. I had just returned to the United States a week earlier from a brief work trip to Israel, and I was in many ways still in Jerusalem. The view from my hotel room in Jerusalem had been familiar. It was also haunting.

After returning home to the United States, I sat in my study recalling the sensation of looking at Jerusalem, breathing the air of Israel, trying to tap into my connections to that place. The hotel had been closer to Arab East Jerusalem than to most of Jewish West Jerusalem, and I knew it was officially on land occupied by Israel in 1967 during the Six-Day War. Hebrew University administrators had put me there. I remember wondering if I should feel something because of the hotel's placement, and then I tried to see if I still felt anything at all for the country, the people, its seemingly irreconcilable competing visions and claims to land and rights. Jerusalem and Palestine—and, really, all of Israel separately and together—are places of violence and disconnectedness. Yet for many years, Jerusalem had been more than a fieldsite for me. Both arriving and leaving were hard. And for me, as for millions of people for whom it is or has been home, Jerusalem was as much a place of vivid connectedness, of intense living, as a place of dying.

Family ties explain nothing in my case. Some acquaintances erroneously assume I am Jewish simply because I learned Hebrew in the early 1980s, or because I seem to "feel things" that feel familiar to many in Israel, but the source of my connection is not so easily explained. I was not born Jewish, nor did I start learning Hebrew in order to marry a Jew, as many do both in Israel and elsewhere. And there is little in the thirteen years I spent in various Catholic schools up and down the Western hemisphere that would provide a logical or meaningful explanation for my affinity for Israel. But I feel a depth of familiarity, angst, caring, even exasperation for Israel and many things in Jewish life—and it is a feeling that does not go away. Of the many places and societies in which I have lived over the past sixty years, Israel got under my skin the fastest, rooted me in ways that other people often find inexplicable— and that never seem to go away. Of all the sites I have cared about while living there, this one ranks very high, with only my natal Cuba having a similar hold on me (and those links seem more explicable, with generations of Cuban minds, hearts, behaviors, laughter, sorrows, smells, and joys preceding me in the most embodied of ways).

I have, of course, cared deeply about other places while living there, studying there, or trying to figure them out as an anthropologist. This was especially true of Montevideo in my teens, and New Orleans in my twenties and early thirties; but the "legs" I grew in these other places eventually grew harder to see and feel. Something about Israel—its landscape, its struggles with peoplehood, its ongoing *shtick*—draw me more deeply, as a person with multiple friendships, a life full of sadnesses, loves, and political reactions, and an analyst of human collectivities and noticed and unnoticed social processes. I think the mix of how my body feels while I am in Israel—alive, complex, comfortable—and what my brain is trying to figure out and say about groupness and peoplehood in human experience through the Jewish case, combine to produce in me a more powerful feeling of place than (with the possible exception of Cuba) any I have ever experienced.

LIVING, DYING, AND THE INTENSE IN-BETWEEN

Thinking back on my long engagement with Israel, two long pieces of writing come to mind—both dated entries spread out over weeks and months, but neither of which I have ever published. I wrote the first set in summer 1982, when I recorded and commented on Israel's invasion of Lebanon; I wrote the second during fall and winter 1986 while watching my Israeli-American partner, E., become terminally ill and then die. I believe I began writing both pieces mostly to keep track of things, and to stay sane. Something told me I would want to remember the details long after the events.

At some point in the writing, it occurred to me that others might want to read them, too—but who, when, and where? Some two to three weeks into the summer of 1982, I sent my first set of "entries" to two acquaintances: someone I knew who worked at the *New Republic*, and a fellow anthropologist in the US whom I respected and who, I knew, had strong though complex feelings for Israel. Eventually, both wrote back. The *New Republic*, I was told, had other sources on the Israeli invasion of Lebanon; they thanked me, but they weren't interested. My fellow anthropologist wrote to say that it was clear I was in the midst of something intense, and feeling it all, but that my pages were not well written.

My writing was no doubt too raw, its detailed documentation overwhelming and puzzling to someone in a calm, faraway place; the rawness of the feelings was probably even off-putting. It was neither journalistic writing nor "creative writing," let alone recognizable anthropological writing. But it was "alive." It was troubled, and it communicated the frenzy and the impatience I saw in myself and in everything around me, and it was what I wanted to communicate to "the outside world." I had a different presence, an embodied and only partly guarded one. It wasn't packaged, formal, conventional, or restrained.

It was writing for myself, but from a world I had joined and thought I could show others, at least in part. Like a good anthropologist wanting to understand a place, its people, its issues, and its debates, I was also a body caught in a whirlwind, buffeted by the wind yet carried by it, kept intensely awake by its power and ubiquity. These were not data entries or logs in field journals, at least not in the common sense of those words. They were full of detail, blow-by-blow entries overflowing with information that came close to excess. They were about war and ceasefires—endless, innumerable ceasefires that came and went—and about following it all, like most others in Israel on the "home front": watching on the TV alone or with friends; listening to the news on the radio, every hour on the hour, along with everyone else on the buses; reading stories almost obsessively in the newspapers; sighing and waking up, eating, not eating, and overeating, worrying and arguing, watching dozens of planes flying north to Lebanon from "somewhere" near friends' homes, public swimming pools, and favorite restaurants.

The first set of notes I wrote while sitting in my apartment in Jerusalem as the Israeli military first bombed and then invaded Lebanon, beginning June 6, 1982. I had already been in Israel for over a year. I had friends and colleagues. My fieldwork was going well—though I had partly redirected it. My initial plan to interview Israelis in "mixed marriages" seemed flat; the interviews I did felt shallow, not capturing the intensity of love, argument, fear, distrust, and being that I sensed all around me. The outbreak of war that June exacerbated my sense that my original research project was beside the point—but I had already begun to feel this the previous fall, when I'd noticed even my assertively secular friends and colleagues paying a great deal of attention to the Jewish High Holidays.[2] My interviews with "mixed" couples just didn't capture the depth I was acquiring in other parts of my fieldwork. I had begun to realize that the frenzied debates, the connectedness, the internal comings and goings, the talk, the writing, the humor, the *shtick* all around me were more interesting than the conception of some marriages between Jews in Israel as mixed—and I needed to figure out how to think about, analyze, capture, and describe all this to others.

The war in 1982 left me with no doubt that my research needed to be refocused. The problem was that I didn't want to write a book on the war—I didn't think I had all the facts, or even that I could get them, and in any case, I didn't want to become a war correspondent. At the same time, I didn't know what kind of book I would write, could write, or wanted to write. Only two things were clear: first, what I was doing in the field was not exactly what I'd promised to do in the grant application I'd submitted to the Social Science Research Council, and second, the "whole" I felt and wanted to understand with some depth, as a person and as an anthropologist, was bigger, more palpable, more multisensual, and methodologically harder to grasp than I had envisioned when I plunged into the research. It was also more embodied and stirring—literally, in my muscles, bones, and skin—than any research I had done before, including an ambitious New Orleans–based project that also refused to limit itself to face-to-face interviews, a neighborhood, or a named "group" of people (Dominguez 1986).

I captured that rawness all too well in the second set of "entries" I wrote some four years later, during the fall and winter of 1986. Anger and love, ad-

---

2. Rosh Hashana, the start of the new year in the Jewish lunar calendar, typically falls in September or October on the Gregorian calendar. The tenth day of the first month, and the most sacred day of the Jewish year, is Yom Kippur ("Day of Atonement"). Sukkoth, a lesser, harvest-related holiday, follows soon after.

miration for some and something close to contempt for others—these were all present in that writing, colored by the inevitable and profoundly personal loss of my partner, which I first anticipated and then very deeply experienced. I was not in Israel when I wrote these notes. But looking back at them now, I am convinced that I allowed myself, in 1986, to write about such deeply felt emotions—the experience of rawness and connectedness, living and dying, exasperation and growth—because of the deeply felt emotions I'd previously allowed myself to write about in chronicling the Israeli invasion of Lebanon in 1982.

Dated entries—one set about killing (institutional), the other about dying (individual). Watching it all, knowing I could be little more than a spectator in both cases, I also knew that I could not avoid total immersion. My writing about both experiences was not so much about *feelings* themselves as it was about being overwhelmed by feelings—and trying to step back, note, record, and hold on to some ground. In the second set of entries, I now read anger, disbelief, expectation, and eventually impatience. When you know someone you love is going to die in the foreseeable future and there is nothing you can do about it, you resign yourself to it, while wondering if you should. Though on a very different scale and distance, the earlier war entries, I now see, are similar. Caught in whirlwinds not of my own making that affected people I cared about, who themselves could do little but be thrust into the vortex, I watched and listened as a way to cope, and I coped because I was there—a participant-observer to the core.

It would be much easier to write about places and "whirlwinds" that had not so completely "caught" me. Those are always easier to describe. They are the ones I do not mind talking about with animation when someone asks me to tell them about "my trip." But I know that I react with quiet impatience when asked about certain other places, and they are all the ones that grew legs for me. They are the ones I know and feel too much about. They are my relationships and their entanglements. They are not postcards or "interesting places" or objects of study or even subjects of research. They are home. They are me.

My relation to these writings reminds me of Susan Harding's experience of being "caught by the spirit" as she worked to understand the appeal of evangelical Protestantism in the United States, and specifically the evangelical church of Jerry Falwell (2000). Surprisingly, Harding's US research had made the earlier, international research that she had undertaken (in Spain) look easier, even though that had required command of a different language, working in a foreign country, and the courage of first-time research. But it is different when one feels "caught."

How many of us have experienced such genuine intensity and immersion in the field that we get speechless when asked "how it is" in our "fieldsite"? More significantly, how many drop out of doctoral programs because they cannot bear the thought of creating enough distance to analyze something and write about it maintaining such distance? Or fail to consider exploring another issue in a different locale, and with people they do not already know, because they cannot bear the thought of reexperiencing the intensity, commitment, entanglement, love, frustration, and rootedness that they had as fledgling anthropologists? Is there room in one's life for more angst, more people, more sighing, more reason to want to be away from the institution that employs us? Some who felt "caught" in their first, long-term fieldwork will relate to the level of intensity I recount from my experiences in Israel (and those of Susan Harding in the US) but forswear the possibility of beginning again elsewhere for fear of developing such a level of intensity all over again. Yet Alma's vision is a vision of rekindling, and I think my Israeli "legs" illustrate that well. It takes courage—and perhaps a bit of folly—to shed light and warmth on things even when we are fundamentally tired or already full of duties, friends, habits of the heart, and habits of the mind . . . but the payoff is worth it.

The stories we tell in this book might well just be good stories about specific people, aging anthropologists with track records that younger anthropologists can see and consider—like good stories told about anyone by those with a knack for storytelling. I remember being there myself—reading Margaret Mead's fieldwork letters (1977) and Bronislaw Malinowski's diaries (1967) much earlier in my career, relishing the details of their everyday lives in the field, their struggles and joys, the stuff rarely discussed as attentively as the finer points of theoretical debates. But I hope that anthropologists picking up this book—in a sense, second-order participant-observers—will assess the payoffs as well as the risks of picking up and starting fieldwork all over again elsewhere. Perhaps the risk is really that of stasis rather than of flightiness or being perceived as ungrounded.

THE RISKS, THE REASONS, THE TANGO

Each one of us takes risks, and each one of us at some level decides which risks to take. Some people see themselves as risk-takers, others as risk-avoiders, but these self-perceptions are worth a second look. As I look back, I know that at least some of my senior colleagues at Duke thought I took too great a risk when I began fieldwork in Israel before getting tenure. I could see eyebrows raised as I began to learn Hebrew at the beginning of the 1980s and then applied for grants to do exploratory research in Israel.[3] I had, after all, been trained as a Caribbeanist, a student of what I have long called the Afro-European half of the Americas—not a student of Jews, nor of Jewish society, nor even Jewish migrations to the Americas; not of Arabs, Arab societies, Arab migrations to the Americas, or Islam; not even of religion in any focused way. Nothing about language, colonial patterns, or historical structures of connectedness and differentiation led me from the Caribbean, even broadly circumscribed, to Israel and the Middle East.

Yet I was not losing my mind. I was picking up a scent of related issues and the chance to experience them framed very differently—most of all, a scent of hierarchy, collectivity, separation, interpenetration, distrust, rootedness, and bondedness, all of which were *not* framed in the language of race. To a product of the Western hemisphere, the intellectual lure was immediate and unshakable. I could see how some scholars might want to exceptionalize the Middle East—to orientalize or primitivize it—and many had (Said 1978). I could see how others might be tempted to see its living and kicking residents as mired in a false consciousness about "race." But the more I read about the region, dug beneath the surface and "tested" it like a good skeptic, the clearer the cost of such a racializing perspective became. I became concerned with the loss of opportunity that a racializing approach to peoplehood in the Middle East represented—for the worldwide intellectual community of thinkers, comparativists, and social scientists, as well as for potential reformers and revolutionaries.[4]

Perhaps only a young PhD—or someone not seeking or expecting a "big"

3. In the summers of 1980 and 1981 I studied at two *ulpanim*, intensive language schools in Israel that were developed to teach modern Hebrew to Jewish immigrants. At the time, many were subsidized by municipalities and the Ministry of Immigrant Absorption. Non-Jews like me—many of them, *kibbutz* volunteers from Europe—also learned Hebrew in *ulpanim*. An initial language course lasted five months and entailed being in class five days a week for four to five hours a day. I had taught myself some Hebrew prior to joining the first *ulpan* and was able to skip the first couple of months of the introductory (*alef-beit*) course. In Durham, I studied with a tutor, Malka Porges, then an Israeli MA student at North Carolina Central University, who became a field assistant the following year in Israel.

4. My interest had also more personal roots. My parents lived in Beirut the whole time I was in college; while visiting them, I'd been to the Lebanese-Israeli border more than once, and had gotten to know some Palestinians who were working for my parents in Lebanon. That, and the fact that many of my friends in college were Jewish, further incited my curiosity. For further reflections on my early involvement in Israel, see Dominguez (1989).

academic career—would have dared consider such a project. But I saw myself pursuing a scent I could not ignore. The incompleteness of the project
of Zionism, which I could hear and smell and feel and read about, kept me
wondering about any claim to collectivity. As I wrote in the book that ultimately came from this project (Dominguez 1989), if a group of people whose
interpersonal and, especially, discursive experience "had legs" for at least two
thousand years could still not be sure that they were, or even wanted to be,
one unfragmented people, what did it mean for much more recent claims to
sameness, not to mention recent claims to difference?

People who know my work on Louisiana may wonder why I am not saying all this about New Orleans and the people I obviously came to care about
there. It is something I have pondered myself, especially in the aftermath of
Hurricane Katrina. I think back to New Orleans and my fieldwork there in the
mid- to late 1970s. Its history had been a pleasure to invoke and explore—first
in my doctoral dissertation, and later in the book that came from it (Dominguez 1986). I had seen Louisiana less as a version of Caribbean people's
history than as a visible and palpable wrinkle in the mid- to late twentieth-
century hegemonic tale that Americans tell themselves about race and class
in the United States. When Katrina hit and the world watched its aftermath
on TV, I could not do much else but watch those scenes, try to contact old
friends, and note the continuing relevance of that hegemonic tale. I have never
written an article faster than the essay I wrote just a few weeks after the hurricane for the Social Science Research Council Forum (Dominguez 2005).
Sadly, little about that tale of race and class had changed in twenty years.

But to a trained Caribbeanist and the child of the Caribbean that I am,
the "discovery" I made about such a tale, and the role of Louisiana in it, was
more expected than surprising. The work seemed valuable—but change,
unlikely. Outside the US South, people have pondered for years "what to
do with New Orleans," and the little I could do would keep most of them
from continuing to exceptionalize southern Louisiana as an outpost of French
and Spanish colonial societies—bringing joy, debauchery, social disorder,
sensuality, fine cuisine, sweat, heat, Catholicism, extremes, and, in many ways,
perceived un-Americanisms to the region. The thought of spending a lifetime
fighting misperceptions of Louisiana—or, more broadly, US perceptions of
difference and otherness drawing on extremely related, if varying, frames of
understanding and habits of thought—depressed me. I could see little sense
of movement in myself or others in the long run, and little use in my own
scholarly work of something I had long valued in anthropology—the possibility of growth through openness to different frames of understanding and

experience, or at least the chance to think differently. Venturing out, going elsewhere, beginning anew meant swapping a plausible professional risk for the chance to think more creatively and more profoundly. Others in this book express related sentiments and thoughts, perhaps especially Alma Gottlieb. Are there risks? Yes. Are they worth it? Yes.

When two people tango, the dance can be refined, the movement intense, and the steps carefully executed—but the dance will remain recognizable and the categories of analysis predictable. When three try to tango, much less can be predicted, least of all what it does to a sensual dance assumed to be for two—one man and one woman. An odd metaphor here? Perhaps . . . but a useful one, nonetheless. Consider the image of three people tangoing at the same time. Two men and one woman? Two women and a man? Alternate pairings? In succession? Do the moves change when the dancers are two men? When the men are heterosexual and not especially homosocial? What, if anything, looks the same, feels the same, and works the same?

Consider the Middle East and the Caribbean. Or even the European/ Middle Eastern nexus that created Israel, and the early- to late-modern Atlantic world that created export-oriented plantation economies throughout half of the Western hemisphere, using and subjugating millions of Africans and benefiting millions of Europeans in Europe and its settler colonies. Although Europe features in both stories, the purpose of my intellectual move was not to highlight Europe but, I might now say, adapting Chakrabarty (2000) in creative ways, to provincialize racialism and the hegemonic racialism I find in so much intellectual work coming out of the anglophone world— including a great deal of self-avowed antiracist scholarship, activism, and pedagogy (for critiques of such work, see Dominguez 1997 and Stoler 1997).

We can ask what Jews have to do with Creoles, or with island countries in the Caribbean and their relation to the United States, and the wonderfully open-minded anthropological imagination could well come up with answers. But that question would not be framed productively or provocatively the way I think I intended it years ago (and still do now). The same goes for the history of Zionism, its internal debates, its tacit fractures and hypervisible ones, and what these might have to do with race, racialism, and racialization in the United States, in the Western hemisphere, and in the Atlantic worlds of the fifteenth through twenty-first centuries. At an empirical level, the answer is not obvious, perhaps not typically thinkable for perfectly good reasons. And the story is no different if we ask what Judaism, Islam, and Christianity, and their obsessions with a small but very specific territory far from the Americas, have to do with the political economy of slavery and the legacies that I was trained to spot and that I have long enjoyed thinking about in comparative ways. Anything, of course, can be seen through the lens of anything else, but my "tango" was not an evasion or evacuation or loss of focus but an insistence on the dance—while challenging its acknowledged genealogies, its hegemonic discourses, its tacit complicity with distinctions and classifications.

In retrospect, the more I'd plunged into comparative histories of racial stratification, color, slavery, and census classifications across colonies, territories, and countries in the Americas, prior to working in Israel, the more "race" had begun to seem too geohistorically delimited. "Race" had been there in my first long-term field project, back in 1972–1973 in New York City, and the resulting long Scholar of the House thesis I had written during my senior year in college (Dominguez 1973). In planning that project, I had not initially anticipated the long historical chapters I ended up including about slavery, race, and color in Cuba, Puerto Rico, and the Dominican Republic. But in trying to make sense of "the Middle Race"—a phrase I coined back then for people who lived in the United States but did not comfortably accept US binary racial classifications—the historical processes that made each society different from the US and even from each other clearly opened my brain to further questions about race and racial classification. Some years later, my doctoral research in New Orleans reinforced this—both in the clear specificity of these social formations, and in the process by which they develop and come to be taken for granted.

But what question was it all really pointing to? Before venturing to Israel, I felt somewhat straitjacketed by discursive communities, their agendas, their intellectual genealogies, and their no doubt unintentional ways of determining the limits of their topics and the outer limits of their object of study. Increasingly I feared that the imperial legacies of the Atlantic world were leading far too many intellectuals, citizens, scholars, and policy makers to assume the universal relevance of race and racial classification, and that this was wrong— missing the boat in important ways that drew me back to Claude Lévi-Strauss, Jean-Paul Sartre, George Herbert Mead, even Kant, Quine, Wittgenstein, and Heidegger, not to mention Fredrik Barth's anticulturalist understanding of "ethnic groups and boundaries" and Lewis Henry Morgan's obsession with the categorization of relatedness. I had never lost interest in some parts of the century-old debates concerning kinship, descent, and alliance that I had learned from Harold Scheffler at Yale and David Schneider at the University of Chicago in my graduate school days—unlike so many of my generation, who deemed the intense debates about kinship that raged in print from the 1940s through 1960s too technical and uninspiring. My interest returned as I tried to sort out the foundation of claims to sameness and difference—ontological or discursive, emotional or political, interpersonal or semiotic, epistemological or phenomenological. In other words, I sought an intellectual framework for understanding sameness and difference not as individual terms or categories but as spatiotemporally developed and sustained systems of social classification, of which "race" was but one. So Israel grabbed me from within, not only my brain but my senses and my heart, in some ways functioning as the transformative fieldsite in my career, even if it was neither my first nor my second.

THE PHYSICAL, THE VIRTUAL, THE CHANGED

But I left Israel, too, for many years—at least physically, if not intellectually or emotionally—and I know my colleagues and friends in Israel noted my absence with varying degrees of knowledge or empathy. I had spent so much of the 1980s there that I sometimes joked I was living in Jerusalem while teaching at Duke. Then I stopped. So when Andre Levy, then president of the Israel Anthropological Association, phoned during the winter of 2005–2006 to invite me to attend the association's annual conference as one of two distinguished speakers, I felt like the prodigal daughter. I was touched—but wondered what it would be like to return after an absence of about fifteen years. That began the journey back. I think the time was right for my head as well as my heart.

I went and have since returned. Each time, my feeling of comfort remains. Each time, I feel alive, I remember living and dying, I wonder why I still remember so much Hebrew, and I fear the inevitable conversations about my physical absence through most of the 1990s and into this decade.

Like Alma Gottlieb, I find myself turning to my old friend Moshe Shokeid's recent essay (2007) on bringing closure to a field project. Moshe asks when to call it quits, or at least what led him to do so in his fieldwork on gay Jews in New York. The question has all sorts of dimensions—ethical as well as intellectual, practical, interpersonal, emotional, and even legal. Moshe's experience of long-term immersion in a gay, synagogue-centered Jewish community in New York made his decision to end the project a sad one, and clearly not one he made lightly. It was largely a matter of realizing the emotional and social distance, the palpable new lack of mutual interest or trust, that had slowly developed between him and the active membership. As with my immersion in Israel, Moshe's immersion in this project had been multiply driven. Not his first US field project (or even his first in New York), it had been motivated by curiosity of the most heartfelt and mind-bending sort. The high point came when his book was published (1995) and reactions in the community and in the scholarly world were mostly positive, though some were more circumspect. But then what? Although Moshe came to the United States often and he visited the community for varying periods of time, I think he was keeping in touch with people he had come to care about more than he was tracking intellectually interesting changes that might push his research further.

I have known Moshe for some time (having first met him in Israel). He hardly needs an interpreter, as he publishes amply, clearly, and courageously. But over the years, I wondered what he was doing each time he returned to "his community." At times, I picked up a kind of sadness in his conversations or e-mails, one I came to interpret as anticipating the loss of excitement, newness of connectedness, novelty of immersion, and sense of intellectual payoff. But to say that one is done with a place, its issues, and its people is to risk feeling or seeming dismissive toward them. I doubt that most sociologists, political scientists, economists, or educational psychologists often grapple with this sort of reluctant regret. In many ways, their projects are more narrowly construed, a data-gathering activity or experimental method defining the contours of the project, as opposed to the emotionally engulfing choice of fieldsite that marks the life of an anthropologist (of the cultural, social, political, linguistic, or economic variety). For Moshe, as for me and many others, the sense of "moving away" is troubling. It can all too easily remind us of childhood friends we lost touch with and family members we stopped interacting with for no special reason, except perhaps the passage of time, the entry of new interests, the busyness of work and our own nuclear families. And suddenly it feels too late to connect, as if no time had passed and no intimacy had been lost.

It takes courage to say goodbye. It also takes courage to reconnect, to return, to rekindle links, even to face the inevitable question a dear old friend asked me in 2006 in Jerusalem: Why didn't you call or write in all those years? "All those years" could be decades or just four to five years—time spent writing rather than researching, running a department or an association, dealing with parental illness and death. Or it could be what happened to me—more with regard to Israel than to any other fieldsite I have worked in, probably because the depth of the connection was greater.

Indeed, when I left Israel in the summer of 1990, I thought I was saying goodbye and, like Moshe Shokeid, I thought it was not out of bitterness but of exhaustion—emotional, interpersonal, and political exhaustion. At some level, I thought it might even be an intellectual exhaustion. Nevertheless, over the course of the 1990s and into the early 2000s, I continued writing about things Israeli, periodically participating in Jewish Studies in the United States, and thinking about theoretical questions through my Israeli lens. All these activities made it clear that the real exhaustion I had experienced, and from which I was trying to recover, was not primarily intellectual.

My partner, E., had died in 1986. I had returned to Israel three times since then. Each time, I had had rewarding moments, productive research time, and experiences of absences—my partner's absence, some people's lack of knowledge, others' absence of feeling, and a fading sense of a future for me in Israel, even as an observer. A life gone, a book completed. Both long processes, rather than sudden events. A physical connection lost, a psychic one unhinged. Like a woman giving birth after the death of her partner, I finished my book about Israel (1989), feeling I was somehow defying death, renewing my commitment to the place, showing the bigger vision of the analytic problem I had spent years studying and the groundedness of the evidence and feeling. My partner never saw the book or even the contract, couldn't help me proof the pages, had no chance to critique it or to celebrate. But it was a book that felt like a birth . . . and under circumstances that were always about dying, living, loving, fighting, defying, and thriving, despite the tears and near despair. No wonder I was exhausted. No wonder I needed a break from smelling, touching, seeing, hearing, arguing about, and thinking about Israel 24/7.

Of course, Israel did not go away, and I could never totally escape. There I was, for example, in September 1993, in Hawai'i in the hours before dawn, glued to the TV set watching Yitzhak Rabin and Yasir Arafat shaking hands on the lawn of the White House. I had been spending reenergizing time at the East-West Center in Honolulu thinking about collectivities, selfhood, cultural policies, and politics with a Pacific and East Asian bent, thanks to the generous collegiality and open-mindedness of researchers and fellows at the Center, who thought that my approach could help spark a reorientation in the work of others there, elsewhere in the United States, and elsewhere in the Pacific rim—and who had noticed my mind-twisting engagement with the issues that Pacific studies and East Asian scholars were addressing.[5] An intellectual environment full of riches and colleagues, the East-West Center had become another home in the early to mid-1990s, and I am proud of the collaborative and individual research, theory, and publications that came out of that period,

---

5. At varying points, this congenial group included Elizabeth Buck, Wimal Dissanayake, Dru Gladney, Geoffrey White, and David Wu.

especially a collection I helped edit comparing the politics of national identity in cultural policies (Dominguez and Wu 1998), and an article challenging the Americo-centric bias marring many discussions of race (Dominguez 1998).

But that September day, three years since my last trip to Israel, I was still glued to the television, this time in Honolulu. Indeed, I had set my alarm to allow me to watch, live, the stunning, nearly unbelievable vision of Rabin and Arafat shaking hands on the lawn of the White House, announcing an agreement between Israel and the Palestinian leadership Arafat represented. Reading about it later would not suffice, nor would watching a replay of that moment, though I knew there would be many.

The connection was just as strong when, back in Iowa City in November 1995, I heard that Rabin had been assassinated. I was aghast, though not altogether surprised. That I was sadly reassured by the news that the assassin was not an Arab was telling as well: I was reassured not only because it reduced the likelihood of negative repercussions for Arabs living under Israeli control but because I had not lost my "touch," my sense of Israel. I had long felt— and even said to friends and colleagues in Israel—that I could imagine civil war in Israel within my lifetime, and that it would not be Jew versus Arab or Ashkenazi Jew versus Sephardic (Mizrachi) Jew but rather war along ideological lines, whether over socialist leanings versus capitalist goals or, more profoundly, over the Jewishness of the state of Israel. So I felt like a minor prophet, still connected, still "spot on."

These moments always brought surprise. I think of them as volcanic eruptions of feeling, reminders of connectedness. While I had followed developments in Israel in detail through the 1980s, I had stopped doing so in the '90s. When I left Duke in 1991 and moved to Santa Cruz, California, I brought many saved Israeli newspapers with me, but I stopped subscribing to them. For a number of years in the 1990s, I subscribed instead to the *Honolulu Advertiser*, as a way to keep track of public discourse in Hawai'i. Following news from the Pacific also let me experience the nonnational and the multinational, and avoid the paradoxical provincialism of the US northeast, the consumption of the *New York Times* as if it were the nation's only truly international newspaper. The *Advertiser*'s coverage of Pacific, East Asian, Southeast Asian, and even South Asian events and concerns was constant and detailed. It made the United States look less like an Atlantic Ocean country than a Pacific Ocean one, and it was a terrific antidote to the hegemonic Eurocentricity of the eastern half of the country. It was, of course, also very, very far away from the Middle East, both in geographic distance and in focus. Yet even from my new perch on the Pacific coast, I could not avoid the Israel that had gotten under my skin.

So what was I, as I sat in my room in the Jerusalem Regency Hotel in May 2008, looking at the striking landscape and skyline of Jerusalem—east and west, no clear line visible to the uninformed eye? Was I the prodigal daughter returning home, or the reenergized scholar once again able to tango, this time with three partners rather than two? Was I the escapee, the one who had gone AWOL and now dared show up again? Or was I "just" the anthropologist—following my nose, choosing to privilege theme or issue over place, culture, and people, as I moved away from Israel, and as I had earlier moved away from New Orleans and, earlier still, from New York City? If so, what was I doing feeling it all over again, in Jerusalem, now after two *intifadas*, after the immigration of a huge number of ex-Soviet Jews and their family members (many of them not Jewish) in the 1990s, after the expansion of both a consumer economy and a software industry that many friends and colleagues thought were changing something fundamental in Israel?

I had missed quite a bit in my absence. I remember noting the ex-Soviet immigration but not dwelling on it. The economic expansion and consumer developments happened over a longer period of time, and I had only paid intermittent attention. The second *intifada* had been more of a defined event for me, but still I had experienced it only through the media and my colleagues' accounts. I remember a volcanic eruption of feeling—coupled with a sense that I just couldn't become immersed in it.

When the second *intifada* began, in the fall of 2000, it found me in Budapest trying to learn Hungarian, preparing to teach at Eotvos Lorand University, and immersing myself in the Hungarian experience of history, nationhood, peoplehood, language, culture, injustice, and desire. My goal that academic year was not to develop another active fieldsite in Hungary; instead, I was there to enact an ethical and intellectual commitment to something I had come to care about deeply by the mid-1990s—engaging with students and colleagues from around the world who specialize in the study of the United States. Teaching American studies and codirecting the International Forum for U.S. Studies, my mental, ethical, emotional, interpersonal, political, and scholarly energy was "taken," and I watched the development of the second *intifada* from a physical and psychic distance.[6]

6. At Eotvos Lorand University, I served as Salgo Professor of American Studies in the School of English and American Studies. Five years earlier, while I was director of the University of Iowa's Center for International and Comparative Studies, I had joined forces with my partner, American Studies professor Jane Desmond, to cofound the International Forum for U.S. Studies with a four-year Rockefeller Foundation Humanities Residency Grant. Subse-

So I had "missed" crucial physical, military, political, social, and phenomenological developments experienced by Jews and Arabs in the city of Jerusalem. Yet I still felt that connection, that warmth, that exasperation, that sense of home. I noticed it again in June 2006, when I was in Israel for about three weeks—and then again after returning to the US that summer. Back home in Iowa City, I found myself constantly following the Mideast war news on US television, online, and over the phone almost daily with my doctoral student Kenda Stewart, then based in Haifa. Israel was at war again that summer, first against Hamas in Gaza and then against the Hezbollah in Lebanon. I felt an intensity and a daily bond very reminiscent of the time in June 1982 when I was living in Israel and keeping a daily log about the endless, failed ceasefires.

To return to Israel is a bit surreal. Exhaustion is real and reenergizing crucial, not to mention fantastic. These are physical as well as psychic things, felt in the body and not just wished away—as any Israeli or Palestinian knows only too well. To deal with them is, I think, both the anthropologist's challenge and the anthropologist's strength, enabled by years of language immersion, social immersion, and sensory immersion that makes return eerily comfortable, no matter how traumatic it is. So *to*-ing and *fro*-ing improves that tango I dance and that I think enhances our insight when we seek depth of understanding of something social, something meaningful, something socially, economically, culturally, or politically consequential.

For me, the continuing thirst I feel as a scholar is for ways of presenting, imagining, and theorizing collectivity and peoplehood on the planet, and I cannot imagine doing it without being constantly thrown a bit by understandings that never quite fit the taken-for-granted, the hegemonic here and the hegemonic elsewhere. And so I wonder if Alma's vision is not that of temporary sojourners who, like pastoralists, have a "region" within which they cycle on a seasonal or periodic basis because it is how they do their work best, grounded while moving?

---

quent grants from the Rockefeller and Ford Foundations allowed us to develop further initiatives, as has our more recent move to the University of Illinois.

From Local to Global Ethnographic Scenarios

Gustavo Lins Ribeiro

Ethnography was what first attracted me to anthropology. In 1975–1976, my last year as an undergraduate student of sociology at the University of Brasília, I took an anthropology course that would change my academic trajectory. The course showed me that field research in anthropology allows for a unique blend of high-level theoretical abstraction combined with a sense of the real world through interactions with people you get to know and listen to, and whose viewpoints are central to the analysis. What I found profoundly appealing in ethnography was that I saw it as a method that would allow me to bring together my intellectual inclination toward theoretical debates and my political preoccupation with the use of knowledge in the service of social justice. It was this sense that social analysis did not have to be reduced to a cold and distant interpretive skill for dealing with abstract models that led me to my first ethnographic experience in 1976. By then, I had given up on being a sociologist and was eager to enter a graduate program in anthropology. But my understanding of ethnography was still mostly empiricist: I took the importance of being in the field as above all related to a need to check theories.

Back in 1972, my decision to study the social sciences had been based on the conviction that knowledge is a powerful tool to promote social and political change. Underlying this belief were two dissatisfactions I had as a teenager—and still have. One was with the great social inequalities within Brazilian society; a few decades later, although inequality has lessened in the country, Brazil remains a most unjust place, with one of the worst income distributions in the world. The other was related to the military dictatorship under which I grew up. I became an adult during the long twenty-one years of authoritarian governments that, starting in 1964, repressed grassroots movements and leftist parties as well as all freethinkers who strove for the reestablishment of the rule of law and democracy. As a graduate student in anthropology in 1977, I myself would be kept prisoner for thirty-one days and prosecuted under the infamous National Security Law. Having experienced authoritarianism in full, I found it completely unacceptable and learned, in practice, the value of democratic liberties.

In the 1970s many Brazilian anthropologists wrote memorable studies of the life of the dominated classes—peasants, rural and urban workers, the informal sector. In Brazil, in contrast to other South American countries (such as Argentina) that were under the yoke of military dictatorships, Marxism was not completely forbidden in the universities, and in fact was in vogue as a theoretical framework among social scientists. In spite of the risk, for many being a Marxist was not only a methodological and theoretical option but also a political identity marker, a sign of opposition to the authoritarian regime. In addition to Karl Marx, Antonio Gramsci and Louis Althusser were common sources of inspiration, to be followed in the mid- and late 1970s by Michel Foucault. Indeed, one might claim that Brazilian anthropologists were making subaltern studies *avant la lettre*. The point was not necessarily to let the subalterns speak, but it was common to find transcriptions of the narratives and "discourses" of ethnographic subjects. In reality, research was meant to perforate the "dominant ideology," to reveal the class contradictions that structured social, political, and economic reality, in order to uncover the "real subjects of history." Marxism provided a certainty that, today, in a post-postmodern era, brings a sort of nostalgia for firmer grounds at the same time that it consolidates a critical distancing from the metanarratives of the nineteenth century. This historical juncture, and my positioning within it, are central to understanding some of the choices I was to make regarding my academic career and my appreciation of ethnography.

DOING RESEARCH IN BRAZIL

I conducted my first ethnographic research as an undergraduate in 1976, writing a senior thesis on a subset of the urban poor—children who sold peanuts and candy at the central bus station of Brasília. It was not easy to be accepted as a researcher by a small group of five teenage boys whose only experience with middle-class men like me consisted of selling them sexual services. This research experience was intense enough to make me relativize my middle-class condition and congeal in my mind the notion that ethnography is done alone. I also concluded that I really wanted to be an anthropologist and would pursue graduate study.

In the seventies, the requirements for a masters degree at the University of Brasília were much heavier than what they are today. I took four years, finishing the degree in 1980, and wrote an MA thesis that was longer than the PhD dissertation I later wrote for the City University of New York. My graduate years in Brazil would deepen my interest in studying grassroots ethnographic subjects. Along with a small group of colleagues, we decided to write our theses on themes that were in the "interest of the Brazilian people." In our minds, we deemed this commitment typical of Brazilian anthropology: to lay bare the causes of inequalities and to search for ways of overcoming them, aiming at the construction of a better nation. With this ambitious goal in mind, I decided to study the experiences of the workers who had constructed the new city of Brasília, which opened as Brazil's new federal capital in 1960.

It proved a pleasant and even easy research project to conduct. People in Brasília were eager to talk about their experiences since they quickly understood that I was looking for "another" history—one that was radically different from the dominant, laudatory records made by politicians, such as Juscelino Kubitschek, the president responsible for the transfer of the capital from Rio de Janeiro. One worker even told me that while he was helping to build the city, he "knew" that one day someone would come to interview him about his pioneering experience.

In my research, I wanted to show how the prevailing discourses on the construction of Brasília were tainted by the nationalism of the elites. These discourses constituted a dominant ideology that served to legitimate both the relocation of the capital and the over-exploitation of the sixty thousand migrants who came to the hinterlands of Brazil between 1957 and 1960 to build the new city. Taking a "bottom-up" approach, my project was a study in both history and anthropology. As a study in history, it reconstructed the daily lives of the tens of thousands of people whose labor defined a reality that is lived today by millions. As a study in anthropology, it absorbed the perspectives of actors who were directly involved in the action, and whose voices had not been registered previously. The exhibiting of these perspectives thus created a displacement of the reader's relation to ossified and naturalized sociohistorical truths.

I believe this combination of anthropology and history is what has conserved the vitality of my MA thesis, "The Capital of Hope," through the years.[1] This felicitous combination expresses itself mainly in the richness of the workers' speeches, which place the reader among the migrants who went to Brazil's Central Plateau to build the new capital. It was the ethnographic perspective that made the difference, much more than the archival work I did. Indeed, it was the ethnographic research I conducted in reconstructing workers' memories that made me look for historical information in the archives, and not vice versa.

This project reinforced my belief in the heuristic strength of ethnography as a method capable of shedding new light on old objects of study, allowing for a renewal of theories and perspectives at the same time that it favored the accomplishment of major political results by bringing new actors and discourses to the scene. By the time I completed my masters research in Brasília, I was starting to consolidate an understanding of ethnography as a double device—both a heuristic and a political tool. The value of other people's experiences, I had discovered, was powerful enough to displace received knowledge, and to open the way for new visions and historical subjects.

Yet academic careers are not necessarily the result of unilineal and cumulative processes. Many years later, my MA thesis would have an unexpected effect on my career. Until recently, I considered my Brasília study to be an early phase of my trajectory, much cherished but almost prehistoric, a step that had led me, as we will see, to more complex and global objects. Decades of interest in the anthropology of globalization have meant that my ethnographic and theoretical interests have taken me farther and farther from home. I was barely an intellectual interlocutor regarding Brasília.

I wrote "The Capital of Hope" in 1980, when I was twenty-seven years old. Since then, the thesis has been read often by researchers interested in a perspective different from that of the powerful agents involved in the construction of the new capital.[2] More than a quarter of a century after I wrote it, *The Capital of Hope* was published as a book in Argentina (2006b) and Brazil

1. The Portuguese title , "O Capital da Esperança," is a play on "A Capital da Esperança," a designation given to Brasília by the French writer André Malraux, who visited the city while it was still under construction. In Portuguese, *capital* may be either a masculine or a feminine noun. *O capital*, the masculine version, has an economic meaning and is the Portuguese title of Marx's classic book, *Das Kapital*. The feminine version, *a capital*, refers to an administrative seat.

2. Soon thereafter I wrote an article on the history of the urban settlement of the Federal District based on the social movements of the migrant workers (Ribeiro 1982). This was the first article I ever published and was later my first work translated into Japanese (Ribeiro 2006a).

(2008a). The publication of the Brazilian edition, in a period of intense expectation surrounding the celebration of the capital city's fiftieth anniversary, generated interest on the part of Brasília's press. As a consequence, I was invited to be a member of a council of the federal agency responsible for the protection of Brasília as a UNESCO World Heritage site. I was also invited to join a committee of the *Correio Braziliense*, the city's largest newspaper, to nominate the fifty most important personages in the history of Brasília; and I was invited to contribute to an edited scholarly volume on the city's urban planning. Prompted by these invitations, I started talking and thinking again about the research I had conducted thirty years earlier and began to consider new topics for research in Brasília. In consequence of this boomerang effect, the return and impact of my early study, I now view the processes involved in selecting research subjects more as spiral curves occurring in different planes, and making up a universe where previous moments can unexpectedly revisit you. A career is not necessarily a straight arrow, where one experience leads to another in a cumulative and logical chain.

While my 1980 MA thesis has produced these recent, unexpected outcomes, it also had more foreseeable impacts that in many ways shaped the next ten years of my academic life, including my ethnographic choices. In the concluding section of my thesis, I posited that the form of production I had chronicled in Brasília was typical of large-scale construction projects carried out in isolated areas. I suggested that it would, in effect, be possible to test this claim by comparing the construction of Brasília with the construction of a major hydroelectric dam, Tucuruí, that the development-oriented military government was building in the Amazon region of Brazil. My theoretical intuition was that the form of production I had studied in Brasília, and that I suspected I would witness at Tucuruí, had recurrent structural characteristics and was linked to the expansion of capitalism. I imagined that comparative research would allow me to identify a form of production structurally similar to that found on plantations. In other words, I was following a theoretical question and I needed to check its viability in another setting. This meant that I never asked myself (to cite the title of the conference session that led to this book), Should I stay or should I go? I felt I simply had to embark on another ethnographic project to extend my exploration of the questions I was asking. In my case, the choices I made in pursuing a new ethnographic study depended directly on the theoretical issues that interested me.

But first I wanted to complete my doctoral training, and I knew where: at the City University of New York, where Eric Wolf, whose work on plantations and other subjects I admired and was teaching. Thus my decision to follow my theoretical preoccupations entailed a change not only of ethnographic scenario but of country.

I had a conversation with Wolf at the beginning of my coursework at CUNY, in 1982, in which I told him about my idea of doing an ethnography of a hydroelectric dam under construction for my doctoral dissertation. He was very supportive of the general plan but made an important suggestion that changed my career. He asked, Why, during your coursework, don't you study the construction of the Suez Canal, or the Panama Canal, or American railroads? At that moment, I went global—I understood that I should open my research imagination to objects located anywhere in the world. I was already disinclined to remain caught in the classic disciplinary One Scholar/One Fieldsite model. Now the world was opening before me—an opening that, luckily, helped me avoid the common trap in Latin America and elsewhere of becoming a specialist only in one's own country, of having the horizon of your nation-state as your most imaginative platform. I proceeded to undertake historical studies of major large-scale projects. From these, I confirmed the existence of the form of production I had posited (Ribeiro 1985, 1987). I also changed my fieldsite to Argentina, where a major dam was under construction in the mid-1980s.

DOING RESEARCH IN ARGENTINA

Conducting long-term ethnographic research for a doctoral dissertation is a privilege most anthropologists will never again enjoy. I spent two years (1985–1987) in Argentina doing research on and writing about the Yacyretá Hydroelectric High Dam that was being built in the northeastern province of Corrientes on the Paraná River, on the border of Argentina and Paraguay. I conducted multisited research for the project: I lived alternately in Ituzaingó, the *pueblo* where the camps and the worksite were located, and in Buenos Aires, where I researched the project's archive and the elite who worked at the headquarters of the binational corporation that owned the project. I also started research in Ayolas and Asunción, Paraguay, but I soon concluded that this would not be a very productive endeavor. At that point, Paraguay was dominated by the authoritarian Stroessner dictatorship, and my presence as a foreign researcher was not welcome.

This time I did not focus solely on the workers' experiences, as I had done during my Brasília research. I did interview workers and union leaders, but I wanted a systemic vision of the project, and that was more accessible through the engineers' and technicians' eyes. From my previous historical research on nineteenth- and early twentieth-century projects, I already knew that large-scale projects were characterized by complex global flows of a technical elite. But I had never met them. They now became the main focus of my ethnographic work at the construction site. I saw these global labor migrants as providing me with an opportunity to discuss multifaceted, fragmented, and fluid transnational identities (Ribeiro 1992, 1995) at a moment when transnationalism and fragmented identities were being discussed only theoretically, if at all. This experience made me highly sensitive to the avatars of international and transnational migration and identities—issues I was to revisit in other locales.

Since my research subject was globalization (which, at the time, was still called "capitalist expansion and integration"), I was never really identified as an Argentinist. Having been trained in an American PhD program, I was a little disappointed that the knowledge I had accumulated on Argentine history, culture, economics, and politics was not much sought after, either in Brazil or in the United States. The fact that I was the only Brazilian anthropologist who had written a doctoral dissertation based on field research in Argentina meant next to nothing to my colleagues in Brazil, where, in those days, almost all doctoral students in any field conducted field research on subjects located in their own country. This is a clear difference distinguishing the Brazilian and American academic milieux. In the United States, when you do field research in a foreign country, you immediately become a specialist in that country and are supposed to develop your career in relation to it (see Nugent 2008b, for the pervasive impact of area studies in the American academy). But I felt a commitment to neither the Brazilian nor the American model of scholarly career. I felt unattached to any specific location—convinced that the social processes I had studied in both Brazil and Argentina could be studied anywhere. I never thought of myself as, or aspired to become, a specialist on the construction of Brasília or of Yacyretá; I knew I would not return to those concrete historical, sociological, and anthropological scenarios. Rather, I maintained my interest in the theoretical and analytic results they provided.

Yet I have continued to keep up with many good friends and colleagues in Argentina. In fact, it is my Argentine colleagues who have stimulated me to think about our two countries comparatively. In the last two decades, intellectual exchanges between Brazilian and Argentine anthropologists have grown consistently, and with the unfolding of free trade agreements among South American countries via the Mercosur (Southern Common Market) process, the importance of deepening mutual knowledge has not only increased but, indeed, become a strategic asset. I like to imagine that I made a modest contribution to this process of drawing together the two nations' anthropological traditions, not only by keeping alive my own social and professional networks in Buenos Aires and Posadas (the latter provincial capital being closer to my research site), but also by publishing my Yacyretá book in Argentina and by editing volumes and writing articles that were consciously directed to enhancing binational exchanges of knowledge (Frigerio and Ribeiro 2002; Grimson, Ribeiro, and Semán 2004; Ribeiro 1999, 2002b, 2004).

During my field research in Yacyretá, I wrote, in Spanish, the only article I ever published on ethnography as a method. It would later become a basic text for cohorts of Argentine undergraduate students in anthropology. Its main argument is that ethnography is based on both objective and inter-subjective exchanges that occur during field research and, as such, is best understood as a series of communicative encounters in which participants are eager to domesticate their mutual ignorance. Crucial for my arguments was the notion of estrangement due to the fact that participants in the ethnographic encounter are typically not reproducing their routine communicative encounters and speech acts: both researchers and researched feel they are living/experiencing awkward interactions. The anthropologist, especially, is out of his or her customary milieu and needs to monitor new relations, exposing him/herself to situations where his or her "practical consciousness"—all the things that actors know tacitly (Giddens 1984)—is temporarily incapable of naturalizing the new people and new environment. This forces the ethnographer to reinforce his or her perceptive and cognitive processes in negotiations with the other people s/he encounters—who, in turn, are also eager to domesticate the prying stranger. Ethnographic experience is thus a series of encounters in a mutual process of negotiation of ignorances and anxieties, the goal of which is to produce a fusion of horizons that will make social life and their daily participants predictable again. When the fusion of horizons is complete and the people you are studying start asking you who they are and why they behave in a certain way, the research is done—it is time to leave. In retrospect, I now see that this conception of the ethnographic experience as a process of negotiation of ignorances is also organic to the idea that ethnography is a lonely experience and that switching fieldsites is a way of keeping your anthropological awareness sharp.

BACK TO BRAZIL

My research in Yacyretá had several ramifications for my subsequent work after I finished my PhD in 1988 and started teaching in the Department of Anthropology at the University of Brasília. First, I came to understand more about engineering and its history as strongly enmeshed with the history of technological advancement; second, I became more interested in global flows of people, information, capital, and political power; third, transnationalism became a subject I knew could be studied ethnographically; fourth, and most importantly, I began work (which would continue for years) on a critical approach to the anthropology of development. The conclusion of my dissertation was that what the economic and political establishment called "development" projects did not really promote anything that could justly be called development since they were directly linked to the interests of expansionist capitalist elites, who kept the lion's share of what was invested. Local populations, especially those that are closer to the projects and suffer their impacts, rarely benefit from such projects. When they do, it is on a much smaller scale than is the case for the powerful outsiders who control the projects. Resources flowing to the local level are usually appropriated by local elites, thus reinforcing preexisting social inequalities. These were the years when major revisions of development ideologies and utopias were under way (Brundtland Report—1987; Rio United Nations Conference on the Environment and Development—1992). Environmentalism became a key force in this political field, and sustainable development a mantra. In such a juncture, my doctoral dissertation won the most important prize in the Brazilian social sciences and in consequence was soon published in Portuguese (1991b) and, later, in English (1994) and Spanish (1999).

In the meantime, I became strongly involved with the Brazilian environmental movement, especially with the defense of the Amazonian rain forest and its "traditional" dwellers (Indians and rubber tappers). Several graduate students who also sympathized with environmentalism came to work with me. The fact that I worked for the environmentalist movement did not hinder me from sustaining a critical view of its metanarratives and goals. I cannot say that my political participation in the field of environmentalist NGOs was an ethnographic experience as such, but it led me to write an essay (Ribeiro 1991a) in which sustainable development was seen as the new ideology/utopia of development, one that necessitated a compromise between the radicals of the environmentalist movement, zero-growth believers, and the typical developmentalists whose world headquarters was located in the World Bank. In 1992, during the United Nations Conference on the Environment and Development, held in Rio de Janeiro, I did another brief fieldwork project, which I viewed as a mega/global ritual of integration of transnational political elites. This notion proved useful when I further developed my interest in the study of transnational political elites and global civil society.

Later, in the mid-1990s, following another theoretical interest I developed from my studies of large-scale construction projects—the history of technology—I was excited by what I posited as important effects of the Internet as a new technology of communication. I did a survey on the use that Brazilian NGOs were making of this tool and on its role during the 1992 UN conference in Rio. Based on Benedict Anderson's well-known interpretation of the relations between "print capitalism" and the construction of "national imagined communities" (1991), I inferred that the new "electronic/computer capitalism" was creating, via the Internet, a techno-symbolic basis that would allow for the development of "transnational imagined/virtual communities" (Ribeiro 1998, 2009b). This analysis was consistent with my ideas on the transnational political elites that were the basis of a developing global civil society.

DOING RESEARCH IN THE UNITED STATES

A firm believer in the role of estrangement in ethnography, I was never comfortable with the idea that Brazilian anthropologists should only do research in Brazil. Indeed, I thought that it was time to use ethnography to study rich countries, reversing the usual power discrepancies involved in the ethnographic encounter, and in anthropology in general. This was the beginning of a line of reasoning that would end with the coining of the notion of "postimperialism" (Ribeiro 2003, 2008b; and see below). I thus started encouraging Brazilian graduate students to do research abroad. To me, the easiest way to open this window was by studying Brazilian migrants in the United States. I hoped this would show students that they could start by studying subjects who are not so distant from them, since they share the same language, for instance, but in a radically different context. I supposed that after this first experience, young Brazilian researchers would gradually become interested in studying other aspects of American society.

As late as the mid-1990s, there had been no field research conducted on Brazilian migrants in the United States by Brazilian researchers. To model the sort of research I hoped my students would conduct, I decided to conduct such research myself. At a theoretical level, the project was consistent with the studies on global flows of people and on fragmented identities that I had done in Yaycretá. Through this ethnographic work, I also hoped that I could contribute to discussions on Brazilian national identity—a debate that, in Brazil, was, to my mind, excessively essayistic.

The insertion of Brazilian migrants in the ethnic segmentation of the San Francisco Bay Area was the ethnographic scenario I chose. In winter 1996 I spent a few months in the area with my wife, Flávia Lessa de Barros, a sociologist. It was the most hectic research I have ever done. Time was short, and the Bay Area is large, yet I had no problem finding people who were willing to talk. Many migrants I met were undocumented workers, but our common national identity helped overcome their resistance to participating in my research. We were helped by Olívia Leão, a sociologist and herself a Brazilian migrant, who opened doors and introduced me to many people. I concluded, among other things, that in the hall of mirrors of the interethnic system of the Bay Area, the stereotypes maintained by Americans about Brazilian national identity were so powerful that they basically reorganized the identities of the migrants—who became, as a result, an ersatz of the stereotyped *cariocas*, people born in Rio de Janeiro (i.e., warm and sexy samba dancers), in spite of the fact that most of them came from other states of the Brazilian federation (e.g., Ribeiro 2000).

My efforts to open the way for graduate students of the University of Brasília to conduct field research in the United States appeared to be succeeding. I supervised one MA thesis on Brazilian housecleaners in the Boston area (Fleischer 2000) and another on the second generation of migrants in Connecticut (Menezes 2002). But that was all. Both Fleischer and Menezes returned to Brazil to conduct their doctoral research. It turned out not to be easy to convince a young Brazilian researcher to conduct fieldwork abroad. Brazilian anthropologists largely consider themselves involved in processes of nation-building—a commitment that propels most young researchers to specialize in local issues that are highly visible in the eyes of Brazilian society, policy makers, and opinion makers. Indeed, our own professional mystique— one that is well represented by the political roles that the Brazilian Association of Anthropology plays in different issues—leads us to long to become public intellectuals. Only recently has conducting research abroad become highly valued.

Back in 1996, I wanted to further extend the notion that anthropologists may do research anywhere, with different kinds of ethnographic subjects, in pursuit of their theoretical interests. After conducting research among Brazilians living in the Bay Area, I took an extended leave of absence from the University of Brasília and moved to the Washington, DC, area, where I lived for a year and a half. As a visiting researcher at the Institute for Global Studies in Power, Culture and History at Johns Hopkins University, I conducted field research on a group of powerful global migrants: officials of the World Bank's DC headquarters. I had already written about the transnational identities of social actors linked to so-called development projects. Now, I was following an insight of Ulf Hannerz (1996), according to which transnationalism also existed in "physical" centers. Once again, I thought that ethnography would be an effective tool for my study of transnational subjects—in this case, to help me understand the ethnic segmentation and cultural diversity of a "transnational center." I was also following another anthropological strategy: go and speak with the real actors, the people who live the experience you want to understand and theorize. Since I was strongly engaged in the debate about development, I knew the World Bank was the Mecca of the global development field (Rich 1994).[3] This globalized institution was a highly interesting ethnographic site, not only because people from more than a hundred countries had to coexist in the same social and institutional space, but also because its *raison d'être*—development—is itself a global discourse on human destiny that purports to be universal.

I chose snowball sampling as my technique to enter the World Bank, since I already knew some officials there who worked with environmental issues and social policies, and who were acquainted with my work on Yacyretá and with Brazilian environmentalism. I spent 1997 visiting the Bank and interviewing officials—sometimes in their offices, other times in the Bank's luxurious cafeteria or in coffeehouses in downtown Washington. I found that many of my "research subjects" themselves held PhDs. Studying educated people who are well acquainted with the nature of research proved a radically different experience from most of my previous studies.

Almost everyone was helpful and open-minded. But toward the end of the research, I met one official who was clearly annoyed by my presence. My interview with her was tense and did not yield any helpful information. A few days later, on a Saturday afternoon in early 1998, I received a phone call at home from a high-level official of the World Bank. He said he had just been informed that I was doing research in the Bank and asked how I had managed to get access to the Bank. I found the question so intrusive and misplaced that I could not avoid answering mockingly, "Through the doorway." I finished the conversation by saying that he should not worry since I had done a piece of academic research that was now finished, and I would be leaving for Brazil in a couple of weeks. He seemed relieved to learn that the research was over.

---

3. In the first half of the 1990s I was vice president of one of Brazil's most influential environmental NGOs, the Instituto de Estudos Amazônicos e Ambientais (IEA; Institute for Amazonian and Environmental Studies). I had also published a critical piece on development as a set of political, economic, and discursive practices (Ribeiro 1991a). In the United States, Arturo Escobar's *Encountering Development* (1995) was a most influential critical book on the issue.

Our conversation ended at that point, and I was never again contacted by anyone from the World Bank about my project.

The phone call episode was a clear demonstration of the power relations involved in ethnographies. Institutions usually do not like to be researched—especially institutions such as the World Bank that are often placed in controversial debates. Until recently, most ethnographies have been done about people who are, arguably, less powerful than the anthropologists who are researching them. However, anthropologists are increasingly interested in pursuing research on powerful institutions and people (although commissioned research still seems to be more common than independent projects). The negotiations necessary to gain access and acceptance certainly vary according to who or what you study. But if someone has to open the doors—or, as in the World Bank, if the researcher has to go through a security check—the negotiations always involve a power imbalance. A simple phone call may prevent a researcher from entering the fieldsite again—although a focused and determined researcher can be difficult to deter: for example, if one cannot conduct research on people within their work environment, one can always approach them outside it. In most situations, the establishment of networks of people willing to collaborate with one's research presupposes both personal skills of the anthropologist and the use of his or her intellectual capital and social networks.

I later wrote an article about the "ethnic segmentation" of the labor market of the World Bank (Ribeiro 2002a; reprinted in Ribeiro 2003). As in my other publications, I avoided identifying interviewees or using sensitive information that could cause them harm. I was acting in accord with the Brazilian Association of Anthropology's code of ethics and with my own understanding that independent research must not be impeded by powerful agents, either by literally closing the doors of their institutions or by attempting to control and censor what will be written. Otherwise, independent "studying up" (Nader 1969) would never be possible.

My research on the World Bank showed that elite migrants shared with poor migrants a series of difficulties, and that both groups reverted to a repertoire of cultural items and rituals to reconstruct and maintain their identities in the new setting. Within the World Bank, for example, several ethnic associations aim to defend their members' interests and showcase their "culture" through parties featuring "ethnic" foods and musical performances. My research also showed that the World Bank is a site of production of transnational ideologies covered by the umbrella of "development" as a master discourse. Its diversified labor force is unified by the Bank's bureaucratic structure, its developmentalist mandate, and above all by the use of the English language.

Indeed, the study showed the power of the linguistically hegemonic English in the structuring of transnational social scenarios and globalized, ethnically segmented labor markets (see Ribeiro 2002a).

These research experiences in the United States reinforced my intention of developing a "postimperialist" viewpoint, a project that presupposes a global south subject position. I then wrote an essay (Ribeiro 2001, 2008b) that included, among others propositions, the need (1) to criticize North American ideascapes; (2) to do research, from a Latin American perspective, on the power centers of the world system and of the empire; and (3) to develop a critique of the central colonizing role that the American academy plays vis-à-vis the rest of the academic world system (which would later converge in a "world anthropologies project"; Ribeiro and Escobar 2006).

BACK TO BRAZIL 2

When I returned to the University of Brasília in 1998, I started a new line of research that I would later call "other globalizations" (Ribeiro 2006c; see also Ribeiro 2009a). I have been working with students ever since on the ramifications of this broad project. They include (1) the study of alternative transnational political elites in mega/global rituals of integration, such as the World Social Forum, and in the field of international cooperation; (2) the study of economic globalization from below (e.g., the trade in global gadgets and "smuggled" goods on a global level and the system it makes up, which I have dubbed a "nonhegemonic world system"); and (3), in a somewhat different vein (because it does not depend on ethnographic methods for its study), the world anthropologies project, motivated by the goal of promoting a more heteroglossic and egalitarian transnational community of anthropologists (see, e.g., Ribeiro 2006c).

As the decades pass, my growing involvement in the politics and management of academia and of anthropology has coincided with a lack of time to do ethnographic fieldwork. But that does not mean my research curiosity has diminished. In reality, it has kept on growing. I now contemplate a project comparing the roles of Ciudad del Este (Paraguay), Panama City, Dubai, and Hong Kong in the structuring of the nonhegemonic world system. In brief visits to these cities, I realized their centrality to the enhancement of the conceptual framework I am currently developing. Maybe I will not be able to do the related ethnographies myself—maybe I will be able to convince Brazilian graduate students to do the fieldwork. In this case, I will keep my passion for ethnography alive through their eyes.

THREE

Field and Home, Self and Memory in Papua New Guinea and California

Maria Lepowsky

One hot August morning, seizing a couple of hours before my mother's hospice nurse arrives, I walk out the door of my parents' tiny apartment, up the arroyo cut by Aliso Creek. I quickly pass an immense, white-barked, heavy-limbed California sycamore. Beneath it is a flat-topped granite boulder—my office—where I sit and write, feet dangling toward the stony creek, a small white egret with large yellow feet picking at the shallows nearby. Just up the hill, another granite boulder, set upright next to the paved path, bears a bronze plaque placed by the local DAR chapter that explains helpfully to elderly exercise walkers, "This Aliso (Sycamore) Was Probably 50 Years Old When the Pilgrims Landed in 1620."

I'm headed farther upstream. I pass the guard shack, staffed by an unarmed retiree, cross Paseo de Valencia, and pick up the dirt road that winds above the creek. Nineteen-eighties-vintage tract houses, painted a uniform off-white, line the tops of the arroyo on both sides. I'm carrying a large hardcover book, a copy of *Chinigchinich*, written around 1825 by Father Gerónimo Boscana and annotated by anthropologist John Peabody Harrington in the 1930s. (It's rare now, selling for $600 online, if you can find a copy.) I peer at Harrington's obsessively detailed notes, particularly his directions from the time he walked upcreek with Acú, the aged mission bell ringer (and shaman and doctor) from San Juan Capistrano, eight miles to the south. I retrace the steps of this odd pair along the old road, left over from when this was the Moulton Ranch. Two more egrets, hunting intently for crayfish, ignore me completely. On a bench of land to my right, Harrington reports, stand the adobe ruins of two houses from the Avila Ranch of the early 1840s. I look, but their eroded foundations are hidden from view under a dry carpet of brittle wild oats.

Dirt road and winding creek duck under the wide carriageway of Interstate 5, passing through a gloomy, echoing concrete chamber. I emerge on the other side into brilliant sunlight. Kalaupa, the double peak known to the Spanish as Santiago, Saint James's Mountain, and to my parents' neighbors as Saddleback, looms dark blue to the east. I come to an abrupt halt. I have (re)discovered the sacred spring of Nawíl. It lies, tranquil, in its grove of sycamores, still a place of respite. During a period of terrible drought, three "aged Indians" testified to Father Boscana, the female chief Coronne and her father led their people southeast from Sejat, Place of Bees. The track they followed, about four hundred years ago, is retraced by Interstate 5. Even in this blistering, global-warming summer, the spring water of Nawíl bubbles freely from a cleft in the rock, surrounded by a lush clump of Woodwardia ferns. Traffic on the interstate thunders north, almost overhead. Another bronze plaque—this one placed by the local Latter Day Saints Ward—commemorates the exact date in 1846 that the Mormon Battalion camped overnight by the spring during the Mexican-American War. There is no one in sight.

Nawíl was a resting place on California's main coastal path for thousands of years. The interstate lies on top of El Camino Real, the King's Highway, which in turn follows the region's longest, most important indigenous trade route. But I had never understood until this moment why the track, the Camino Real, and the interstate all passed alongside this exact spot. All three routes link together the most reliable year-round springs and water sources up and down California's Coast Range valleys.

My faculty position is in a distant American state. My current ethnographic research returns me, physically and emotionally, to the region where I grew up, to landscapes imbued with my childhood memories. The process of doing this research activates multiple, situational strands of personal identity. I am at home in the place where I helped care for my dying mother, the place where my father still lives, the place to which my sister finally came home.

The apartment my parents found, when they retired and moved south from Hollywood, sits on a high bank of Aliso Creek. It perches directly above the ethnolinguistic boundary that Alfred Kroeber drew in 1925 (based, again, on the counsel of old Acú, the mission bell ringer and shaman from San Juan Capistrano) between Gabrielinos to the north and Juaneños to the south. Their descendants prefer today to be called Tongva and Acjachemen, respectively. The Acjachemen named the creek, as did the Spanish, centuries later, for the sycamores that dot its banks.

Strands of personal and intellectual biography are woven more visibly into ethnographic research projects than they are those of other disciplines, paralleling the complicated, variable interweaving of participation and observation of our principal research method. Our initial choices of setting and topic connect directly to our senses of self as beginning scholars. A long, first-fieldwork immersion begins to fragment, and then only partially reconstructs, our core senses of self and person.

Second, or later, projects further disarrange and fragment professional and personal identities, laying bare the false dichotomies between the two. Elements of biography, passage through life stages, lead us to newer fieldsites. These are often places we think of, however partially, as "home." We experience more recent fieldwork through the expectations and responses—not fully conscious—of our initial fieldworking personas, our selves-in-the-field. These fieldworking selves, generated by formative experiences with persons and places increasingly distant in time, are filtered through complicated layers of memory and reflection as we observe, interpret, and write. After each new research project, as at each life stage, we work to reconstruct and reintegrate ever more complex layers of experience, to make psychic sense not only of our ethnographies but of our multiple, layered selves.

A few pioneering anthropologists have reflected on the fieldworking self and its multiple relations with others, from Zora Neale Hurston ([1942] 1969) to Hortense Powdermaker (1966) and George Devereux (1967). The last few decades have featured extended anthropological conversations about the self and the fieldwork encounter: reflexive, dialogical, stressing the self's partiality, its gendered surfaces and depths, the deceptive ease of fictive kin relations. These conversations have illuminated the multiple strands of selfhood engaged in field situations and the regression, dissolution, and reconstitution of self during immersion into other ways of life with their troubling webs of meaning, their baffling expectations for interpersonal relations.[1] I've been reading, or rereading, these works lately, pondering the shifting, interpersonal negotiations of self and identity that lie at the core of fieldwork and its cross-cultural discourses, trying to make sense of my own more recent moves into contrasting realms of field experience.

Midcareer ethnographic projects are often unconstrained by geographical

---

1. Notable works include Behar (1993), Bolles (1985), Briggs (1970, [1970] 1986), Clifford and Marcus (1986), Crapanzano (1980), Frank (1985), Geertz ([1974] 1983), Golde ([1970] 1986), Kondo (1986, 1990), Kracke (1987), Marcus (1998c, 2009), McLean and Leibing (2007), Narayan (1993, 1997), Rabinow (1979), Shostak ([1981] 2000), and Stoller and Olkes (1987).

distance. No longer punctuated by the early-career need to file dissertations and get degrees, they blur boundaries of ethnographic research and personal life, home and field, to a greater extent than those of our graduate student days. This raises basic questions. What counts as fieldwork? What counts as ethnographic writing? Who is an ethnographic subject? How do you document the (partially) familiar? Where is the field? When is the research done? Can I come home now? Where is home, anyway?

Cultural anthropologists often meet skepticism when launching "second projects." Colleagues, tenure committees, funding agencies, and editors sometimes wonder if what we are doing, or planning to do, is "real anthropology." Later work is sometimes suspect—as dilettantish, unserious, merely convenient—especially if we are accommodating the demands of a current life stage, such as the needs and desires of dependent children, elderly parents, or romantic partners. Second projects are sometimes judged by our peers as lacking in intensity and depth—unless we hie ourselves off once again to some distant continent, and do so for longer than a summer break.

We have to humble ourselves to begin, almost anew, if we were not trained professionally in the literature of our new field, if it is a world region that we have not formally studied before or published on. We lose a considerable part of our expert status, networks, professional credibility. Finding research funding becomes a challenge.

We may face condescension, or rivalry, from new, interdisciplinary subsets of professional colleagues. If we are lucky, we also gain new intellectual companionship, form new friendships among the people we study and within our new scholarly circles. I've experienced all of these outcomes myself in recent years in the course of my immersion in a "second project." If we try to engage more centrally or intensively in new or different methodology—archival research, analyses of sound recordings, ethnographic film—we have to arrange our own training, often on the job. If the new project is multisited, or located in part in the disembodied, placeless electron streams of the Web or television and film, our struggles for renewed professional validation are compounded.

Still, there has been a secular change, a paradigm shift—even if only a partial one—over the last couple of generations, concerning what ethnographic research is most highly valued, what conveys the most prestige and cultural capital, what translates into academic positions and research funding. Since the antipositivist challenges of the mid-1980s "crisis of representation," social/cultural anthropology has become notorious (in social sciences, science studies, and the academy more generally) for its—our—relative lack of agreement on what constitutes high-value, original research. The issue has blown apart major departments of anthropology, generated quantifiable disagreements in peer review panels, and so on (e.g., Guetzkow et al. 2004; Marcus 1998b; Plattner, Hamilton, and Madden 1987). A notorious example is the scoring of research proposals by NSF cultural anthropology review panels, which has a wider range than in any other "scientific" field, with the same proposals scored anywhere between 1 and 5 by different reviewers. The Society for Humanistic Anthropology, sponsor of the American Anthropological Association panel for which some of the essays in this volume were originally generated, is itself an institutional response to this (partial) paradigm shift, this ongoing lack of agreement about the ethnographic project.

As George Marcus (1998d) pointed out over a decade ago, those of us who hold the (increasingly rare) privilege of a tenured academic position, garnered by successful publication of earlier research, become freer to experiment ethnographically in topic, method, and analysis. We hold the professional privilege of bending rules, often unstated, for designing, carrying out, and writing about ethnography without the fear of losing our jobs and livelihood.

Midcareer and senior anthropologists have so far tended to be the ones who essay multisited or "global" ethnographies, incorporate media or textual analyses, or do intermittent fieldwork over months or years. We are the ones who can more likely get away with conducting fieldwork "at home" while still maintaining some academic credibility. More than 50 percent of American social/cultural anthropology dissertations in recent years may be based on field research in North America (according to statistics compiled in the "Guide to Departments in Anthropology" published by the American Anthropological Association between the late 1990s and early 2000s). But it is still much harder to obtain funding, or to secure a tenure-track position, without going to another country to do research. Although this may be slowly changing, especially for researchers with an urban or transnational focus, North American scholars with North America–based dissertations seem to have a lower academic employment rate; in the United States, most AAA job listings still specify another world area.

Midcareer or senior scholars also tend to be those who foreground narrative, subjectivity, or reflexivity in their writing, yet still manage to get it published and, critically, accepted as part of their scholarly output. The issue of whether anthropologists who are even more senior to us, or our peers, find us to be scholarly enough, to be producers of "real anthropology," has already been adjudicated, based on our earlier, more conventionally written academic projects, by dissertation, tenure, promotion, and manuscript review committees.

ISLAND HOME

I started out as an anthropologist by journeying to one of the ends of the earth, a Coral Sea island a couple of hundred miles southeast of the main island of New Guinea, to carry out the kind of ethnographic research most characteristic of early modernist anthropology. In fact, after months of casting about for a site that met all of my criteria—Pacific island, never before studied, remote, matrilineal—I finally located "my" island by returning to Malinowski's map of the kula region in modernist anthropology's foundational text, *Argonauts of the Western Pacific* (1922). My type of ethnographic project—the holistic study of a small-scale, nonliterate society in a nonstrategic world area, a society never previously documented ethnographically—was decidedly out of fashion by the time I was a graduate student at Berkeley. The dominant anthropological research paradigm was by then positivist, hypothesis-testing, problem-focused. The expectation was that your research would be funded by the National Science Foundation, or by an area studies–based grant tied to a part of the world relevant to Cold War–era government priorities. This largely meant, in practice, Southeast Asia or Latin America, and definitely not the Pacific Islands, which had been firmly secured as an American zone of influence and military control by the battles and occupations of World War II and its aftermath.

Trying to figure out a testable hypothesis that might win me an NSF grant yet still allow me to do a holistic study of an unknown culture, I ended up surfing early swells of what retrospectively became known as second-wave feminism. I postulated that women's position in this obscure matrilineal region was high and that, if so, island women as well as men would be prominent in ceremonial and interisland exchanges cognate to kula (Lepowsky 1993).

My first research project was old-fashioned in scope, method, and setting, if not in its research topic: the dynamics of women's—and men's—lives in an egalitarian society. But it was old-fashioned in a way that turned out to have lingering prestige in the late twentieth century and into the twenty-first. It was the first study of a culturally conservative place where indigenous ways of looking at the world contrasted radically with the Euro-American mainstream. Part of a new wave, then in formation, of what became known as gender studies, my topic, coupled with an old-school research site, eventually secured me an academic position, access to publishers, and scholarly credibility.

This was the result of luck, plus ongoing Hegelian cultural synthesis—not calculation. I wasn't trying to maximize a future academic career. If I had been, I would have trained to work in a world region, such as Southeast Asia, that had an active Communist insurgency and, thus, better domestic funding streams and future hiring possibilities. (A similarly career-minded ethnographer these days would do well to study Arabic.)

Instead, I was following my own personal and intellectual inclinations. But these were embedded in the (counter-)cultural milieux I lived in, which included a contrapuntal matrix of anthropological sensibilities—romantic, antimodern, critical—that had drawn me into the discipline in the first place. My South Seas research reflected some of California's utopian and counter-cultural values as well as its distinctively Pacific senses of place, which are simultaneously geographical and emotional. I wanted to go live on a Pacific island as remote from Western influences as I could find, among people who grew and foraged and bartered for their food and sailed around on outrigger canoes. I wanted to live among people, if there were any on the planet, whose customs and philosophies didn't devalue women or valorize male aggression. What I found, and documented ethnographically in a dissertation and a book, was Vanatinai, the Motherland, one of the world's most gender-egalitarian societies (Lepowsky 1993).

Utopian, feminist ideals, and the move of publicly discussing one's subject position as researcher and author (including its unscientific, emotional dimensions), are still not fully part of the social science and humanities mainstream today. But they are far less peripheral and marginal in the "decentered" postmodernist landscapes of the twenty-first-century academy than they were in my student days. My recently completed memoir of my first ethnographic field experience in the islands was acquired by a major New York publisher (Lepowsky, in press). Over years of writing and rewriting the memoir, I've had plenty of colleagues inform me, dismissively, that I was writing "popular" anthropology. The clear subtext was that it therefore could not be taken seriously, that I was in the process of making myself into a scholarly lightweight. This professional scorn is one of long standing (see, e.g., MacClancy and McDonaugh 1996 and Gottlieb 1997, as well as Lutkehaus 2008 on Margaret Mead as media celebrity). At least these days I can confidently expect that a different, and significant, fraction of my disciplinary peers will accept this frankly subjective and autobiographical work as a kind of ethnography, a contribution to a substantial subgenre of ethnographic writing—the field memoir, which dates as far back as Frank Hamilton Cushing ([1883] 1970). The often painful experience of writing the memoir, of reliving the most intense experience of my life, has made it even more clear to me now than when I first left the islands to return to California that I will never be completely whole again, that I long ago left part of my self on Vanatinai, the island claiming me, and I it, as my home.

CALIFORNIA

I've also used my accumulated academic capital in recent years to return to an even earlier intellectual interest, to do research in the place where I grew up. I'm no longer on a global periphery but in a planetary center. My reflections on multiple ethnographic selves and layers of memory are generated by my experiences, still ongoing, of triangulating my upbringing, my island sojourns, and my (hopelessly intermingled) life and fieldwork in twenty-first-century Los Angeles and its hinterlands.

In the process of attempting to understand the cultural histories of Los Angeles's indigenous inhabitants, I've come to see that contemporary indigenous Southern Californians and I routinely cross borders of personal identity and cultural practice, including the borders of ethnographic research and political action. We are each doing different yet interwoven kinds of anthropologies at home.

California Native descendants bluntly reject the sly, subordinate-sounding anthropological role of "informant." Separately and together we have sought traces of the young Tongva shaman Toypurina and the revolt she led in 1785 against Mission San Gabriel, just east of the new pueblo of Los Angeles. Some indigenous Californians I've encountered have puzzled, as I have, over the century-old fieldnotes of Alfred Kroeber, the brilliant and erratic John Peabody Harrington, and the self-taught ethnographer and Indian activist Constance Goddard DuBois, tracking down scratchy wax cylinder recordings of sacred songs in dialects now extinct, and learning from traditionalist elders, still very much alive. (*"Ehove!"*—we are still here—as the Tongva dancers, who live a short walk from Mission San Gabriel, call out at the end of all their public performances.) Meanwhile, overlapping alliances, and sometimes competing factions, of Native descendants have been pushing for cultural and spiritual recovery and revitalization, building cases for federal recognition, and protesting desecrations of ancestral sites. These are cultural phenomena to which I'm currently bearing ethnographic witness.

In the landscapes of my childhood, my multiple adult identities as ethnographer, archival researcher, part-time resident, daughter and caregiver, friend, historic preservationist, environmental activist, Native rights advocate, and angry citizen have irrevocably blurred. My professional identities have become blurry as well. I won funding from humanities institutions to do archival research on California histories and cultural transformations years before any outside agency supported the ethnographic side of the research. My university stepped into the breach at several points and offered modest funding for ethnographic fieldwork as well as archival prospecting. (The first time I applied, though, my faculty peer interviewer, a political scientist, told me I should have applied instead for funding to go back to New Guinea. I didn't get funded during that round.) I was finally licensed to commit ethnography by the University of Wisconsin's Institutional Review Board, whose federally designated mandate is to protect the "human subjects" I might subject to anthropological research. My research was officially declared "exempt," in fact, although I am obviously far from exempt from an array of ethical, moral, and professional constraints as ethnographer and in my other, overlapping California identities.

I spent slow years getting to know people and working in the archives before trying to publish anything related to my California research. My scholarly papers and public talks, tracked on the Internet, have already begun to influence some of the revitalization movements I've been studying. That was not my original intention. Naively, I never expected that a hyperlinked ethnographic reflexivity would have an impact upon my research subject or field methods. But Web-based communications, texts, and images have since become part of my (distributed, decentralized, overlapping) ethnographic fields. By now I see this recursive dimension as an inevitable aspect of twenty-first-century participant observation in and around a world city. These engagements, both in public and off the record in the personal domain of friendship, shape my verbal, written, and visual representations (and what I leave out of them) of Southern California's largely subterranean transcultural histories.

I'm an urban anthropologist now, among other things, studying a world city as well as its coastal, mountain, and desert hinterlands. For my first California book, I'm still studying the traces of small-scale societies whose ancestral philosophies and cultural practices contrast—or in some instances, used to contrast—radically with those of Euro-Americans and other Californians. But I'm also looking at multiethnic political alliances and environmental protests, spending time with Sierra Clubbers, surfers, MeXica antigang activists, ecofeminists, and New Agers, as well as Native Californians with a wide range of social backgrounds and worldviews. I'm situating indigenous Southern California within global flows of persons, objects, and ideas, at a key nodal point on the continent, in a region where small-scale societies have been swamped and reconfigured over two and a half centuries by just these kinds of transcultural flows.

As an anthropologist officially at home, confident in my American citizenship, my self-designated right to speak out about public affairs in my home state, I write polemics, deploy my PhD to speak as a self-declared "expert," and testify at public hearings. I started at first by responding to the requests of individual Native descendants that I give testimony at City Hall in the old mission town of San Juan Capistrano. A friend also asked me to give a public talk, as community outreach and education, to submit a written statement to attach to a Draft Environmental Impact Report on a proposed development, and to write letters to the editor of local papers. Other indigenous descendants made it clear to me that using my education and cultural capital in this way was what I ought to do, and could most usefully do, as their ally and sympathizer. Doing so has helped make me, not an insider, but not a complete outsider either.

I have acted as a political advocate on my own initiative as well. When I got a "foreign researcher" visa to do anthropological work in Papua New Guinea, I had to sign a document stating that I agreed not to get involved in national politics. At Los Angeles City Hall, I went through a metal detector, took the stairs to the ornate, echoing rotunda, and saw someone I knew, Chief Anthony Morales of the Tongva–Gabrielino Mission Indians of San Gabriel. We walked in to the council chambers together, deep in conversation. I looked up to find myself sitting on a polished mahogany bench between Chief Morales and a short, bearded man, a former classmate from Hollywood High School. Each of us waited to testify against the wholesale desecration of Tongva ancestors, downstream from City Hall along Ballona Creek, the old course of the Los Angeles River. Los Angeles as urban village. My village.

I take part each year in vigils at Tongva and Acjachemen ancestral sites that are threatened by destruction. By now I see protest and advocacy, in the version of native anthropology I am enacting, as ethical, compelling, and inevitable components of participant observation, not separate or apart from it, something professional as well as personal. What I'm doing is not new. The late 1960s and early 1970s saw calls for action anthropology, activist anthropology, "studying up" (to those in power), and condemnations of political collaboration by anthropologists, with our own or foreign governments, against the interests of local people we study. That is where the AAA Code of Ethics comes from. It implies that sometimes it's unethical *not* to act in support of the interests of the communities we study against those of political officials or governments. Of course, it's never that simple. Who are the locals? What are their interests? Whose interests, exactly? In my current version of anthropology at home, I have to make my own moral judgments about how to cross and recross blurred borderlands of anthropology and advocacy. It's much easier to do this where I have a personal history, local knowledge, and the legal rights of a citizen.

Still, in the course of doing this research at home in Southern California, I've transgressed many of the core edicts and customs I learned from my anthropological elders a generation ago at Berkeley, some of whom had themselves been advocates for the rights and dignity of the people they studied. My teachers, and their teachers, who mostly traced their lineages to Boas or Malinowski as apical ancestors, had good professional reasons for passing these core edicts down to us. They told us above all to remain neutral observers in the field, to avoid being aligned with one faction over another, to stick with pure research, to publish quickly, and not to get involved in local politics.

What, then, are the implications of all these disciplinary border crossings and transgressions of hegemonic disciplinary customs in twenty-first-century anthropologies at home, like mine, for thinking about ethnographic research methods, representations, identities, values, and ethics? These are issues I continue to explore through the lens of my participant observation in controversies over several key sacred sites in Southern California.

SACRED SITES

Some outsiders can easily grasp the idea that a snowy mountain peak, a year-round spring, or a grove of ancient sycamores is sacred to an indigenous people. This kind of religious philosophy evokes the kind of all-American, nineteenth-century transcendentalist thinking that brought us John Muir, the Sierra Club, the modern conservation movement, and our national parks. (Other Americans are actively hostile to this kind of thinking, finding such a pantheistic, animist worldview deeply disturbing and, specifically, un-Christian.) But what about a vacant lot, a former rodeo ground, an abandoned orange grove edged by willows where transients sometimes drink and camp next to the interstate? What happens when someone's sacred lands underlie a world city and its relentlessly expanding exurban edges? Studying the history and politics of indigenous sacred sites in this kind of milieu raises questions that are fundamental to anthropology and history. What counts as sacred, and who has the right to say so? Whose histories will be memorialized or erased, and by whom? These contests over rights to place reveal overlays of cultural memory on landscapes of one of the world's most populous, ethnically diverse regions, long dismissed by outsiders as a country of migrants and a place without history. Taking seriously the ongoing struggles over sometimes unprepossessing stretches of earth, rock, and trees, what happens to them, and what they mean presses us to ground, remember, and valorize California histories that are largely hidden from view.

Movements to protect Southern California's indigenous sacred sites are complicated by the fact that Indians of the Los Angeles region were long ago described, and not just by Anglo settlers, as having vanished from their homelands. I know Native Californians who will never forgive Alfred Kroeber for pronouncing in 1925, in the *Handbook of California Indians*, that the Gabrielino (the Tongva) were already extinct. But they still value the painstaking detail of Kroeber's records of ancestral custom, language, and song.

The prehistoric village and ceremonial center of Puvungna is now the campus of California State University at Long Beach. Puvungna, and the Cal State campus, sit on a rounded knoll above the spreading wetlands formed by the mouth of the San Gabriel River, which drains the ten-thousand-foot snowy peaks of the range, fifty miles inland, that rims the Los Angeles Basin. The Pacific shoreline used to run just below the bluff at Puvungna, before the massive land reclamations and real estate booms of the last century pushed the sea a couple of miles to the west. Construction of the state college in the mid-twentieth century unearthed thousands of artifacts and hundreds of human remains. Puvungna's remaining grassy open spaces, marked by the mounds of six-thousand-year-old, above-ground tombs, remain under the threat of construction of new dormitories and (of all things) a strip mall, originally proposed in the 1990s by the university administration to generate revenue to replace the state support for higher education that has drastically eroded in the last two decades. Puvungna is remembered by Tongva and Acjachemen as home to Weewyot, or Wiyot, who is one of the First Beings and was their sacred chief. Much later, within the last few centuries, Puvungna was home to the newly risen god and chief Chinigchinich and the birthplace of a regional prophetic movement. Puvungna means Gathering Place. Since ancient times this regional ceremonial and trading center has drawn people across ethnolinguistic boundaries. Its sacred space is still used for ceremonies to celebrate the solstice, honor ancestors and the recent dead, and share and sing indigenous songs both old and new.

A drainage ditch for a giant project in West Los Angeles that developers call (in real estate Spanish) Playa Vista, in a place environmentalists for the last twenty years have called Ballona Wetlands, has disturbed over four hundred burials and the Tongva village of Sa'anga—which is about twenty miles up the coast from Puvungna, just north of LAX, one of the world's busiest international airports. It lies along Ballona Creek, which runs from near downtown Los Angeles to Santa Monica Bay through Culver City, not far from Sony Studios and the old MGM backlot. Sa'anga means Place of Tar, a reference to the asphaltum seeps old-time Tongva used to caulk their planked oceangoing canoes for trips across the channel to the sacred island of Pimu, twenty-two miles away. (Spanish voyagers renamed the island Catalina, after Saint Catherine, to commemorate the saint's day on which they first landed in one of its deep coves.) At Pimu's prosperous villages and hamlets the mainland Tongva exchanged asphaltum and other goods for quarried soapstone, round and pierced disks of white shell currency, abalone shell, and sea otter skins. Some island goods later circulated, via the Mohave and other inland exchange partners, as far east as the pueblos of what is now New Mexico. The islanders of Pimu were Tongva as well, speaking a different dialect, celebrated for their skills as seafarers, renowned and feared for their shamanic powers.

Sa'anga is a key place in the landscape of Southern California, one of its indigenous capitals. The hundreds of burials laid down over thousands of years continue to bear witness to this, one by one, as they have been unearthed during the construction of high-priced condos, technology office parks, and massive shopping malls. In the early 1800s the last resident Tongva were moved inland by Spanish soldiers from Sa'anga to Mission San Gabriel and to ranchos throughout the region, where they worked as laborers, often unpaid. Shortly after Mexican independence in 1821, Sa'anga (and much of West Los Angeles and Santa Monica) was granted by the governor of Alta California to the Machado family. The family has only recently sold off its last major holdings to developers. Much of the land around Sa'anga, in the spreading floodplain of Ballona Creek, remained in row crops until the 1960s. When I was a child we used to drive the two-lane road past the MGM lot, the lima bean fields, and the sprawling green hangar that housed the Spruce Goose, Howard Hughes's giant wooden airplane, to buy fresh corn and tomatoes at the Machado family's rickety wooden produce stand.

Legal systems codify dominant ideologies and customs. California statutes offer no protection to Sa'anga's ancestral remains. The 1865 California Cemeteries Act, passed not long after the wave of murderous violence, wholesale persecutions, and removals of Indian people that followed statehood in 1850, is quite specific. Six or more burials in the same location constitute a cemetery and should by law remain undisturbed—as long as the burials took place after 1850. The statute neatly excludes all indigenous Californians buried (or cremated) before their land became part of the United States, denying the sanctity of their burial grounds, reclassifying them as real property subject to sale and private ownership when duly recorded in county courthouses. The act was challenged in the early 1980s by Native activists and their allies, but they were defeated in the California Supreme Court.

Since the early 1990s, an alliance of indigenous and environmental activists has been protesting at Sa'anga and testifying to city commissions. Native descendants have led dozens of vigils, praying and singing to Tamáayawut, Earth, and other sacred beings. After an Anglo environmental activist's hunger strike, film director Steven Spielberg finally changed his mind about building his Dreamworks Studio at Playa Vista, which would have been the first major film studio built in Los Angeles in a generation. Nevertheless, construction continues on what development supporters call the last large "buildable" parcel of land in Los Angeles. Phase II of Playa Vista went before the City Council again, opponents filed a lawsuit late in 2005 to block it on environmental grounds, and the issue remains before the courts.

To the southeast, a day's march away, as the Spanish used to measure distance in their faraway province of Alta California, lies the famous Mission San Juan Capistrano. At the confluence of two creeks north of town, twenty-nine acres of coastal sage scrub and willow swamp were recently scraped and leveled. This part of coastal Southern California is recognized by federal and state officials as a biodiversity hotspot and by environmentalists as containing some of the most endangered ecosystems in the country.

The city of San Juan Capistrano finally, despite years of protest, approved the building of a large gymnasium, a performing arts complex, and a swath of football, baseball, and soccer fields, the expansion of a private, nondenominational Christian high school. The new school is named after Father Junípero Serra, founder of the Franciscan missions of Alta California, beatified by the Vatican, a candidate for sainthood—and architect of genocide to many indigenous Californians. The actual classrooms sit across the street in buildings left over from a failed office park. Virtually all the students enrolled to date are Anglos who come from suburban communities outside of San Juan Capistrano. Nobody, including me, has uttered the words "white flight" in public testimony, though development opponents did point out that the school would not serve the town, would increase traffic congestion and pollution (every student drives in, or is dropped off by a parent), and had very few "minority" students. Few could afford the yearly tuition, which is well into five figures. The school's backers promised to provide some scholarships for local students.

San Juan Capistrano is notably browner than any city in Orange County south of Santa Ana, twenty-five miles up the interstate. It has a unique mix of Acjachemen descendants, Californios whose ancestors built their adobe houses, still standing, in the 1790s or 1840s, Anglos with deep roots in the ranching days as well as newcomer suburbanites, plus a population of Mexican ancestry whose forebears came north at some point between the 1880s and last year. Saying that the majority population of the town is Spanish-surnamed fails to capture its dynamics, tensions, and alliances. Quite often, an extended family—or even a single person—could be fitted into most of these ethnic and historical categories. San Juan Capistrano also has the largest and most active—and most ethnically diverse—local history society in California.

The site of Serra High School's new athletic facilities has been known for hundreds of years as Putiidhem, the ancestral village of the Acjachemen people. There are an estimated five hundred direct living descendants of this village, which was inhabited into the 1770s. *Putiidhem* means a navel sticking out. Acjachemen today, and their ancestors in the early nineteenth century, have recognized this as referring to the navel of Coronne, the female chief who, with her widowed father, the old chief Oyaison, led her people there from Sejat after a catastrophic drought. The migrants stopped first for a generation at the sacred spring of Nawíl after her father returned home. At Putiidhem, Coronne's fertile body (the Franciscan father Gerónimo Boscana was told sometime before 1825) burst open during a great celebration (Boscana [1933] 1978). The early ethnologist John Peabody Harrington ([1933] 1978:218–20), in his meticulously documented annotations of Boscana's manuscript, notes that a prolific spring—whose name, Paal Putiidhem, means "navel spring," according to old Acú—flowed into the creek next to the village. (Boscana spelled it Putuidem and Harrington spells it phonetically.) The spring, whose waters long supplied San Juan residents, was by 1933 on the property of Aaron Buchheim, whose descendant recently sold the land to the J. Serra School for development.

Coronne's people dispersed from this navel of the land to the other historically known Acjachemen hamlets. Evidence of origins at Putiidhem comes from family stories, Franciscan baptismal and marriage records, and the surviving manuscript and correspondence of Father Boscana, who labored at Mission San Juan Capistrano from 1814 to 1826 and who documented Acjachemen customs and religious philosophy. His account was translated and published fifteen years after his death as an appendix to American resident Alfred Robinson's *Life in California* (1846). Boscana's ethnological researches are a uniquely rich record of indigenous California life in the late eighteenth and early nineteenth centuries. His manuscript corroborates both Acjachemen oral traditions and archaeological research to a remarkable degree, as I was able to testify at San Juan Capistrano's City Hall.

Putiidhem was both a year-round village and a religious center. Its soil contains ceremonial burials and cremations, as well as shamanic artifacts. These include crystals for divination, sacred pipes, and stone scrapers used during rituals in sweat lodges. They also include bone fragments from golden eagles and condors, raptors whose relics are sacred to Chinigchinich, the recently ascended spirit being and prophet from Puvungna, to the northwest in Tongva country. These objects and avian relics were essential for the ceremonies that Chinigchinich prescribed, probably in the late eighteenth century, and that spread throughout indigenous Southern California over the next 150 years (DuBois 1908; Lepowsky 2004). Archaeologists estimate there are two hundred burials beneath the soil around Putiidhem. Smaller sites, thousands of years older, lie closer to the sacred spring that still bubbles up near the creek.

At the core of the alliance opposing development at Putiidhem were Acjachemen descendants, members of two out of three competing tribal organizations. Prominent as well were environmentalists and nearby condo owners, most of them Anglos. The local chapter of the Sierra Club contributed funds and volunteers. Several local archaeologists, who formed a concerned scientists alliance with Acjachemen preservationists, wrote letters opposing the project in response to the Draft Environmental Impact Report (required by California state law), gave testimony at San Juan Capistrano City Hall, and helped file a federal lawsuit with support from the Sierra Club. A few cultural anthropologists teaching at colleges in Los Angeles and Orange County allied themselves with the preservationists as well, sending letters to local papers and contributing comments to the DEIR.

Other archaeologists (some local, some from out of state) and at least one cultural anthropologist were working under contract to developers at Putiidhem as others had been at Sa'anga, in Los Angeles, excavating the sites, writing technical reports, recommending mitigations that would allow development, and testifying in support of the developers at public hearings. In other words, there were also factions among the anthropologists.

Not all Acjachemen descendants in San Juan Capistrano opposed developing Putiidhem. The third and smallest tribal faction actively supported building the new Christian school facilities. Its leader, who has gained lucrative consulting fees and will likely continue to do so for years, has been designated by the developers as the MLD (most likely descendant), a requirement under California state law. He was thus empowered to observe construction and rebury any disturbed human remains. During a break in one of the hearings, he explained his position to me. Development was inevitable. He had been fighting it for years (as a former chief of the original tribal group, ousted some time ago in a bitter dispute). He had lost so many battles that he had given up. This time, he told me, he might as well see that the development was "done right."

The key person behind the development at Putiidhem was the owner of a Toyota dealership, located up the old road a few miles, past the In-N-Out Burger, in the next town, Laguna Niguel—named for the sacred spring Nawíl by way of the title of a nineteenth-century Mexican land grant. Rumors spread among development opponents that the whole thing was a giant tax shelter for this multimillionaire businessman, as well as a monument to his love of team sports. But prominent members of the city Cultural Heritage Commission and the San Juan Capistrano Historical Society, Anglos, Californios, and devout Catholics—San Juan Capistrano is still very much a mission town—were allied in support of expanding the private school's facilities.

"How can a vacant lot be sacred?" one leading figure demanded into the microphone in the council chambers. In the crowded lobby afterwards I overheard one older Anglo woman talking to another.

"How can they worship a bunch of old bones?"

I thought immediately of saints' relics, but wisely kept quiet.

The other woman snorted derisively. "They should just go to church."

Nearby, a white-haired man in a well-cut business suit, also Anglo, leaned in close to me, explaining emphatically and in detail why my public testimony had been mistaken on all points.

"That place was just a hunting camp—it's not sacred," he finished loudly. "Or if it is, then all the land around here is sacred!"

A stately Acjachemen woman in her fifties who was making her way past us, someone I didn't know, heard his last comment.

"Yes, all the land around here is sacred," she answered him. "But some places are more sacred than others."

So whose vision of the sacred counts as religious belief and practice in a famously conservative, militantly monotheistic region? This was Orange County, birthplace of Richard Nixon, the John Birch Society, and several of the world's largest evangelical churches (including the Crystal Cathedral, currently in bankruptcy, and the more recently founded Saddleback Church, named, ironically, after the sacred peak of Kalaupa). Orange County had for several generations been the most reliably Republican county in the United States. Still, Acjachemen descendants who championed indigenous religion and ancestral remains found plenty of allies. This was also twenty-first-century California, a birthplace of the modern environmental movement and of New Age spirituality of every sort. Southern California is also home to active and vocal civil libertarians and minority rights advocates, some of them wealthy and willing to fund political action.

Acjachemen who opposed the new development at Putiidhem organized e-mail alerts, letter writing, leafleting, talks, and public hearings, as well as protests, vigils, and ceremonies. Groups of young, self-described MeXica (Mexican indigenous activists) garbed in striking red and black T-shirts, led by veteran pro-Aztlán activists now doing antigang, cultural empowerment work, came down in support from Santa Ana and the majority Latino cities of southeastern LA County. They performed songs and dances of Mexico's *indigenas* by the side of the old two-lane road that runs between Putiidhem and the creek. Native Americans from elsewhere in California and across the United States prayed too, offering songs and protesting at the chain-link fence that encircled the site. A year later it was still festooned with sun-faded prayer ribbons and bundles of sacred tobacco. Putiidhem became a stop on the annual Honor the Ancestors pilgrimage, led by Acjachemen descendants, in which a hundred people, Native Californians and their diverse allies, hold vigils, pray, and sing at threatened sacred sites (Lepowsky n.d.).

Toward the end of the hearing process, a few recent Mexican immigrants from a huge nearby low-income apartment complex came to testify at City Hall. Speaking in Spanish, with a friend interpreting, they declared that they too were *indigenas* of the Americas, that it was important not to disturb the land. In the final hearing, several Anglos and Latinos testified that they had opposed development to protect sensitive wetlands and open space (the environmentalists) or because of increased traffic and noise (the condo owners). But they had learned, each of them said, in slightly different words, that honoring and protecting this ancestral Acjachemen sacred place was the most important reason to preserve it.

"This is all of our history," one of them testified. "This is all of our California."

The Acjachemen, the Tongva, and their indigenous allies made precisely the same point.

Epic winter rains mired the earth-moving equipment at Putiidhem in deep mud. The ancestors were angry that their resting place was being disturbed, one of my Acjachemen friends said. The City of San Juan Capistrano, in approving the new development, made some minor concessions. The developers had to forego the tennis courts, avoid building on already identified burial sites, and include a one-hundred-square-foot memorial (in the athletic complex, on private land not accessible to the public) featuring a plaque and a bronze sculpture of the female chief Coronne by a Native Californian sculptor who lives in San Diego. When I drove by recently, Anglo kids in shorts and numbered jerseys were playing soccer between the new buildings on a grassy field that now overlies Acjachemen ancestral remains. I've heard several times from indigenous descendants who opposed the private school expansion that additional human remains and grave goods were uncovered during the new construction and privately reburied in a secret location, under the supervision of the leader of the small prodevelopment tribal faction.

CALIFORNIA SEMI-NATIVE

I'm neither a California Native (with a capital *n*—a descendant of indigenous inhabitants with thousands of years of history in the state) nor a California native (with a lowercase *n*—simply born in the state). I'm a California semi-native. This phrase, which I've appropriated as the title of one of my book projects, comes from a bumper sticker I used to see around. It seems perfect for Southern California. The phrase is multivocal, satirizing the nativist, xenophobic, potentially racist implications of California Native (a much more common bumper sticker and T-shirt slogan, one sported by Anglo residents and less often by indigenous Californians). Yet each phrase simultaneously claims California with pride as home, as a site of personal and collective memory.

My family moved to Los Angeles from New York City when I was four years and one day old, after my father was blacklisted during the McCarthy era and fired from his job as a teacher in the New York City schools. We came west looking for a new start, like so many others before and after us. I remember the lima bean fields where the San Diego Freeway is now, and coastal valleys and uplands carpeted in gold poppies under the snowy front range of the San Gabriel Mountains. I remember when we drove down to San Juan Capistrano and on the way saw the Matterhorn at Disneyland, topped with fake snow, under construction, just before the freeway turned into a eucalyptus-lined road through seemingly endless orange groves.

The climate was drier then. "It's a dry heat," people used to say when the Santa Ana winds blew down the mountain passes and the temperature rose toward a hundred degrees. They said it so often that it remains a local in-joke today. There was less evaporation from fewer lawns and golf courses, swimming pools and air conditioners. I remember grunion runs, Pismo clams, late-night driftwood fires on the beach. I also remember the sky to the south lit up by flames the hot August night the Watts riots started. I remember the old lady down the street in Hollywood correcting Yolanda and me—"Don't say Mexican, say Spanish. It's more polite"—even though Yolanda's parents came from Mexico. I remember the coyote that ran alongside the runway on the grass at the Los Angeles airport, mouth open, tongue out, when my one-way flight to college in Berkeley took off toward the ocean.

I went to elementary school on Sunset Boulevard in a neighborhood so tragically hip in recent years that it's now sometimes declared "over." I remember my fourth-grade teacher at Micheltorena Street School (named after an unpopular 1840s Mexican governor of California) telling us that California Indians were so lazy and ignorant, they didn't even know how to plant crops; they just dug their food out of the ground. And that's why, she said, we call them the Digger Indians. I remember telling this to my father, because it didn't sound right to me even at age nine. I remember that he got angry, although not at me. The next weekend we drove our secondhand '48 Dodge to the Southwest Museum of the American Indian, LA's oldest museum. You enter through a long dark tunnel, lined with miniature dioramas, built in the side of a steep, dry hill. I was especially taken with the one of life beside the Los Angeles River. We saw baskets with zigzag designs woven so tightly they could hold water. That's where I bought my first book, a paperbound copy of *California's Gabrielino Indians* (1963), by Bernice Johnston, for three dollars. I'm still reading that same copy, its pages yellowed by decades of Los Angeles smog. That's where I first decided I wanted to be an anthropologist. Now I'm guest-curating an exhibit at the Southwest Museum, based on my research on the shaman Toypurina and her cultural legacies, including movements to protect indigenous sacred sites. The museum itself has a new incarnation, merged with the Museum of the American West, founded by cowboy star and multimillionaire Gene Autry.

All of this is part of my idiosyncratic version of (semi-)native anthropology in Southern California, where I'm studying not only indigenous Californians but the people who have moved onto their lands over more than two centuries. A translucent film of remembered cultural nuance, regional and personal history, and, critically, memories of fieldwork in the outer islands of the Pacific filter my understandings of recent experiences in the field "at home." When I discovered, in the archives of the Huntington Library, an account of Toypurina, a Tongva woman in her twenties, a shaman, a person who, her neighbors testified, had the power to kill just by thinking of it, who inspired and helped lead a revolt against the Spanish at Mission San Gabriel in 1785, it sounded strangely familiar to me. I thought immediately of the magical powers and the

ritual violence against colonial forces that characterize the cargoistic philosophies and histories of my former island neighbors on Vanatinai.[2]

There are major differences, obviously, between these two cultural regions
and their inhabitants' responses to colonial hegemonies, but I inevitably see
the second I encountered as an anthropologist through a lens ground by
my long experience with the first. I try to take that into account as I think
about Native California and the California frontier. I value the unique insights
granted me by a previous long residence with islanders whose elders, most
now long dead, mistook me for an ancestor spirit and who attributed to me, in
spite of my denials, all kinds of magical powers that I (unfortunately) do not
possess. I also work quite self-consciously not to think about, or represent,
ancestral Tongva and Acjachemen as some kind of mainland, California version of the islanders of Vanatinai. Nevertheless, the personal resonances for
me of Toypurina's story, because of my earlier fieldwork on the far side of the
Pacific, have meant that she has taken over the book I'd originally intended to
write about indigenous California landscapes, early encounters on the California frontier, and the history and politics of sacred sites in Southern California. My book in progress is now framed around the shaman Toypurina and
her cultural legacies.

ANTHROPOLOGICAL SELVES AT HOME

My childhood attachments to the landscapes of Southern California, their
deep emotional meanings to me, will never make me an indigenous Californian. But they do give me certain kinds of insights: historical, cultural, personal. They also give me the confidence to speak out as citizen and anthropologist in support of what I, and the people I've been spending the most time
with, view as social and environmental justice. The dominant mid-twentieth-
century modernist ideal of an objective, detached, ideologically neutral
ethnography that does not alter the community under study has in recent
decades become progressively harder to square either with current anthropological theory or the messy pragmatics of fieldwork. This is especially visible

2. Classic accounts of Melanesian cargo cults and cargoistic philosophies include Williams
([1939] 1977) and Worsley ([1957] 1968). See Lepowsky (2004) on cargoistic movements on
Vanatinai and nearby islands, and on my own unwitting involvement in them. I also document
the deep regional histories and continuities among Melanesian cargoistic movements, including those in the Vanatinai region, and contrast them with indigenous revolts and ritual violence
on the California frontier.

in the writings and conversations of younger cohorts and scholars who are non-European or members of racial/ethnic minorities. Most anthropologists have by now acknowledged the discipline's origins in, and sometime collaboration with, colonialism and imperialism, including the internal colonialism of Euro-American expansion and settlement. Those of us who are Americans tend to be aware of the aura of power, wealth, arrogance, and desire that our nationality confers. Many ethnographers face the relative poverty and powerlessness of hosts; initial suspicion or heightened deference; requests for blue jeans, watches, school fees, or intercession with local officials. We notice our small, often inadvertent, cumulative influences over young people's dress, speech, aspirations, or selective resistance to local customs.

Popular, or accessibly written, ethnographic findings, visible in modernist anthropology since the 1920s heyday of Malinowski and Mead, had increasingly lost favor by midcentury as social and cultural anthropology adopted a more scientistic model of research design, funding, and reportage. More recent countertrends, growing in influence, of a reflexive or a politically engaged anthropology arose as responses to the positivist and objectivist direction of the anthropological mainstream (Lepowsky 2011; cf. di Leonardo 1998; Lutkehaus 1995; MacClancy 2002). We have seen the increasing influence over the last three decades of initially separate, later merging streams of anthropological thinking about disciplinary knowledge-making and authority, reflexivity, gender, and subjectivity. Many of us now routinely acknowledge that we write from a particular subject position as unique, although culturally shaped, persons; that we engage our ethnographic consultants at particular junctures in their, and our, histories. We often feel obliged to describe these intersections in our books and articles, if briefly.

Still, the ideal of objective research (the most hegemonic of the models of ethnographic practice and analysis I was socialized into at Berkeley) continues to exert powerful influences. Adam Kuper (1994, 1995), Roy D'Andrade (1995), and others champion objectivist research, arguing that our research findings should be written mainly for other anthropologists. This position can be counterposed against the insistence of Nancy Scheper-Hughes (2005), for example, that the "primacy of the ethical" means anthropologists have a "responsibility to be public intellectuals" and to act as advocates for the people we study. Scheper-Hughes (2004) argues not just for an "engaged" but an "enraged" anthropology, on behalf of the exploited and the powerless.

But "pure research" still has a far higher prestige value than applied. It is dramatically more likely to win a younger scholar an academic position, a major research grant, and tenure. Assistant professors and graduate students who engage in public advocacy on behalf of their research communities are still warned by senior colleagues that they are "anthropologists, not social workers." It's far more difficult to get an article about social policy, cultural advocacy, environmentalism, or applied research published in the most prestigious anthropological journals.

Yet the research and writings of some of the most influential contemporary anthropologists, such as Scheper-Hughes and Paul Farmer (e.g., 2001, 2003), directly address social injustices and seek to effect change and influence international public opinion. The University of California Press has in recent years launched a series of books on "Public Anthropology," addressing anthropological ethics and engagements with host communities. Anthropologists whose research on cultural minorities living within nation-states of the global south is widely admired, such as Terence Turner on the Kayapó of Brazil and Sharon Hutchinson on the Nuer of Sudan, are internationally visible as advocates for the political and cultural rights of their ethnographic subjects.

Leaders of the American Anthropological Association, openly concerned about anthropologists' relative invisibility as opinion-shapers, offer to send us to media boot camp to learn how to talk to reporters or write an effective op-ed piece for our local newspapers. The AAA now encourages us to write press releases about our research and offers to hook us up, at the annual meetings, with curious journalists and editorial writers.

Of course American anthropologists have used ethnographies to address American social problems and influence public opinion since Lewis Henry Morgan advocated for the Iroquois in the mid-nineteenth century and Franz Boas wrote against racism and ethnic prejudice in the early twentieth. Anthropologists have been doing ethnographies in their hometowns since at least 1927, when Zora Neale Hurston drove back down to Eatonville, Florida, from Columbia University, and Ella Deloria took the train back to Standing Rock reservation in South Dakota.

Our sociologist colleagues have a tradition as well, almost a century old, of combining ethnographic research in American subcultures with advocacy and political critique. This is most visible in the work of Chicago School urban sociologists and their present-day intellectual descendants (e.g., Anderson 1923; Duneier 1994, 1999; Zorbaugh 1929). Katz (2006) makes a case that this intellectual tradition of ethnographic sociology among, and advocacy for, marginalized groups in one's own society (virtually as old as sociology itself) is currently endangered, driven largely underground through prior restraints on speech and research imposed by university institutional review boards, as mandated, or so they maintain, by federal statutes. Anthropologists, too, face intensified surveillance by university administrators and faculty committees who mistrust the imprecision and lack of objectivity of ethnographic methods and research designs. As a direct result, they sometimes question our professional ethics (cf. Bradburd 2006; Lederman 2006).

The climate in which anthropologists do research, in the global south and among minority subcultures in metropolitan countries, is still marked by suspicion of our motives, allegiances, and power. Many of us, for intellectual, political, and personal reasons, turn our anthropological attentions to our own societies. But the disciplinary prestige of anthropology at home remains lower, research funding and academic positions harder to obtain.

The question of who or what is a native anthropologist has been elegantly addressed by Kirin Narayan (1993), who points out that we all, as persons, have multiple strands of identity. We and those we study activate or recognize relational strands of identity in ways that shift and transform with flows of interpersonal dynamic and social situation. Those we hope to study, our would-be consultants and interlocutors, may deny or reject the strands of common identity or allegiance we proffer, whether of co-residence, nationality, gender, or political sympathy. It remains easy for the more privileged (the educated, the wealthier, the lighter-skinned) to imagine, to project social and emotional ties with the marginalized, who may not want our sympathy and may actively resist our identification with them.

Self-delusion is a constant methodological and ethical danger in studying people whom you think of as part your own community, or even your own country. Who has the right to speak, either for them or about them, after all? I recall in this connection a major reason that I did not do dissertation research under the live oaks of a back-country California ranchería: the time a delegation from the American Indian Movement, then protesting federal policies by occupying the former prison island of Alcatraz in San Francisco Bay, accepted Professor William Simmons's invitation to address his undergraduate lecture class Anthro 155, Indians of North America. Taking a small boat to the Berkeley Marina (successfully eluding the FBI), they arrived in Dwinelle Hall in full regalia, where Russell Means (I believe it was) exhorted us all to stop exploiting American Indians and get out of anthropology immediately. The point of view, widespread in Indian Country, that anthropologists are visible and essential tools of government oppression and chicanery was eloquently expressed in the writings of the late Vine Deloria Jr., nephew to Boasian anthropologist Ella Deloria (e.g., 1969; cf. Biolsi and Zimmerman 1997).

I took their point to the extent that I did not train to do ethnographic research in Native California. But I didn't agree enough to get out of anthropology. Instead I groped my undergraduate way toward the conclusion that some of my indigenous Californian friends succinctly express these days as "There are good ones [anthropologists and archaeologists] and bad ones." The AIM delegation's visit helped shape my goal of becoming one of the "good ones."

When we do some version of anthropology at home, we face much more starkly than when we do research elsewhere the problem of formally distinguishing ethnographic work from the rest of our lives. This is plain when we try to justify and explain research to, or avoid scrutiny from, our university's institutional review boards (Lederman 2006). It is also plain when we try to explain our research design and methods in applying for funding. These are not venues where we want to foreground our partisan actions as citizens, advocates, or protestors. But when we work in our own society, turn our attention and training toward categories of persons co-resident in the country where we hold citizenship, the community in which we live, how can we separate out our interactions as citizens and neighbors from our ethnographies? Do we have to? Who says so? Our disciplinary peers, funding agencies, manuscript reviewers, IRB committees?

What counts as home? And who gets to say? These are classic questions for the ethnographer. They can also be explosive and divisive: home is an emotionally, ethnographically, and politically loaded concept. What can the process and practice of doing ethnography at home in the United States during these uneasy first decades of the new millennium reveal about the state of anthropological methods and philosophies of research, and about where our profession is going? What business is it of mine to intervene in a local political dispute, and to take the side of one faction (two, really) of Native Californians against another? What gives me the right? Who do I think I am? This is the fundamental question. What kind of anthropologist does this make me?

I am, again, activating multiple and situational strands of identity, at home in the region where I grew up, where I live part of the time, where I cared in these last years for my dying mother, where my father still lives, the place my sister came home to. I have the rights of a a citizen. I was taught, in Los Angeles public schools, that we Americans should participate in civic life, educate ourselves about public issues, and vote. I have a right to speak out without getting thrown out of the country and having my research permit revoked, which I didn't have as a foreign researcher in Papua New Guinea. Here, in theory at least, I'm protected by First Amendment rights of freedom of speech and freedom of assembly.

I grew up in this part of the country. I have seen much of coastal California paved over in my lifetime, oaks cut down, poppy fields decimated, strawber-ries fields replaced with giant malls and SUV dealerships, coastal strands lined with trophy houses. The Cattle on a Thousand Hills—the evocative title of a classic local history book (Cleland 1941), derived from a biblical phrase—have been replaced in my lifetime by the condos on a thousand hills. My own ancestors are buried in Kiev and the obliterated shtetls of Ukraine and Lithu-ania, places I have never seen. I feel a deep identification, a kinship, with the desecrated remains of ancestral Tongva, brutally dislodged by bulldozers from their resting places under the ground where the Machado bean fields once ran, under the Westchester bluffs, during my own Los Angeles childhood. I am distressed, and angry, when developers try to ram a toll road through a state park in one of the few remaining undeveloped valleys on the Southern California coast, dooming the steelhead trout run in San Mateo Creek, and ruining a famous surfing beach under sandstone cliffs at San Clemente, a place we used to drive down to during my high school years. Construction of the toll road would uncover the remains of my Acjachemen friends' direct ancestors, as documented by Franciscan missionary genealogies, at the ancient village of Panhe.

I have taken sides, in this anthropology at home, when I've seen a compel-ling moral and ethical reason to do so. Yet I still feel a professional reluctance to ally myself with one side again another. So far I've managed, with some effort, to maintain cordial relations with key members of the several factions of Tongva in Los Angeles (even when one brought suit against another in federal court) and with members of all the Acjachemen factions (even though I testified against the position of the smallest group at San Juan Capistrano City Hall). I make an effort to understand and report the prodevelopment point of view in my writing. This is cultural relativism, good ethnography, and basic human courtesy. I'm unlikely to die of poison, sorcery, or violence because I've aligned myself with one faction or another.

But there are personal and anthropological costs. People I respected, whom I wanted to continue working with, supported the new development at San Juan Capistrano and were unhappy to see me testifying and giving public talks for the other side. I had to work to repair and maintain friendly relations with several people who were, to use the phrase of an early anthropological era, key informants. One was the head of the local historical society, widely known around town as El Presidente. He had invited me to join the historical society, hosted me with notable cheer at Rancho Mission Viejo barbeques and society fundraisers, spoke at length with me about his family history, and once tried to set me up with his unmarried cousin (the cousin and I politely declined). El Presidente was a descendant of Spanish soldiers who arrived in Alta California in 1769, of the sister of a Mexican governor of California, an Englishman, and an Acjachemen great-great- (etc.) grandmother. But he and I, it turned out, had very different ideas about what counts as history.

Many Acjachemen and Tongva descendants have their own ethnographic projects: to recover knowledge about ancestral cultural practices, villages sites, sacred songs, and sacred places. Some have asked that I help them locate and repatriate songs and indigenous knowledge recorded by earlier anthropologists. They use aspects of my work to augment their own, to revive ceremonials, relearn crafts and names of places, and press claims for federal recognition. Descendants do their own anthropologies at home with elders, archives, and the Internet in order to practice spiritual healing: of the land, plants, animals, the sick, alcoholics, children who don't know their heritage. It's terribly important, they say, to learn the names of things and places. The Internet is a great (although highly imperfect) leveler in standing in for aspects of higher education and professional training, helping Native descendants locate resources, people, documents, genealogies. Yet anthropologists and archaeologists can be useful allies—if we don't go to work for the other side. We have expert knowledge of earlier ethnographic writings and where to find them, research skills, and the status, credentials, and entrée of a person with an anthropology PhD. It's not as difficult for us to locate, contextualize, and translate Kroeber's or Harrington's or DuBois's fieldnotes into plain English.

Contemporary Native Californians tend to take a more nuanced, pragmatic view of anthropology than that AIM delegation at Berkeley did a generation ago. We have our uses as researchers and strategic allies. Knowing that they'll be reading what we write, which is now virtually immediately via the Web (cf. Brettell 1996), challenges us both ethically and intellectually. It presses us to be aware of our work's potential and conflicting meanings and uses, now and in the future, to the people we study, their descendants, and outsiders or institutions using it for their own ends. We can use our professional, "expert" status to testify to the powerful, and maybe they will listen. Or maybe not. Our books, research reports, museum exhibits, and films can communicate basic messages on behalf of the people we study: we are (still) here, we and our cultural beliefs and practices are worthy of respect, we hold this land as sacred, and we want our rights.

In an appropriately postmodern irony, the kind of globally framed, multiethnic, multisited, (partially) urban research I am doing in California now seems to be more highly valued in anthropology, and in the broader transdisciplinary domain of cultural studies, than studying custom in small hamlets on remote islands (cf. Marcus 1998d, 2009). Some of my more recently PhD'd colleagues from around the globe, who've done ethnographic studies in the Pacific Islands, are still struggling to find long-term academic positions.

My latest research combines and reflects both longtime personal interests and the contemporary zeitgeist: Native shamanism, California landscapes, hometown Hollywood—but also globalization and its discontents, transnational media flows and celebrity fetishism, environmentalism and planetary crisis, yearnings for heroic figures among women and people of color, multiethnic quests for "authentic" spirituality. All of these are far more widespread, and mainstream, fixations, fears, and desires than when I first encountered each of them in my own youth in 1960s California.

Fieldwork on and in Southern California—personified indigenously as Tamáayawut, Earth, female First Being—is a return to my earliest anthropological fascination, from both my childhood in Los Angeles and my undergraduate years. As with my fieldwork in the islands, this project returns me to one of modernist anthropology's first fields of study, a legacy this time around of American internal colonialism rather than British imperialism. I perceive and write about California today through multiple filters of memory laid down by my earlier selves. Being in the field evokes, simultaneously, my childhood ties and my anthropological training at Berkeley, from freshman to PhD, studying with, among others, Alfred Kroeber's students. I'm now reading, analyzing, and writing about Kroeber's carefully archived California fieldnotes. Berkeley, Cal, Kroeber Hall, is the place where I first found "my" South Sea island on Malinowski's hand-drawn map of the kula ring.

My ethnographic field in Southern California is fractured, multiple, discontinuous, encompassing modest postwar tract houses and sacred sites in remote canyons, the revolt against Mission San Gabriel led by a young female shaman, and the Honor the Ancestors Walk this past season. My sense of a fieldworking self is fractured as well. Native Californians and I routinely cross borders of personal identity and cultural practice, doing very different, yet interwoven, anthropologies at home. In these landscapes of my childhood, and theirs, my personal and professional identities continues to blur.

A long-time colleague, senior to me, who began research in Papua New Guinea some years earlier than I did, asked me at the AAA meeting whether I'd given a paper, and what it was on. Second projects, I said. Beginning research midcareer in a new field, California. He smiled pleasantly at me.

"Traitor."

I feel I have to defend myself to my Pacific colleagues, and to myself, to explain that I'm still working on my Pacific material; that I haven't abandoned it, or them; that I'll return to the islands when my family situation and elder care responsibilities have changed; that I have written a memoir and I'm working on another book, an anthropological history of the Coral and Solomon Seas.

In my California project, I have managed once again to choose an orphaned geographical and ethnographic area, Native North America—orphaned, that is, in terms of funding possibilities and area studies institutional support, perhaps even more so than the Pacific Islands. Indians were brought, forcibly, under American government control several generations ago, if not longer.

I have chosen not to write about whole domains of what I initially thought of as ethnography, as participant observation, including in this chapter, because the friendships I've been lucky enough to grow into mean that I've become the guardian of my friends' privacy. I don't want to sacrifice friendship because of my ethnographic material, no matter how remarkable.

I have kept people's secrets in the islands, too, plenty of them, and cherished friendships with islanders. But I find it harder to separate out the academic and the off-limits when the ethnographic enterprise includes mutual visits to my own elderly parents and to theirs, when the research and the friendship go on over the course of many years, at home. The personal and professional have overlapped far more than I expected when I began this project.

Even in the twenty-first century it can take weeks to get to the outer islands in the Coral Sea. There are no scheduled planes (or boats), no Internet, no cell towers, no cars or trucks, only canoes and narrow tracks through forest and swamp. (Since I know where to look, these days I can trace some of these paths, faintly, on Google Earth.) Most of the islanders remain nonliterate, without access to air letters or bird of paradise airmail stamps or the spare coins to buy them with. Leaving the island after a stint of fieldwork was always a clear punctuation mark.

There will never be such clear punctuation to my California research. My understanding will, as with all ethnographic fieldwork, remain partial, situated, fragmentary. It will be harder to attribute this to practical circumstances. Thanks to webs of transport and communication, I can fly to Los Angeles for a long weekend to attend a ceremony or political vigil, walk on the beach at San Clemente while discussing repatriating sacred songs recorded by Kroeber on wax cylinders, prospect in yet another collection of objects or documents at the Southwest Museum or the Huntington Library. I sometimes hear about a bear ceremony by way of e-mail or a website.

When, exactly, will I be ready to finish a book manuscript? When is an ethnographic study complete? When is this research project going to be done? (Alma Gottlieb and Virginia Dominguez pose similar questions in their chapters in this volume.) Where are the borders to the field this time? And does this matter? After all, I am placing borders and contact zones, their fuzziness and cultural ferment, at the metaphorical center of this research. Doing ethnography on an island was hard enough, despite the neat stereotype of beaches as boundaries. My island neighbors tended to depart without notice for the other side of the island, or sail off to other parts of the archipelago for weeks, to attend feasts or search for kula necklaces and stone axe blades. Kroeber himself used to say that an anthropologist should spend a full year in the field so that he (the pronouns then were invariably masculine) could observe the full round of life, the changing of the seasons—or so I was told by one of his students. (Of course, Kroeber rarely did this himself, nor did his students, at least in the early decades of the twentieth century.) I am by now many years past Kroeber's full round of life/one-year mark. But how can I judge the endpoint of my California fieldwork when I'm not sure what counted as its starting point? Doing it full-time while on research leave? Writing fieldnotes? Being funded?

Doing research at home in California shatters disciplinary illusions of methodological coherence and ethnographic completeness that I hadn't realized I still shared. My current, more open-ended, indeterminate ethnographic and historical research is set in a region simultaneously familiar and strange, dramatically changed since my childhood. It is a landscape almost unimaginably altered since 1769, when the Anza Expedition, fresh from their first encounters with the Acjachemen, traversed the northern reaches of their country, stopping for the night by the spring Nawíl, on the banks of a sycamore-lined creek a few miles from the ocean. The kind of ethnography I'm doing now more closely approximates the messy, unbounded realities of human cultural life, its endless transformations from one generation to the next. Sensing my own, partially recovered layers of self and memory leads me to reflect on the far deeper, more numerous layers of cultural and historical memory, tied to place and homeland, that I am writing about.

My father, then ninety, put a red, black, and white "Stop J Serra, Save Putiidhem" bumper sticker on his Cutlass Ciera shortly before he decided to stop driving. My sister has joined me on the annual Honor the Ancestors Walk, which ends at the sacred site of Puvungna, on a knoll near the mouth of the San Gabriel River. She went back to school a few years ago to work on a science education teaching credential. We both call her new alma mater, located on that same coastal knoll, Cal State Puvungna.

When I lived in the islands, I used to dream, repeatedly, yet always unexpectedly, of Los Angeles. I hadn't lived there, at that point, in years, since I left for Berkeley as a freshman. But in the islands I used to see, night after night, the darkened silhouette of the Hollywood Hills against the sky, a faithful dream image of the view to the north out the window of the bedroom my sister and I once shared. Now I see life on Tamáayawut through layers of island memories: how mountain peaks and ancient groves have names, powers, and spirit identities; how shamans heal or afflict; what people were thinking when Europeans first appeared on the land. My perceptions of present-day Los Angeles and its hinterlands, street grids, buildings, neighborhoods, canyons, beaches, and transverse mountain ranges overlay imagined, indigenous sacred landscapes of Southern California. These are in turn refracted for me through lingering traces of childhood and adolescent dramas, memories tagged to specific places. I am not fully conscious of them. They come back to me gradually, in a rush of sensation, as I move along Hollywood backstreets and dry-season mountain trails, attend ceremonies downcoast, walk the Southwest Museum's high, dim halls, share a Salvadoran lunch with a Native leader in a Figueroa Street café, catch the scent of sage along the arroyo after the first rain.

ACKNOWLEDGMENTS

Research in and on Papua New Guinea has been funded by the National Science Foundation, the Chancellor's Patent Fund of the University of California, Berkeley, the National Institute of Child Health and Human Development of the National Institutes of Health, the Wenner-Gren Foundation for Anthropological Research, the American Philosophical Society, the American Council of Learned Societies, and the Graduate School of the University of Wisconsin, Madison. Research in and on California has been funded by an Andrew W. Mellon Fellowship held at the Henry E. Huntington Library; Dora and Randolph Haynes Foundation grants distributed by the Historical Society of Southern California; the Autry National Center for the Study of the American West; the Wenner-Gren Foundation for Anthropological Research; a Henry Vilas Associate Professorship and a Vilas Trust award, held at the University of Wisconsin, Madison; and the Graduate School of the University of Wisconsin, Madison. I am deeply grateful for all of this financial support over many years.

I thank Kirin Narayan for her insightful comments on earlier drafts. Sections of early drafts of the larger work from which this chapter is drawn were first presented in 2005 at the American Ethnological Society annual meeting, San Diego, California; the 2005 American Anthropological Association annual meeting, Washington, DC; and in 2006 at an invited lecture at the University of Illinois, Urbana-Champaign. I thank Rena Lederman, Alma Gottlieb, and members of each audience for their comments. Parts of an early draft of this chapter were presented in 2007 at the American Anthropological Association annual meeting, Washington, DC, in the session "Should I Stay or Should I Go? The Challenges—and Pleasures—of Switching Field Sites." I again thank Alma Gottlieb, as well as other session participants and contributors to this volume, for their valuable comments and suggestions. Special thanks to Rebecca Robles, Rhonda Robles, Louis Robles Sr., Louis Robles Jr., Chief Anthony Morales, Andrew Morales, Cindi Alvitre, Craig Torres, Chief Dee Dominguez, and the late Juan Antonio (Tony) Forster for their insights and generosity.

FOUR

Two Visions of Africa: Reflections on Fieldwork in an "Animist Bush" and in an Urban Diaspora

Alma Gottlieb

OPENING THOUGHTS

The silver sedan screeched to a stop inches before me as I dashed across the well-marked crosswalk. After catching my breath and turning to catch a glimpse of the Portuguese driver who had nearly killed me, I remembered the word for "run over"—*atropelar*—which I had just looked up yesterday, after seeing it mentioned numerous times in the local newspaper. Suddenly a series of stories I'd barely glanced at the past week made sense, and I made a mental note to pay more attention to what I now suspected might become a theme in my stay in this city—and that, I worried, might even be a theme endemic to the Portuguese psyche.

After twenty-five-plus years living among, working with, and writing about the Beng, a small, rural, "animist" community in the rain forest of Côte d'Ivoire, I recently began research in a radically different space—the European capital city of Lisbon—as the jumping-off point for a new research project with Cape Verdeans, a deeply diasporic population dispersed across Africa, Europe, and the Americas. Some anthropologists move easily from one fieldsite to another; that was not my profile. Loyalty had kept me attached to the Beng long after the point when I could visit them safely, and a good decade of indecision had kept me from committing to a new fieldsite. My hesitations had both scholarly and personal foundations. In this chapter, I use my own case to think through broader trends and themes that characterize our disciplinary expectations for the model professional career.

When I last conducted fieldwork in a small Beng village in 1993 with my husband, writer Philip Graham, I started having doubts about the One Scholar/One Fieldsite model that I thought our discipline regarded as normative (see my introduction to this volume). That summer, the Beng endured poverty even more extreme than what Philip and I had observed during our previous stays, in 1979–1980 and 1985. Globalized forces far from their purview had taken their toll—from declining coffee prices on the world market, and unrealistic requirements imposed by "structural adjustment programs" as part of huge loan packages proffered by the World Bank, to outrageous mismanagement and plundering of the country's finances by government officials. As a result, the West African nation's small-scale farming communities were in crisis. Buses rarely ran in the countryside, and when they did, few villagers could afford the fare, stranding the ailing far from the town's health center. In any case, the dispensaries contained no medicines—and sometimes no staff. Nor could villagers afford to buy the few medicines that the pharmacies actually stocked: the price that government traders offered the farmers for their coffee harvest—their major source of cash—had fallen so low that the Beng had chosen to watch coffee berries fall to rot on the forest floor, rather than invest time in collecting them to sell for an insulting pittance that couldn't even cover their costs (for further reflections on that stay among the Beng, see Gottlieb and Graham 2012).

While Philip and I despaired for our Beng neighbors, I also weighed whether our growing family could withstand another long-term residence in these relatively remote, medically underserved villages. During our last stay, we had brought our six-year-old son Nathaniel with us, and in three short months, he'd lost 12 percent of his body weight. While Philip and I wanted to give Nathaniel a sibling before long, bringing another young child to the Beng region any time soon seemed an increasingly distant option.

Yet my fieldwork had always been *en famille*. Inspired by the rural African parents I have known—who keep their children by their sides as they work, hold meetings, celebrate, and sleep—I have tried to blend the parts of my life that our society tells me I should separate. Never having considered doing fieldwork without my husband and child(ren), I felt in a quandary.

While I agonized over how to keep both my family and my career healthy, our small household expanded in ways that simultaneously brought us closer to, and farther from, Bengland. When we'd last lived in Côte d'Ivoire, I had hired Bertin Kouadio, then a Beng college student and the now-grown son of one of our village hosts, as my research assistant. By the end of that summer, Bertin confided to us his fears and frustrations as the nation began scaling back its commitment to education—and canceled most college scholarships, including his. That fall, we managed to sponsor Bertin as a student at our university in Illinois, and he brought a thick slice of Africa into our American lives.

Welcoming Bertin into our home and family meant honoring the promise we had made his parents that we would in effect become Bertin's American mother and father. I had to resist the temptation to practice my Beng and forced myself to speak English with him—to improve his chances of passing the English language test that stood between him and the scholarship that our university had provisionally committed for him (see Gottlieb and Graham 2012). Though Bertin kept us close to the Beng community despite the ocean separating us, another reality made returning to Bengland any time soon improbable: Ivory Coast's political system was fissuring.

Shortly before Bertin moved to the United States, Côte d'Ivoire had lost its long-standing president, and his successor introduced the politics of ethnic resentment, religious schism, and regional divide. The possibility of our returning receded farther into the distance when our daughter Hannah entered our lives. A healthy baby, Hannah clarified our travel options. Living in remote villages in the West African rain forest where reliable medical care was many hours away was now impossible for another six years at the least.

I also started having doubts of another sort. Was it advisable for me as a scholar to devote the next decade or two of my professional life to these villages? Would I keep finding enough new issues to write about, or was I in danger of writing version after version of the same anthropological story for new audiences? The topics I had treated over my career to date had been heterogeneous, as I had deliberately sought novel issues to ponder, fresh bodies of literature to delve into. After producing six books and dozens of articles, how many notable scholarly contributions might I still make, inspired by the Beng? Painfully, I forced myself to consider that most anthropologically heretical of thoughts: The Beng and I might not have that much more to say to one another.

Anthropologist Moshe Shokeid acknowledges such a quasi-taboo possibility. Reflecting on his long-term involvement with a community of gay Jews in New York, he recently wrote:

It dawned on me that my ethnographic mission had been accomplished: I have exhausted my professional interest in that particular field. At the same time, it seemed that I could not contribute any more to the people who now maintain the social and cultural scene of "my" fieldwork site. (2007:220; and cf. Shokeid 1995)

Yet even as I began to grapple with my own sense of such an inevitability vis-à-vis the Beng, I wondered: Was a switch to a totally new research area academically acceptable?

I felt heartened when I recalled that my first college mentor, Irving Goldman, had in a sense changed fieldsites: after doing extensive fieldwork with the Cubeo in the Colombian Amazon, he had completed two more books, each set on a different continent—one about ancient Polynesian political organization, the other about the Kwakiutl *potlatch* (Goldman 1963, 1970, 1975). Although the latter two works were based on extensive library research rather than fieldwork, I remained impressed that, in midcareer, my beloved teacher had mastered two new, entirely unrelated and extensive bodies of literature, two new sets of cultural mindsets, in carrying out these ambitious studies.

My other major undergraduate mentor had also switched research agendas in midstream. After conducting extensive fieldwork in the Himalayas with the Sherpa (1978, 1989, 2001), Sherry Ortner had "returned home" to conduct fieldwork in and about her native suburban community in New Jersey (2005). One of the most celebrated and brilliant scholars of her generation, surely her peripatetic imagination was worth emulating.

Indeed, the more I considered it, the more I realized that nearly all the anthropologists I admired had moved at least to a second major fieldsite and, in some cases, to far more than that. During the years that I worked with him, my graduate mentor, Victor Turner, had branched out well beyond his celebrated work among the Ndembu in Zambia, conducting research in Brazil, Japan, and Israel. Rayna Rapp had begun her career studying life in French villages and was now doing research in American doctors' waiting rooms, while Emily Martin had moved from rural China to geneticists' labs in Baltimore. In my own department, my revered senior colleague, Edward Bruner, had started his career working with Native Americans, made his name based on research in Sumatra, and then began globe-trotting in places as far-flung as Ghana, Kenya, and Hong Kong, constructing an anthropological approach to modern tourism (see chapter 7, this volume).

And it wasn't only my elders. In my own generation, some of my scholarly friends and contemporaries were beginning to chart major research moves—from Niger to "African New York" for Paul Stoller (see afterword, this volume); from Guinea-Bissau to Williamsburg, Virginia, for Eric Gable; from Melanesian villages to scientists' offices for Rena Lederman. All of these scholars switched scholarly gears, and continents, in midlife, and the moves had hardly crushed their careers. Quite the opposite—the changes had reinvigorated them as scholars. Clearly, my old-fashioned One Scholar/One Fieldsite idea was, at best, outmoded.

And so, while waiting who knew how many years for the possibility of returning safely to the Beng, I decided to consider conducting research in another region of the world. But where, and on what? Suddenly I felt liberated to revisit my original motivations for becoming an anthropologist.

Raised in a politically engaged household, and active in a variety of political movements from the age of twelve, I had found myself drawn to anthropology in high school as a way to think about alternative models of creating a society that reduced imperialism, racism, and patriarchy. While my youthful idealist self acknowledged more subtleties and complexities over the years, I have always retained a basic commitment to looking for ways to improve some corner of the world through my writing and my teaching. A new project in a new place might allow me to renew my aspirations to contribute to social change through my scholarship and my pedagogy. I began imagining myself in other parts of the planet, analyzing different issues, even learning new languages.

Francophone Africans living in New York? After some twenty years of internal exile to the flat middle of the country, that plan appealingly combined my long-standing interests in francophone Africa, and my knowledge of French, with a return to the city of my birth—a city I'd missed so much that after I left it for graduate school, I wrote my MA thesis about its early colonial history (Gottlieb 1978). With a project based in a slice of "African New York," I could see my hometown through new eyes. At a scholarly level, I could contribute to wider conversations gaining importance in the United States surrounding race, class, and immigration. Still, I found the idea of urban fieldwork challenging. Having thoroughly charted the intersecting genealogies of every resident of the first Beng village in which I'd lived for fourteen months, its population under three hundred, what methods would I need to craft to find informants and identify "communities" in a global city such as New York?

Tribal rituals of Wall Street stock investors? This project would also bring me back me to my native city. And at the scholarly level, it would allow me to undertake a new research agenda with enormous relevance to just about everyone on the planet. Viewing the bastion of capitalism as a primitive tribe complete with irrational, magical practices, I could apply the cultural and interpretive approach I had honed in my writings about rural African religions to an arena normally subject, instead, to macroeconomic analyses by neoclassically trained economists. With such a project, I might illuminate hidden realities and contradictions of the capitalist world system, and chip away at the easy confidence so many in the modern world have in it. Politically, such a project could not only critique the absurdities of capitalism but could also serve to combat widespread prejudice against non-Western peoples who supposedly maintain a monopoly on "magic" and "superstition." Yet I might need to read thousands of pages of economic theory simply to participate in conversations with my informants, and their conversations with one another; I feared these texts could prove either intellectually offensive, incomprehensible, boring, or all three.

Francophone Africans living in Paris? This option would allow me to bring my French and Africanist training to bear on immigration issues in Europe. The prospect of frequently visiting, and perhaps living for a long period in, my favorite city in the world offered a further advantage. (As a graduate student, when I first told my family of my intention to conduct research in the rain forest of francophone Africa, my worried mother had responded quite seriously, "Don't they have culture in Paris?" I laughingly dismissed her suggestion as both impractical and anti-anthropological. Perhaps she was ahead of her time.) With my commitment to avoiding translators, however, a Paris-based project might require me to study some new African languages, as the francophone West African diaspora in Paris included no Beng speakers. Was I up to learning Bamana, Songhay, or Wolof?

Lusophone Africans living in Lisbon? In my life as an Africanist scholar and teacher, I had given short shrift to lusophone Africa. This project would offer me an intriguing way to deepen my understanding of the African continent and to compare the French and Portuguese colonial projects. It would also delight my husband, long infatuated with all things Portuguese, who had faithfully followed me to France and francophone African villages for over twenty years, and who cowrote *Parallel Worlds* with me, our memoir from Côte d'Ivoire (Gottlieb and Graham 1994)—all while longing to enjoy the *sh-sh-sh*s of European Portuguese. With my knowledge of French, I imagined it shouldn't be too hard to learn the equally Latin-derived language of Portuguese . . . though there was an ancient linguistic score I'd have to settle, from back in 1971.

That first year in college, a Portuguese classmate had, in my mind, polluted a French literature seminar I was taking. The daughter of a diplomat, she was far more worldly, better educated, and more impeccably dressed than I (improbably wearing Coco Chanel outfits to every class). But, just turned seventeen, I was still working on a pretentious Parisian accent, and I ethno-centrically graded all spoken French on a Parisian scale. Absurdly, my Portuguese classmate received a failing grade in my private, Paris-based test, and her Portuguese-inflected French set me up for three decades of unabashed prejudice against the sounds of European Portuguese. I'd have to set aside this silly but long-standing bias against the nasalized tones of the Portuguese language.

Sephardic "Crypto-Jews" and descendants of "New Christians" living in Portugal? While drawing on my expertise in religion, this plan would dramatically expand my ethnographic gaze historically, linguistically, and geographically. At the same time, it would allow me to connect with a somewhat submerged aspect of my own identity. Though as far as I knew, my family tree contained no ancestors from Iberia, encountering Sephardic Jews would offer an exotic means to connect with my own Ashkenazi biography. And, being based in Portugal, such a project would thrill my lusomaniac husband.

But the scholarly demands of this plan scared me. Not only would I need to learn that problematic language of continental Portuguese, I might also need to learn to read Hebrew, and I would surely have to engage with a huge chunk of Iberian history as well as with Judeo-Christian ritual practice. Could I possibly imagine such a linguistically and historically ambitious project at this busy stage in my life? Even if I had the time, was my aging brain capable of it? Maybe it was no coincidence that most of the midlife fieldsite switches I knew about brought my colleagues closer to home—not farther away. And except for an absurd rumor I could scarcely believe about Michael Herzfeld becoming fluent in Thai in midlife (see chapter 5, this volume), no colleagues' fieldsite switches I knew of involved learning even one new language, let alone two.

Autographing rituals among authors? This idea grew out of another submerged aspect of my identity. Before becoming a social scientist, I had fancied myself a writer. In high school, I had cofounded and published a literary magazine; in college and graduate school, I published some poems and even won an award for one of them. Since then, I had gained my literary pleasures vicariously, by hanging out with my writer-husband and his social circle. Pursuing this project would allow me to actively bridge the humanities/arts/social science divide. As such, it would be family-friendly in a different way from the Portuguese-based research I was contemplating: it would allow me to become professionally engaged in my husband's literary world, interviewing his friends and colleagues. As with the Wall Street scheme, I could apply an interpretive approach to a contemporary, urban ritual, shedding light on Western forms of magic to challenge the easy Western condemnation of non-Westerners as superstitious. But was there enough of an idea here to make this into a long-term research agenda that might produce a book and not just a charming article or two?

Despite the drawbacks that potentially compromised each of these projects, I relished the prospect of pursuing any and all of them. As the possibilities multiplied, I felt heady, like a first-semester freshman selecting classes in college. So many new places to travel to, vocabularies to dip into, issues to contemplate. . . .

Yet I was also nervous. Any of these choices would mean mastering new bodies of scholarly literature and, in some cases, one or more new grammars and dictionaries; making my husband and children adjust to new places; forging relations with dozens of new colleagues I had yet to identify. . . . As a researcher in search of a new fieldsite, was I any less pathetic than the title group in Pirandello's absurd *Six Characters in Search of an Author?* Part of me was happy to postpone the difficult choice as long as possible.

I also remained ambivalent about abandoning the Beng, much as I realized the risks involved in returning to them. I felt forever close to my former Beng friends, neighbors, and adopted family, and I still loved writing about them. As I seesawed back and forth between proliferating options for new fieldwork and unrealistically imagining ways to travel back to Côte d'Ivoire, I spent ten years writing two new books based on my previous research in Bengland (DeLoache and Gottlieb 2000; Gottlieb 2004). I was finishing up the first book and getting back to the second when, in 1999, Côte d'Ivoire suffered a military coup. In 2002, full-scale civil war broke out, and brokered truces preceded broken truces; my distress about how my old Beng friends and neighbors were faring in this new nightmare could find no safe outlet. The time had definitely come to choose another fieldsite for myself and my still-young family. My years of productive procrastination were over.

A NEW RESEARCH AGENDA

In the end, I chose a project that I thought offered the greatest intellectual payoff, speaking to the widest set of scholarly issues. An offshore outpost of Africa that allowed me to draw on my Africanist training yet keep my family in a malaria-free zone, Cape Verde also opened up new worlds of historical intrigue and contemporary significance. On the surface, Cape Verde might appear an outlier, exceptional—and an especially odd choice for a francophone Africanist. These islands, 385 miles off the west coast of Africa, are so geoculturally liminal that the nation established a unique "special partnership" with the European Union in 2007 (Vieira and Ferreira-Pereira 2009), following a proposal seriously introduced in 2005 by a former prime minister of Portugal, Mário Soares, that Cape Verde ought to enter the European Union; and the possibility of Cape Verde joining NATO, while rejected by government officials, was also seriously raised recently by journalists (FORCV 2010). At least one scholar has suggested that the archipelago's racialized, cultural, and linguistic history bears more resemblance to the island nations of the Caribbean than to mainland Africa (Batalha 2007); another has pointed out that the islands' cultural riches, especially in literature and music, are almost a "miracle of uniqueness" in the face of the nation's extreme economic poverty and few natural resources (Pratas 2007).

But the more I read of the archipelago's history, the more I became convinced that these nine islands—while largely unknown in the English-speaking world, and rarely addressed in scholarly works even by Africanists—represent the epitome of modernity. Before the Portuguese occupation beginning in the 1460s, the islands were uninhabited, so the first generations were largely a mix of Europeans (mostly men) and West Africans (both men and women). Strategically located in the middle of the Atlantic—a rollicking space of pirate- and storm-laden danger through the eighteenth century—the islands served as the first major stopping-off point for ships bound from Europe for the Americas bearing all manner of cargo—including slaves. Serving as the Atlantic's major slave depot for the first century of the trans-Atlantic slave trade, the Cape Verde islands became instrumental in forging early triangular ties among Europe, Africa, and the Americas. As such, the worldview of the population that became Cape Verdean—in effect, the state of being Cape Verdean—was tied up from the inception in a modern mix of populations—in other words, in hybridity, travel, diaspora. As the historian Tobias Green has recently suggested, Cape Verde may well be the place where "we" became modern (2007). Given the singular historical and cultural positioning of the islands, my own move from working with a relatively isolated group in the rain forest to a diasporic population at heart excited me for all the theoretical and historical issues with which I could now engage.

Beyond offering me an ambitious foray into five hundred years of globalization history, my choice of a Portuguese-speaking nation thrilled my husband. We found a Brazilian tutor and began studying Portuguese together, setting aside a grand total of one hour on those Sundays when we could spare the time. During some lessons, the semester's relentless claims on my sleep caught up with me, and I'd catch myself dozing off on our couch as our patient tutor explained for the fifth time the rules for which syllable to stress in a word. Between lessons, Philip and I spent spare moments drilling each other on verb conjugations as we drove to pick up our daughter Hannah from school or sauntered down the aisles of the supermarket in search of the week's groceries. Many weeks, overwhelmed by our writing projects, students' papers, committee work, and parenting, we remembered to start our homework only minutes before our next lesson. By the following Sunday, we'd forgotten the new prepositions we'd started learning the week before. I joked with our tutor that we must be her worst students ever. Knowing French did help me learn to read Portuguese—but got in the way of learning to speak it. I despaired that I'd ever get a quarter as comfortable in Portuguese as I felt in French. Still, learning a new language in midlife proved a great adventure; eventually, while Nathaniel was off at college, Hannah joined the family study group.

When Philip and I combined our sabbaticals with some grants for a year's leave, I was able to begin my new project in Lisbon, where I planned to locate Cape Verdean immigrants now living in the postcolonial metropole—though I hadn't yet decided which aspect of the Cape Verdean diaspora to research. I knew that race, class, gender, and religion were all critical to Cape Verdeans' lives, but this time around, I wanted to avoid a serious misjudgment I had made in my first research among the Beng, when I settled on a research project before contacting the community, based on theoretical issues I had identified from scholarly literature. The difficulties that resulted from that act of hubris formed the continuing theme behind the memoir I coauthored with my husband (Gottlieb and Graham 1994). Determined not to repeat this mistake, I deliberately kept my project open-ended, applying for "seed grants" that would allow me to identify a suitable topic in a new fieldsite.

I spent the first several months meeting Cape Verdeans across class, race, and gender lines and getting to know scholarly colleagues who specialized in Cape Verde. Secretly, I expected to carry out what I imagined as the easiest of the projects I had sketched out: a study of children. With infancy in rural Africa the focus of my research and writing about the Beng over the previous decade, it made sense to draw on the thematic expertise I had already amassed and take it to a new context. Of course, the new context was hugely different, but that made the project exciting: the comparativist's payoff seemed tremendous. As I discovered, though, other scholars of Cape Verde had also found the childhood project appealing, and I found myself disappointed to consider researching a topic that colleagues in several fields had already tackled.

By contrast, no one knew of any research on another topic I had considered: Cape Verdeans who had Jewish ancestry. In studying the archipelago's history from the fifteenth and sixteenth centuries, I had read that the earliest European settlers on the uninhabited islands included Iberian Jews fleeing anti-Semitism in both Spain and Portugal . . . but I had yet to read about any contemporary Cape Verdeans who could trace their family line back to that moment, or who even knew about it. Would I find any live Cape Verdeans who cared about this subject?

From my first days in Lisbon, I started tentatively mentioning this potential topic to colleagues. My Cape Verdeanist colleagues all knew of the early Jewish era of the islands and encouraged me to pursue it, optimistic that I would find some Cape Verdeans who traced their ancestry back to those early Jewish immigrants. So I started asking the Cape Verdeans I met about this. To my surprise, they, too, knew about the Jewish history of their island nation, and urged me to focus on this line of inquiry. But they didn't know anyone who actually descended from those Jewish immigrants. Not being a historian, I wanted a living community to work with. If I couldn't find any living Cape Verdeans who counted themselves as Jewish—or who at least acknowledged the Jewish branch of their genealogy—I wouldn't take on this project. My quest to find Cape Verdeans with Jewish ancestry eerily echoed another quest on which I had unintentionally embarked over a quarter century earlier, when I had spent a month roving across Abidjan in search of a single member of a tiny minority ethnic group, the Beng, whose lives I had arrived to study. Was I doomed to choose obscure groups hiding in invisible corners of complicated ethnic landscapes?

One day, I spotted a notice in the Lisbon newspaper advertising a book signing for a study about Portuguese Jews by a local historian. ("Book launches" held in shopping malls are a favorite pastime of the Portuguese, Philip and I had discovered to our delight.) Might I spot some Cape Verdeans in the audience? If I did, would I have the courage to approach them and introduce myself?

In the bookstore section of the department store where the signing would be held, I eyed the empty seats and led my husband and daughter to a row from where I might glimpse everyone entering the open area. Soon enough, two men entered who I guessed were Cape Verdeans. Although the "phenotype" of Cape Verdeans is strikingly variable—thanks to the diversity of groups that mixed to create the islands' population—I'd had good success so far in identifying Cape Verdeans when the opportunity arose. What if I stumbled now? The thought of embarrassing myself publicly kept me in my seat.

Luckily, the two men sat down in the row directly in front of us, and I was close enough to eavesdrop. Straining my still-poor understanding of Portuguese to the limits, I managed to catch enough of their conversation to be convinced that my hunch was right: they were Cape Verdean. And since they were at a lecture about the history of Jews in Portugal, was it too much to assume that they might have Jewish ancestry themselves, that they had ventured out on a cool night out of curiosity about their own family histories?

As the author of the book began his short lecture, I found my attention commuting back and forth between his summary of his research, and the occasional whispered comments in front of me. Suddenly my project felt alive, feasible . . . mine.

Just as suddenly, the prospect of actually shaping a project around Jews in Cape Verde seemed daunting. The doubts and concerns I had already cultivated about beginning a new research project assailed me as my first two potential consultants sat, unknowingly, in front of me.

Still, by the end of the talk, I found the resolve necessary to approach the men. I introduced myself with some small talk about the lecture, then declared my professional identity and asked if they would be willing to participate in an interview some time. Both men nodded eagerly, then scribbled their names, cell phone numbers, and e-mail addresses in my notebook.

Whatever doubts and anxieties I might still have, it was too late for them to claim me now. My research project had begun in earnest.

*

Choosing a project theme because it intrigued and excited the community—rather than appalling them, as my first research on traditional religious practice had done with the Beng so long ago—was the beginning of what I hoped would be a more egalitarian, hence more ethical, basis for my new research project (cf. Lamphere 2004). But beyond the many intellectual pleasures that the project offers me, it has entailed several tectonic shifts for me as a scholar. While in Lisbon, the most immediate difference was the task of pursuing consultants across a city of almost three million—rather than finding curious neighbors standing right outside my front door in a village of a few hundred. In Ivory Coast, once I'd finally found a Beng student in the nation's capital, he'd sent me a letter of introduction to his uncle up-country, and Philip and I had moved into the uncle's compound for a few weeks, then into another village down the road. From then on out, "the Beng" surrounded me as neighbors.

In Lisbon, the space of research proved quite different. Cape Verdeans live spread among many neighborhoods on both sides of the Tejo River, and Cape Verdeans with acknowledged Jewish heritage are even more dispersed, only partially an acknowledged group even among themselves. The first two men I met led me, one by one, to friends and family all across the metropolitan area, taking me on new subway lines, to new neighborhoods, as I followed their widespread ties. My challenges in identifying a somewhat hidden and dispersed community may not be endemic to all urban anthropology projects. Many cities do contain bounded neighborhoods in which relatively homogeneous groups live—working-class Mexicans in Chicago, second-generation Chinese-Americans in New York, Korean-Americans in Los Angeles. . . . But such is not the case with Cape Verdeans in Lisbon.

Indeed, although I grew up in New York and considered myself a "city girl," doing ethnography in a European metropolis often left me breathless. For my first few months in Lisbon, I wasn't even sure if, or when, I'd actually "started fieldwork." In recent years, a growing number of cultural anthropologists have pondered their own version of such "Where does 'the field' start and end?" conundrums, and I had even taught some key texts on the theme.[1] But reading and teaching articles, and living their lessons, were two entirely different endeavors—as countless generations of students and scholars before me have well known. Did learning to find my way through the metros and buses of a new city constitute "ethnography"? Or figuring out which pronoun to use (or not use) when greeting people? What about knowing when to predict that the car speeding up the hill was likely to screech to an unlikely stop at the crosswalk, rather than run me over?

And then there were the evenings. Just two weeks into our thirteen-month stay in Lisbon, Philip and I celebrated our thirtieth wedding anniversary by going to a concert by the great Cape Verdean musician Tito Paris, who lives in Lisbon and was playing at a downtown club. Could I claim our anniversary celebration as the official beginning of my project, or was that personal ritual too intimate to share the discursive space we call "research"?

Scholars such as Behar (1996, 2007), D'Amico-Samuels ([1991] 1997),

---

1. For an intelligent selection of such writings, see, e.g., Amit (2000); Anthropology Matters (2004a, 2004b); Dresch, James, and Parkin (2000); Gupta and Ferguson (1997); Marcus (1998d); Ortner (1997); Rasmussen (2003); Stoller (1997). In this volume, Lepowsky, Seligmann, and Stoller also reflect on this issue.

Stoller (2004), and others have wondered aloud whether the search for boundaries between our personal and professional lives even makes analytic sense (cf. Hanisch [1970] 2006 for an early feminist articulation of this position). Likewise, I came to see my fieldwork in Portugal as a complicated space suspended between domestic and scholarly entanglements. I might spend one hour helping my daughter study for her sixth-grade history test (in Portuguese) about the Portuguese colonial empire in Africa, the next conversing with our Cape Verdean housekeeper, the next meeting with a Cape Verdean diplomat . . . all the while plotting in my mind how to ask for paper towels the following morning at our grocer's, using minimally decent-sounding Portuguese (cf. Murano 2007).

To be sure, from our first days in Lisbon, any time I interacted with anyone—filling out bank forms to open up an account, buying pots for our understocked kitchen, making arrangements for an Internet connection in our apartment—I struggled to expand my fledgling Portuguese by mentioning my plan to conduct research with Cape Verdean immigrants in Lisbon. From such casual conversations, I observed a range of people's reactions to the project. Some whispered tedious warnings to "be careful" in "those neighborhoods," which were notoriously "crime-ridden." Others offered to introduce me to their Cape Verdean house cleaner, or brother-in-law, or colleague. No matter what the reaction—from crypto-racist to supportive—everyone had an opinion about my planned research with Cape Verdeans, and that fact itself was of ethnographic interest.

Contacting Cape Verdeans meant an initial telephone conversation or e-mail note—both communications in Portuguese, a new language with which I was still doing mighty battle (cf. Graham 2009). In striking contrast to a range of expertises to which we may have become accustomed in middle-age professorship, a midcareer fieldsite switch may produce a shocking but ultimately welcome reminder that we are always students at heart, that the business of learning is as important to our careers—as scholars and as professors—as is the business of teaching.

After two decades with relatively firm collegial networks, I am enjoying forging relations with new colleagues in several arenas of scholarship (including Jewish studies, lusophone studies, migration studies, and European studies). Then, too, my project has me working with people along the "race" spectrum, who have complicated relations to their own racialized positions (rather than with a single group of people easily classified as "black"). I am now reading in critical race theory to approach issues that were previously relevant to my research more as background than foreground.

The class position of my consultants has also changed drastically from that of my previous research group. I am now largely working with middle-class professionals and highly educated elites—rather than farmers trained in the oral tradition; this shift to "studying up," as Laura Nader first termed it (1969), produces its own challenges.[2] In the short term, I struggle to iden-tify appropriate goods or services to provide, in exchange for my consultants' precious time. The dried fish or bar of soap that was richly appreciated by a peasant Beng woman would be an insult to the Cape Verdean elites I inter-view. Beyond offering coffee or lunch in a café as we chat, I anticipate that a copy of an article I have written that draws on our interview will be the most appreciated gift for many of my consultants; for others, a digital copy of a photo I took of them, or a reference to an obscure publication about Cape Verde, is the best gift. Moreover, I find it much harder to maintain the fiction of expertise in the face of my "informants'" education (they can often draw their own genealogies faster than I can, using their own visual shorthand), and their desires to read everything I write about them. Of course, they merit this right, but I am just beginning to foresee the complications that may turn my writing into more of an ongoing conversation than a last-word publication "when they read what we write" (cf. Brettell 1996).

My new project also entails studying a highly mobile population spread across four continents—rather than a highly rooted community with endur-ing ties to place, as the Beng were. The new generation of anthropologists is trained to work with such diasporic groups from the get-go; catching up with my students' techniques is exciting . . . and humbling.

The breadth of my consultants' lives in space is matched by their depth in time—a new source of knowledge for me. Among the Beng, written records were few and far between: I once spent two weeks in the French colonial archives and managed to find only a single document mentioning the Beng region in passing. By contrast, both Cape Verdeans and Jews have richly doc-umented histories. My new project compels me to master a daunting array of historical eras in Jewish and Cape Verdean histories and diasporas. Indeed, over the course of my year in Lisbon, the project asserted itself by popping out in new directions, taking me to new continents, new centuries, new litera-tures at a dizzying pace. In this lifetime will I ever be able to claim expertise in all these fresh paths of discovery?

2. For more recent discussions of anthropological work with elites, see, e.g., Carter (2007); de Pina-Cabral and de Lima (2000); Fumanti (2004); Ignatowski (2004); Marcus (1992, 1993, 1998a); Marcus and Mascarenhas 2005); Ortner (2010), Shore and Nugent (2002).

For example, initially I thought my theme was relations between Portuguese Jews and Cape Verde. But many of the "Cape Verdeans" I have met are not fully "Cape Verdeans," though in some contexts they claim to be. The life story of one woman I met early in my stay in Lisbon, Maria, pushed me to expand my definition of "Cape Verdean." Born on the Cape Verdean island of São Vicente, Maria moved to Guinea-Bissau with her parents at the age of five. There, she later married a man born in Guinea-Bissau, whose parents had also emigrated from Cape Verde. Despite considering themselves Cape Verdean, the couple lived for the next thirty or so years in Guinea-Bissau, where they bore and raised their seven children. After independence, the family managed to attain Portuguese citizenship, and they all moved permanently to Lisbon. Soon after they moved, they felt prosperous enough to finally plan a vacation: Maria, now a grandmother, "returned home" to Cape Verde, where she spent a month getting to know her homeland for the first time since her early childhood. Her children and grandchildren have never been to Cape Verde—indeed, they live dispersed across several countries and two continents. Nevertheless, at least one of this couple's grown daughters, who has never set foot on the islands, considers Cape Verde "home" and says she feels enormous nostalgia and homesickness—*saudade*—for the islands whenever she hears music from the homeland of her grandparents.

Since hearing about this family's history, I have discovered that their life course is quite common. I had already read about epochs in which ties between Cape Verde and the nearby continental former Portuguese colony of Guinea-Bissau were especially active. My readings had focused on the period immediately preceding and following independence from Portugal, in which the charismatic, Cape Verde–born leader, Amilcar Cabral, had united the island and mainland colonies in a political struggle that earned him, first, international fame and honor, then assassination (Chabal 1983). Now I discovered that the connections linking the mainland and island communities ran far deeper than Cabral's biography and political struggles, and had existed for far longer than I had realized. Reading the history of the past half millenium taught me that studying Cape Verdeans necessarily means studying Guinea-Bissau as well.[3]

As I seek out Cape Verdeans with Jewish heritage—and Portuguese Jews with experience in Cape Verde—I find that the two diasporas, of Jews and

3. Several chapters in one scholarly volume document the extensive, and often competing, nature of these ties between Cape Verde and Guinea-Bissau, dating back to the early sixteenth century (Santos 2001).

Cape Verdeans, are both so persistently mobile that neither stands still for me (Gottlieb 2007). For example, early in my Lisbon year, I met a Portuguese Jew who was born and raised in Mozambique. Although she had no ties to Cape Verde, her network and her stories led me to other Portuguese Jews—and other Cape Verdeans—who did migrate, sometimes for short periods, sometimes permanently, from Cape Verde to Mozambique. To trace the networks of these peripatetic lives, I can now contemplate fieldwork not only in Cape Verde and Guinea-Bissau, but in São Tomé, Angola, and Mozambique—the other outposts of the former Portuguese empire in Africa—and, farther afield, in Brazil and even Goa, where some of my consultants also have relatives. A different historical era could take me in yet other directions: to Morocco and Gibraltar, where another group of Cape Verdeans trace their "Sephardic" ancestry to Jews who fled from Morocco's nineteenth-century economic and political woes to Gibraltar, and thence to Cape Verde; and to other European cities where sizeable groups of Cape Verdeans now live, including Paris, London, Rome, and Rotterdam.[4]

Closer to home, the project is also taking me to New England, the site of a robust Cape Verdean population that can trace its origins to the first group of African Americans to arrive in the United States as free migrants (rather than as slaves), via the nineteenth-century whaling industry. I have recently begun engaging with the Cape Verdean community in New England, now over a quarter-million strong, and consider the Providence-Boston corridor as my major fieldsite for the immediate future (Gottlieb 2010).

CONCLUDING THOUGHTS

When I contemplate my career to date, I am struck to realize how my field trajectory embodies that of the discipline writ small. From the malarial zone of West Africa to the flu zone of western Europe . . . from a small village to a capital city . . . from a local, ancestor- and spirit-based religion to a conjoined Judeo-Christian monotheistic one . . . from an insistently isolated and localized population to an insistently diasporic and mobile one . . . from a singular racial identity to a complex multiracialized one . . . from the neoco-

---

4. The project is also pushing me to question the easy divide between Ashkenazim (Jews with origins in Eastern and Northern Europe) and Sephardim (Jews with origins in Iberia, Turkey, and North Africa)—a dichotomy on which Jewish historians routinely rely. The transcontinental routes taken by Cape Verdeans with Jewish ancestry cross-cut these two geographic zones and challenge such a neat division (for a related critique, see Kaye/Kantrowitz 2007).

lonized south to the former-seat-of-empire north . . . from a single fieldsite
to a multisited community . . . from peasants raised in the oral tradition to
economic and political middle-class workers and even elites . . . the list of
transformed, and transformatory, themes in my professional biography, as in
the discipline's, goes on.

In short, as cultural anthropology has come to terms with a globalized
world, so have I—and, as the other contributors to this volume suggest, so
have many colleagues in midcareer, in their varied ways. The discipline itself
continues to challenge its models, methods, and modes of thought—just as
we, as individual scholars, continue to develop our own intellectual paths.
In trading midlife expertise for second- (or third-) time-around neophyte na-
iveté, we lose claims to authoritative knowledge . . . but we regain that sense of
wonder that drew many of us to anthropology to begin with—and that, both
as scholars and as teachers, we lose at our peril.

ACKNOWLEDGMENTS

I presented an earlier version of this chapter at the 106th annual meeting of the
American Anthropological Association in Washington, DC, where I received
lively and inspirational comments from copanelists and audience members
alike. An expanded version was presented to a doctoral seminar ("Illinois Anthropology") in my home department, where students and the course's co-in-
structors—my delightful colleagues, Virginia Dominguez and Ellen Moodie—
further provoked my thinking with their incisive questions.

For support of my year in Lisbon, I am grateful to the National Endow-
ment for the Humanities (for a Summer Faculty Award) and several units at
the University of Illinois at Urbana-Champaign (the Research Board/Humani-
ties Release Time Award; International Programs and Studies/William and
Flora Hewlett Award; the Research Board/Arnold Beckman Award; and the
Department of Anthropology and the UIUC campus/sabbatical leave). For my
current research in New England, I am grateful to at the University of Illinois
at Urbana-Champaign's Research Board and College of Liberal Arts and Sciences. Expert transcription and translation of my interviews, and a variety of
other forms of research assistance, has been ably provided by Bryan Anderson
(Urbana), Jose Carlos Cabral (Lisbon), Tholani Hlongwa (Urbana), Renato
Lima de Oliveira (Urbana/Rio de Janeiro), Laura Marks (Urbana), and Giulia
Mazza (Urbana).

For the rich welcome they have offered me to their lifeworlds, I am grateful to too many Cape Verdeans to name in Lisbon, Santiago, Mindelo, Provi-

dence, Boston, Paris, and elsewhere in the Cape Verdean diaspora. A special *obrigada* to Gershom, Gabrielle, and Yehuvah Barros for hosting me, an initial stranger, in Providence, Rhode Island, for week-long stays in what has quickly become a home away from home thanks to their extraordinary hospitality. I owe a further debt to the many Cape Verdeanist colleagues who have generously shared their contacts, advice, and wisdom with this newcomer to their professional world. Among these, Luís Batalha, Catarina Costa, Marzia Grassi, Fernanda Pratas, and João Vasconcelos deserve special thanks for their extraordinary support and friendship.

Finally, for introducing me to the many pleasures of the lusophone world, from Cesaria Evora to grilled sardines and port wine, I offer my deep and enduring *obrigada* to my husband, Philip Graham; and for plunging with grace into an un-asked-for year in Europe and emerging far more fluent in Portuguese than I can ever hope to be, I have more admiration for our brave daughter Hannah than I can say.

Passionate Serendipity:
From the Acropolis to the
Golden Mount

Michael Herzfeld

Early in my career as an anthropologist, I let it be known that there were three things I would never do: become an activist, make ethnographic films, and work outside Greece. Some three decades later, with two films on Rome already in distribution and another on Bangkok in production, after working with evictees in Rome and with an entire community facing collective eviction in Bangkok, I find myself wondering, "What other lies did I tell—myself, as well as others?"

They were not really lies, of course—just terribly inaccurate predictions, based on a rather priggish intellectual purism in the case of the films and the activism, and a conviction (perhaps a little more modest!) that I would never achieve the same degree of intense acquaintance with another country that I already had with Greece. They illustrate aspects of my intellectual upbringing that are worth mentioning, especially as I think they are widely shared.

So let me tell this story from the beginning, more or less.

As a schoolboy in England, I usually did really well in only one class: French. Whether because I was fortunate enough to have a teacher both talented and tolerant, or because this language sat on the higher margins of my German-Jewish refugee family's cultural domain, I found the class exciting. It allowed me to escape the constraints of English without having to surrender to a family language tradition to which my parents were never especially devoted. Be that as it may, my teacher realized that I could race ahead of the rest of the class and encouraged me, when I had exhausted the possibilities of the textbooks prescribed for us, to work on my own and learn additional languages of my choosing. Meanwhile, my desire to be an archaeologist had landed me in the classics stream, which meant studying advanced Latin and ancient Greek. Italian and modern Greek did not seem like unscalable heights, and I persevered. (My school reports often said, "He must persevere"; but that was about classes I decidedly did *not* enjoy.) Travel with my parents as well as school groups helped me to consolidate my knowledge of both languages, which remained an important element in my enthusiasm for both countries. As a university student, I traveled in Crete with two friends, Greg Eaves and Paul Atkinson (now a well-known British sociologist), in search of the songs of the White Mountains and surrounding areas; received my first education in nationalist folklore when a radio show announcer told me that songs that referred only to village events were not really historical songs at all; and acquired a smattering of the Cretan dialect, a new linguistic adventure that was soon to stand me in very good stead.

So there was a philological basis to these beginnings. When I graduated from Cambridge, where I did my undergraduate degree in archaeology, I had already acquired near-native fluency in Greek. I was bored with archaeology as it was taught—it seemed to be all about classification and stratigraphy—and hung out with linguistically generous Greek friends, on some days speaking far more Greek than English. In one sense, venturing into Greece for ethnographic research at that time was not particularly courageous; I might as well have done it in my native England. Well, not really—especially as I grew up with a German-accented mother who declared frequently that we were not English but British, and who (understandably, as a Jewish refugee) bristled any time others dared to suggest she might be German! I do not think I would have found much excitement in doing fieldwork "at home," either in England generally or among people of similar background in particular. But I did speak Greek well by the time I saw my career path opening up, and that was a decisive factor.

There was something distinctly German-Jewish-bourgeois about my passion for the classical lands, which included an early and incurable infection of Verdi-mania. (It has gotten steadily worse, and my bathroom warbling has continued to test my musically talented wife's tolerance to the utmost.) Modern Greece drew me as a cure for my ennui with classical texts; it had all the antiquities, to be sure, but this was the time when Mikis Theodorakis, he of *Zorba* fame, was creating marvelous music, and my memory (from a school trip to Greece) of the spirited Athenian taverna trio who dashed off "Varka sto yialo" ("A Boat on the Seaside") remains as vivid as that of the extraordinary passion that a spectacular performance of *Nabucco* had inflamed in me during a family visit to Florence two years earlier. As I recall that earlier epiphany,

I did not want the magnificent overture to end, because that meant that the whole opera would end; and with that came the realization of a more encompassing mortality. Little did I know that Ettore Bastianini, who sang the title role and was surely the greatest Verdian baritone yet, was to meet his own end a scant seven years later at the age of forty. But I was discovering the awful corrosion of time, conceivable only as the loss of great beauty; at fourteen, I was just starting to grow up, and anthropology lay in ambush.

What I discovered during these voyages during my high school and undergraduate years was living people. I was still fascinated by classical ruins; but I could taste, smell, hear, and see the cultures of the living (though the ancient stones had a distinct olfactory effect as well, to be sure). The sizzling lamb fat and oregano of roadside souvlakia and the pervasive furniture-polish smell of the wealthier parts of Athens; the celery-tinted smells of early-morning cooking in Italian restaurants; even the mixture of gas fumes, seaweed, and octopus roasting on a Greek island—and then all that *music*, and the shattering roar of a caique's engine or the clatter of a mover's van, the colors made more intense by the bright sunlight—all these seemed to reproduce, in crazy variations, the tuneful operatic arias and the bouncy songs of these extraordinary places.

And Rome! There, truly, my senses overloaded almost beyond bearing. As I happily struggled with a language I quickly came to love for its cadences and its rhetorical flourishes, I could appreciate the monuments precisely because they were part of the fabric of everyday life. Rome was perhaps not the first place in Italy to warm my being; but its massive, contradictory, and ultimately irreducible presence made it the place that can still, in an unguarded moment, wring from me the eye-stinging tears that come, unexpectedly and with embarrassing force, only from the desperate beauty of gloriously shattered ruins madly entwined with a raucously undisciplined present. Once while still a schoolboy and on a family trip to Rome, my father had me ask a policeman if we could park the car on a certain street, and the impressively uniformed official replied, "It's not allowed, but"—smiling—"it *is* allowed!" What an introduction to the easygoing "accommodation" I later discovered Romans attributed to themselves!

By the time I went to Cambridge to study archaeology and fell in with some of the Greek students, I had worked briefly as a travel courier to Greece and could, still a little haltingly but very enthusiastically, speak my new friends' language. I put Italy aside for the time being and became an aficionado of things Greek. I played the bouzouki in a Greek Cypriot restaurant, danced Greek dances with my friends, and gradually became familiar with the culture. Then came the colonels' coup. Although I did join in one demonstration, I am ashamed to say that I was politically much more conservative in those days and did very little to support the anti-junta movement; later, after spending a year at the University of Athens that greatly sensitized me to the capillary workings of petty tyranny (the police spies were said to be identifiable by marks left on their heads by their uniform caps), I started veering toward a more critical position. To be honest, I think that growing up in a refugee family that tended not to want to be politically involved initially led me to turn a blind eye (which I regret now); but later, when I could no longer ignore what was going on, my family background sensitized me in exactly the opposite way—and prepared the way for the kind of anthropology that I really only began doing after I left Greece (and yet also involved me in some political shenanigans with Greek overtones after I had moved to the United States in 1978). But I was, politically, a slow learner.

My relative conservatism, at that early stage, also led me to resist the siren call of anthropology. Not only did it seem like a sometimes frighteningly radical discipline, but I remember feeling very strongly that I would feel uncomfortable prying—as I felt the discipline required—into the lives of ordinary people. Moreover, my old friend Paul Atkinson's enthusiasm for reading anthropological theory both fascinated and terrified me. Was I too lazy, too immature, or just not as inclined to theoretical gymnastics as he was? When I started living in Greece and reading what anthropologists like Ernestine Friedl and John Campbell had to say about local culture, that perspective changed; Greeks, it seemed, were like anthropologists all the time. They were certainly not averse to prying, and they made it clear that anyone who *failed* to snoop was rather a fool. So at least there would be some reciprocity.

Among a series of events that led me from archaeology to folklore and thence to social anthropology, perhaps the most important was a meeting with another anthropologist, Peter Allen, who was doing fieldwork in the Mani peninsula of southern Greece at the time and told me that if I wanted to be an anthropologist (which was how I was beginning to define myself), I should certainly go to John Peristiany's conference on Mediterranean family structures in Nicosia in the summer of 1970 (see Peristiany 1976). My parents enthusiastically supported the project—as refugees who had both lost academic careers, I think they still hoped I would land on my academic feet, although they never pressured me. In Nicosia, I met my future mentor, the gentle, wise, and infinitely perceptive John Campbell, as well as several other anthropologists who have remained good friends and colleagues ever since. I remember being overwhelmed—once again—by the theoretical sophistication of others, this time by people who could talk airily about "FBD marriage" and the like; but the die was definitely cast.

As a result of my faltering start as an unsuccessful undergraduate archaeologist, I later heard there was some hesitation about admitting me to Oxford. But I had meanwhile spent a year in Greece and gone on to write a master's thesis on Greek folklore under the generous and knowledgeable supervision of Margaret Alexiou, and the late Edwin Ardener—to whose memory I will always be grateful—evidently decided that I looked like a good risk, and so I got my second chance. Campbell—who had, it appears, enthusiastically endorsed my application—could not supervise me during that first year because he was not technically a member of the Institute of Social Anthropology, and so I was assigned to Ravindra K. Jain—another great teacher—who was generously supplemented in my fourth term, when Campbell was on leave, by the late Maurice Freedman. The logic of that first-year arrangement was that, since no one in the Institute "did the Mediterranean," Indian ethnology—Jain's specialty—seemed the best fit.

All this was formative of what was to come later because, in an Institute already dominated by Evans-Pritchard's insistence on the centrality of comparison in social anthropology, I was pulled at an early stage away from the narrow country specializations that became ever more frequent subsequently as bibliographies swelled, the permitted time to degree completion shortened, and funds became scarcer. But back then I was blissfully unaware of such complexities. I read a lot of African ethnology, managed to annoy the great "E-P" by disagreeing with him in the Institute students' house journal,[1] was so enraptured by the complexities of Indian kinship and the elegance of formal reciprocity that I started looking for parallels in Greece, and generally felt that at last I had found my true calling. That feeling, at least, has never weakened. I suspect that the frequency with which anthropologists turn out to be refugees from other disciplines—even, as in the cases of Edmund Leach, Ed Bruner, and Akhil Gupta, from engineering—presages the tendency they sometimes display, later in life, to wander outside their geographical areas of primary specialization.

I wrote my doctoral thesis on categories of inclusion and exclusion in a

1. See Herzfeld (1973). At the party held to celebrate the first-year students' successful completion of the diploma requirements, Godfrey Lienhardt came over and told me that "E-P would like a word." In the only encounter I had with the great man—he died shortly afterward—I got a rather severe dressing-down for, he rather trenchantly claimed, failing to understand his arguments in my article, which had originated as a paper for one of my weekly "supervisions" by Ravi Jain.

village on the island of Rhodes—a fairly classic, structuralist-oriented exercise—and it was far from an unqualified success. This was partly because I had been all *too* successful in terms of "participant observation"—about halfway through my projected year of fieldwork, I got kicked out of Greece by the colonels' regime, apparently at the instigation of an ambitious policeman who managed to get two or three locals to accuse me (precisely of what, I was never told). My wife and I were newly wed at the time, so we decided to take advantage of our eviction and honeymoon in Rome, rather than doing fieldwork. Who could have predicted that twenty-five years later, we would return to Rome for, precisely, fieldwork? By the time I got back to Greece a few weeks later, with some political help that was itself redolent of Campbell's description of patronage (see Campbell 1964: vii, 213–62*)*, I was in a very different mood politically, although it still took some years for this to become apparent. Meanwhile, unwilling to embarrass the decent citizens of that Rhodian village—or to confront the potential hostility of those few who had probably been responsible for my expulsion—I decided to work in Crete instead, and found myself in the village that I later came to describe in *The Poetics of Manhood* (Herzfeld 1985*)*. The thesis that resulted from this unplanned multisited fieldwork was a contrived affair, a strange essay in rather forced comparativism that I never published but "cannibalized" into articles each of which then took on a life of its own. Once again, near-disaster turned into something that for me, at least, proved beneficial.

This might be the appropriate moment to broach the complexities of my wife's role. Cornelia (Nea) Mayer Herzfeld, an American trained in classical philology and working for a junior-year-abroad program in Athens (where we had originally met), continued to share many of my field experiences with enthusiasm and commitment. Not an anthropologist by training, she often nevertheless showed herself far more adept than I was at organizing information about kinship and other abstrusely anthropological concerns. She also proved herself a remarkable photographer, as the published account of our time in the mountain village I have called "Glendi" demonstrates to the full—especially in her ability, striking in someone so characteristically quietly thoughtful and unassertive, to engage the affectionate but always respectful gaze of even the toughest and most swashbuckling of the animal-rustling shepherds with whom I consorted much of the time. (It perhaps did not hurt that one of her distant maternal ancestors had been hanged in England for nothing other than sheep theft!) She has continued to add depth and affect to my relations with informants in all my fieldsites, becoming a pedestrians' rights activist (what I called a "militant pedestrian") in Rome, and sharing moments of real terror in potentially dangerous moments in our Bangkok friends' struggle against collective eviction while also contributing her organizational flair to their efforts. But now I am running ahead of my story.

In 1978 I moved to the United States and to my first full-time job, at Vassar, after which I moved to Indiana University in 1980. For most of this time, I felt no real intimation of desire to test my ethnographic skills anywhere other than in Greece, so we can fast-forward to 1989–1990, when the first stirrings of rebellion against my self-imposed cultural isolationism began. Indiana University had a distinguished tradition in Turkish studies, and to take advantage of campus resources, I decided to investigate the fate of the Muslim Cretans—who, designated as "Turks" because of their religion, had been forcibly transferred to Turkish territory during the population exchange that followed the Turkish defeat of the Greek military in 1922. And so I went to Ayvalık, a seaside town on the northwest coast of Turkey, on a brief prospecting trip to the most famous concentration of these refugees and their descendants.

There followed scenes of mutual astonishment. By this time, I spoke fairly creditably in the Cretan dialect—which happened to be the intimate language of the community. In Ayvalık, I recall one old woman who spoke barely a word of Turkish. But these Cretan Muslims were no less surprised to encounter a British speaker of a dialect that had by now become fairly diluted in much of Crete but was still strongly preserved in "my" village—a rather lawless place, to be sure, but for that very reason culturally conservative in important ways that included not only animal theft but also the ineluctable obligations of the blood feud. I had begun learning a little Turkish, but it proved less useful during those two weeks or so than my knowledge of Cretan Greek. Soon thereafter, however, I discovered that a Greek graduate student was already working in the community—although I was told nothing about her by the residents and had only the vaguest idea that someone from her university might be working in the area. I opted to leave the field open to her, because at that point, Italy seemed like an interesting alternative, and I already spoke that language. So I stepped back from a possibility that had been a very alluring mixture of the familiar and, for me, the culturally novel—a different religious system, a new language, and a political system that was intriguingly teetering between aggressive secularism and new trends leading in exactly the opposite direction.

By now, I had moved to Harvard (in 1991), and something in that change of location may have added to the desire to change field location as well. I toyed with a number of possible sites; my wife, ever both sensitive to my interests and imaginative in her sense of the possible, demanded why Rome was not high on my list. She was, of course, absolutely right; and Rome was where we went.

In my turn to Italy, there was no direct connection with Greece, although my colleagues regarded this transition as relatively understandable. Here, they thought, was the other classical land, a European place in "the Mediterranean." So everything ought to be rather familiar.

This did not seem quite right. Dimly at first, then with increasing clarity, I sensed that Italy was in one important respect the precise opposite of Greece. Whereas Greece had seemed a very unified land, with tiny ethnic and religious minorities and a policy of not recognizing the specificity of ethnic difference at all, Italy was clearly fragmented in all sorts of fascinating ways. Romans themselves spoke a dialect that not only was distinguishable from the "standard" Italian usually taught to foreigners, but was clearly despised by most other Italians—and even by bourgeois Romans, who insisted that there was no such thing and that anyway, if there had ever been a real Roman speech mode in the heyday of the dialect poet G. G. Belli, it no longer existed but had been dragged down to the depths by the cultural depravity of poorly educated and partly foreign youth. Such language ideologies are by no means uncommon, but it was startling to encounter this particular stance in the capital—the self-designated *caput mundi* ("head of the world") of ancient times, and still the core of what is arguably the world's oldest global religion.

I began my Rome work with some exploratory encounters with artisans, thinking that perhaps I could pursue the kind of work I had already done with artisans' apprentices on Crete. That remains a possibility, although the number of apprentices has become vanishingly small; social security costs and the allure of more prestigious modes of learning have effectively put an end to craft apprenticeship. So my interests soon shifted toward another theme familiar from my Greek work—the impact of historic conservation on the lives of local residents—and I came to Rome in 1999 for a full year's sabbatical research on the topic.

That was when my original self-view really began to fall apart. My earlier reluctance to work outside Greece had arisen from a feeling that I could never match the level of linguistic competence that I enjoyed in that country: fluent standard modern Greek, a good grasp on a dialect or two, a working knowledge (based on my high-school classical Greek) of the neoclassical *katharevousa* used in the universities, the media, and all public pronouncements until the fall of the colonels. In fact, it turned out, not only was my Italian quite workable, but I was so charmed by the local dialect and accent that it quickly invaded my speech (to the later amusement of some of my Italian students and colleagues), and a language I had viewed as appropriate to opera and friendship suddenly became a manageable fieldwork tool as well. To make matters even more delightful, it transpired that Romans might have invented themselves for the benefit of anthropologists; they described themselves as "chatterboxes" (*chiacchieroni*)—and energetically lived up to that self-portrayal. It would have been hard *not* to learn the local accent.

Meanwhile, I began to discover just how pernicious the rash of evictions from homes and workplaces then plaguing Rome was proving for my increasingly numerous friends in the neighborhood (Monti) where I had chosen to work, and this led me to a growing involvement in questions of housing rights. These questions were certainly complicated. The nation's far right, for whom I had no political sympathy, were filling a gap created by the increasing complacency of a heavily intellectual and ideologically purist left, presenting their local faces to the evictees as staunch supporters of the marginalized lower middle class in their struggle to retain a foothold in the increasingly gentrified historic center of the city. Some of those facing eviction were tempted to accept the help of the neofascists, with disastrous results; while the rightists were more than willing to help erect and maintain barricades against the authorities who came to enforce eviction orders, this was a clearly local ploy that did not fully disguise their party's much more prochurch and probusiness orientation, and their local interventions alienated many of the old leftists from those few who succumbed to the allure of this support. Since I knew one member of the then center-left government (a neighbor who was both an anthropologist and an active member of the Green Party), I was able to help one group of people facing eviction to organize a press conference with a much wider spectrum of political representation than they might have managed on their own. Very few ordinary people actually came to the press conference; some local observers also suspected that the newspapers, at least one of which was under the control of a magnate with close ties to the major banks, had deliberately ignored the occasion. But at least for me as an observer, the political dynamics revealed at that press conference helped to make sense of the apparent disjuncture between the national and local levels of ideological action.[2]

I got into the habit of videotaping such events. Meetings are notoriously hard to follow, even in a culture where people are more inclined to take turns speaking rather than, as in Rome, to erupt in raucous and highly dramatic

2. This fieldwork is represented most fully by a book (Herzfeld 2009b) and a film (Herzfeld 2007), the latter to be discussed below.

arguments at frequent intervals. Sound recordings are also resistant to easy decipherment after the fact. So I had begun to videotape all sorts of meetings—street gatherings, meetings of local activists, formal seminars, demonstrations, even a condominium meeting (which turned out to be richly suggestive of intergenerational tensions over whether it was better to be corrupt and save money or follow the rules and face the rapidly billowing expense of living in Monti). My video camera did not go unnoticed. A neighbor—a hairdresser who had a great deal more experience than I possessed in using a video camera, and who used much more sophisticated equipment—pointed out that I was obviously doing a lot of filming; and so, said he, why not make a film about two brothers who ran a newspaper stand in the district square and who had a stock of great stories to relate?

As it happened, I had recently acquired a video editing program, so I decided to experiment with it. The result, which departed in various ways from the project originally suggested by my neighbor, was the first version of what eventually became *Monti Moments*—a film about the artisans and shopkeepers who, while desperately trying to resist the pressure to move out, recall the hardships as well as the good fellowship of an earlier age. A rough cut was aired in the main square, but the film underwent many more revisions as I learned about editing on the job, much as I had learned the Italian language many years before.

A few years later, videotaping meetings was also to be an important component of my research in Bangkok, where it enabled me to provide evidence that Pom Mahakan, the community with which I was working, needed to convince a United Nations commission that it had democratically decided to request that commission's intervention in its struggle to stay in place.[3] But now, once again, I anticipate myself. Linear narrative does not best serve these interweaving dimensions of a complex trajectory, but some sense of sequence nonetheless remains important for understanding the links among them.

Why Bangkok? Most of my colleagues accepted that shifting from Greece to Italy was somehow natural—such is the force of area studies conventions. From one Mediterranean country to another, they seemed to think—and this,

3. The United Nations intervention came as the result of an appeal to the Committee on Cultural, Economic, and Social Rights of the UN in Geneva. The committee requested evidence that the decision to approach it had been taken by the community as a whole, which I was able to provide in the form of a brief description of a videotape I had made of the meeting at which that decision was taken despite strenuous efforts to make sure that any possible objections were given a hearing. In Rome, I briefly encountered another United Nations entity, a fact-finding group investigating the housing crisis. Both are reported in AGFE (2005).

despite my already well-known criticisms of the Mediterraneanist paradigm. But there was, to be sure, something quite quixotic about the shift to Thai-land.

One of my oldest and closest friends, someone I had known as a schoolboy in England, is Thai. When I had the opportunity to go to Hong Kong for a conference in the spring of 1997, it seemed like the perfect opportunity to visit Prudhisan Jumbala, now a political scientist and recently retired from Chulalongkorn University in Bangkok. I had not seen him for nearly three decades. A rapturous reunion and a talk at his university, at which he introduced me to a few very interesting colleagues, began the process of my involvement—cemented by my finding, on my return to Harvard, that I could take an undergraduate class in the Thai language. Who knows what subconscious calculations were pressing me in that direction? One of the Thai scholars I met, Paritta Chalermpow Koanantakool, remained in e-mail contact with me, and after a wonderful exchange of ideas spanning several months, she suggested I return to Bangkok to conduct a short seminar with her. The die was cast.

One of the world's most distinguished scholars of Thailand, Stanley J. Tambiah, was still teaching in our department while my interest in things Thai was beginning to stir; he initially avoided hearing my professed intention to start fieldwork in Thailand. One day, thoroughly exasperated, I finally confronted him, and he admitted to worrying that I might be abandoning my work comparing Greek and Italian nationalisms. Soon, however, especially after hearing me speak Thai one day, he came around to the idea that I was actually going to do the Thai work as well. His support from that point on, as generous and selfless as his earlier concern over my inexplicably reckless lurch into the unknown had been, was certainly vital. Another colleague, Mary Steedly, meanwhile reassured me that, if I focused on issues I had already examined in Europe, I should be able to produce something worthwhile. Such collegiality has been my great good fortune at Harvard, and I owe an enormous debt to all the people I have mentioned here for helping me overcome my own doubts and inhibitions as, parachute-less, I swerved blindly over the edge of the cliff.

It turned out that there were some points of resemblance between my interests in Thailand and those I had pursued in southern Europe. I had already worked on historic conservation and its impact in both Greece and Italy. Saipin Suputtamongkol, then a student of mine (and the first Thai anthropologist to do field research in Italy, or indeed in Europe), drew my attention to the crucially important Rattanakosin Island project, a plan to develop the area of old Bangkok as a monumental complex in honor of the ruling dynasty. This area is rich with tiny communities, each with its own origins, ethnic composition, and professional identities. Some are middle-class; many are dilapidated and neglected. What they shared was uncertainty about a future dominated by a series of master plans, each of which would erase the complex palimpsest of populations long attached to temples and markets in favor of a bureaucratic demarcation of monuments to the past—at once a large-scale diorama, an iconic display of national unity, and a simplified vision of Thai national identity.

My first, stumbling attempts at fieldwork in Thailand were not very productive. Although I had studied Thai for a couple of years in anticipation of this research, the language I encountered on the street seemed very different from what I had formally learned in class. People, especially in the market communities, were very busy, and most of them had little time or patience for a strange foreigner who was often clutching at thin air for the right words and phrases, and whose Italian-inflected gestures were vaguely menacing. My own depression at this state of affairs was hardly helped by the constant, and inevitable, comparison with my fluency in Greek and Italian; this new language seemed distinctly less accessible. Gradually, however, and then more suddenly at one catalytic moment, as I became a more familiar presence, and especially as my gestural comportment adjusted to local norms, I began to make more sense to others and to be able to produce something that sounded moderately understandable as well.[4]

It is worth pausing for a moment to consider the impact of the anthropologist's own professional trajectory through real time on the actual content of field experiences. When I began work in Greece, I was a student; and, as a student (especially at a time of right-wing dictatorship), I was insignificant, possibly a nuisance, and certainly ignorant. I could be refused access to information, snubbed, and, as eventually happened, kicked out of the country, all with impunity. By the time I arrived in Thailand, I was even more ignorant and personally still quite insignificant. But I was now also a professor from a prestigious university who had acquaintances in high places and—or so many Thais seemed to think—powerful patronage up my sleeve. In the market, people responded poorly to my broken speech because they had no time to waste in putting aside their commercial activities even for a few minutes, and because they did not necessarily know that I was not a weird tourist who had wandered away from the flock at the Grand Palace. But others,

---

4. The unexpected allegation that I "looked Thai" sprang, not from my physiognomy, but from a rather sudden change in my bodily comportment (see Herzfeld 2009a).

who knew what institution I represented, decided to take a more active hand. Some of these people proved very helpful. In particular, the mysterious "Mr. Tortoise," known to most of the foreign anthropologists who had spent any time in Bangkok, proved to be extraordinarily well connected and willing to share his contacts with me.

And then, one day, came the most important stroke of good fortune. I had already attended a small demonstration launched in a public area by a tiny community, Pom Mahakan, against its collective eviction by the authorities, who were threatening to move imminently against the residents. Some while later, an NGO activist of my acquaintance suggested that I accompany him to another demonstration the community was holding on its own territory. At first, I was not very enthusiastic. I thought this community was too small and too closed to be of interest, and I did not see its problems as related to my current obsession with "historic conservation." I should have known better. Such serendipitous encounters often produce the best contacts—as when, decades earlier, I had gone to the wrong bus stop and ended up in the Cretan village where I went on to do research on reciprocal animal theft and masculinity.

The Bangkok encounter, it later transpired, was actually not quite as serendipitous as it seemed at the time. I learned a long while afterward that the NGO activist and the residents had discussed whether a certain Harvard professor who was doing research in the area might usefully be co-opted into the struggle against eviction. Apparently they thought it was worth a try. My own initial reaction was correspondingly casual; I thought I had nothing to lose by going along for a couple of hours. And so began one of the most intense engagements of my life.

The demonstration itself was certainly arresting. In the front area of the community's space, located beneath an imposing white, late eighteenth-century citadel set in the original city wall, two individuals—a man who was the community's effective president and a woman who was a housing rights activist—held a "conversation," using microphones to amplify the sound, about the history of the place and the rights of the residents to remain. Since I saw how busy they were, I left my business card with them, then moved away—only to hear the activist say how the visit now of a professor from Harvard proved that their cause was getting attention for the historical significance of the place and the community. A microphone was then thrust at me, and I was asked whether I would support the community in its struggle. Struggling with my inept Thai, I explained that I would not make promises because I was not a politician but that, if the residents helped me get information about their situation, I would decide later whether I should help; that in general I favored allowing communities to remain *in situ*; but that each case had to be decided on its merits. Much later, when my language skills were evidently somewhat improved, a community leader told me that the residents had found it hard to understand what I was saying. Apparently, however, they liked what they were able to extract from my remarks, because, very quickly, they came to see me as a friend and a supporter, as indeed I was and am.

Initially, my interest in their cause arose from their very palpable engagement with history. That they were poor and few in numbers gave them an advantage with which the then governor of Bangkok, Samak Sundaravej, had clearly failed to reckon: while he may have thought that they would have been the easiest group to sweep away, their effective leadership and almost completely unified stance effectively blocked what turned out to be a much more comprehensive plan to evict enormous numbers of people in communities all along Rajdamnoen Avenue, the broad ceremonial street that leads down toward the old palace grounds and that was destined, according to a much-mocked plan that emerged at about this time, to become the "Champs-Elysées of Asia."

That plan was the most recent manifestation of a curious Europhilia that seemed to support, not only the inclusion of much that was of Western origin in architecture and town planning, but even the architectural representation of "Thai-ness." One of my first associates in my Thai ventures, Vimalin Rujivacharakul, now a specialist in Chinese architectural history at the University of Maryland but for a brief while my research assistant at Harvard, wrote a paper showing how such modeling of Thai architectural features actually followed the dictates of a Western-inspired model of cultural identity (Vimalin 1999). That insight coincided in an important way with my growing realization of one (perhaps retrospective) factor that had led me from Greece to Thailand.

That factor was the curious circumstance that both countries, while historically never comprehensively placed under official colonial rule, had become modernist nation-states in the image imposed on them by the colonial powers, and continued to manage the image of their respective national cultures largely in accordance with the colonial powers' expectations. I laid out my first systematic account of this remarkable—but hitherto largely unremarked—phenomenon in an article commissioned by the Mexico-based Indian anthropologist Saurabh Dube (scion of a famous family of Indian anthropologists), who wanted to bring together a group of scholars who were as impatient as he was with the conventional binarism of colonies and colonizing powers. Another happy piece of serendipity thus allowed me to articulate my ideas at a relatively early stage in my explorations in Thailand. And I was then fortunate in the generosity of another great scholar and old friend, Thai historian Thongchai Winichakul, who in turn spoke of these ideas to an audience that included a Thammasat University Women's Studies student, Woranuch Charungratanapong; she in turn wrote an important piece about their impact on the architectural designs of Rattanakosin Island and of the new restoration project of "crypto-colonialism" (using Thongchai's translation of the term into Thai as *anaanikhom aphraang*). When I read that article, I realized that the connection between my Greek and Thai work was indeed viable (and was relieved that I had followed Mary Steedly's advice so closely!). I felt even more elated when, once I had started working at the Pom Mahakan community, a Bangkok weekly trumpeted "crypto-colonialism" over a photograph of me with video camera in hand, apparently surveying the space around the Golden Mount Temple that towers over the community.[5]

I have been asked, notably by Paritta Chalermow Koanantakool, whether I have always followed friendships in exploring new avenues of research. Certainly, by now, it should be clear that this has been an important factor. It has given some degree of coherence to the twists and turns of my intellectual path, and provided a sense of staying connected over a world stretched ever wider afield; at various times, for example, I have reconnected both professionally and personally with Paul Atkinson, Ravi Jain, and Prudhisan Jumbala. Maria Minicuci, an Italian anthropologist who teaches in Rome, has been a powerful influence, as much through her consistent friendship as through her combination of intellectual rigor, theoretical curiosity, and deep ethical commitment to her students and her craft. And it is surely neither irrelevant to the theme of friendship nor coincidental to the way I have worked that my wife and I met in Greece, share a deep passion for Rome, and developed an affectionate curiosity about, and ethical commitment to, our shared friends in Bangkok as well as in the places of our other field adventures.

So I think that I would now phrase the answer to the question about friendship as follows. First, friendship both motivates and enables what I do; it is the affect that also brings a sometimes astonishingly powerful emotion to all my dealings with the people at Pom Mahakan, where it is palpable in the very un-Thai-seeming embraces that galvanize my arrivals and departures to tears of pure joy but also of corrosive worry about my friends' security and happiness, and in the burning anger I still experience when I think of big

---

5. See Anonymous (2004); Herzfeld (2002); Woranuch (2002); and cf. Thongchai (2001).

capital evicting decent people from their homes, whether in Bangkok or in Rome. Friendship is the paramount value of what it means to be a human, an *anthropos* in Greek (or *manut* in Thai). Without that irresistible current of attachment, anthropology, the intimate study of human relations, seems pointless and arid. And second, I see no reason to distinguish between those affective relationships and those I have been privileged to enjoy with teachers, present colleagues, and students. All are my mentors, because their affection and commitment constantly open my senses to new understandings.

Friendship has thus also deeply informed how I respond to what I have encountered in the field. This point is linked to a methodological issue. I have followed the letter of some projects as originally proposed; other projects have deviated because my friends showed me that those original conceptions were either infeasible or less interesting. I did not *intend* to study Pom Mahakan. I did not *intend* to get involved in that community's struggle (Rome seemed a slightly different proposition inasmuch as, being a European Union citizen and now also part-time resident there, I have some legally protected participatory rights). But the ineluctable fire that drives my fascination with the revamping of history and ignites my own fury at the way history has been used to justify genocide burns even more intensely when I am watching people sign away the physical sites of their lives to impassive lawyers and rapacious contractors, or when bureaucrats sweetly announce that there is nothing a community can do to save its collective soul because a nominalistic reading of the law can be invoked to force the residents into an unknown future. That much I do now know; and I understand why, over the years, my near-indifference in earlier years to the plight of people facing dislocation from their homes has gradually transmuted into a helpless inability to refuse engagement. Helplessness: there it is—the one sensation that perhaps can enable us to experience, however partially, what our friends feel when they are faced with the brutality of eviction, prejudice, and suppression of their most treasured values.

That experience of intersubjectivity, which for me is tempered by a well-trained and even slightly puristic resistance to claiming to understand others' innermost feelings, has also given me another important insight. The nation-state, as we know it today, is largely the product of Cartesian and positivistic impulses, and the creation of capital cities follows and reflects those impulses. It is thus a curious irony that some scholars, among whom Thai social scientists allied to the dominant political establishment are not atypical, should invoke the Cartesian ideal of objectivity in asking me how it is possible to do good research and yet be so involved in community politics and so obviously committed to the residents themselves. It is an irony because these purveyors of objectivism, to use Bourdieu's apt term ([1972] 1977),[6] do not appear to realize that they are also involved—as purveyors of an ideological position, that of the state and the academic establishment. But there is an even simpler answer, which is the one I usually give: that without that deep involvement, I would never be privy to much of the information I possess now, information that shows how inaccurate the official portrayals of the community have been. Even from the perspective of older intellectual traditions that treated objectivity as unproblematic, access to greater expanses of data increases, rather than undermines, the observer's ability to offer a realistic picture.

And so the generosity of friends has been a guiding force in much of what has happened to me professionally over the past two decades. That seems not only acceptable but logically fitting in a study of human predicaments—of what another good friend and colleague, Arthur Kleinman, so appropriately calls "local moral worlds" (2006:219; see also Kleinman 1999:90). These are not necessarily "local" in some Malinowskian sense of a bounded place; none of us is an island, none could do the work we do without the friendships that give it meaning.

Even in a more technical sense, the idea of locality needs stretching, as a number of anthropologists have been arguing, to new possibilities. From an early point, in my work in the mountains of Crete, I was in effect working on an ethnography of the state—not through its offices and institutions, but through a group of people who gave it meaning through their very opposition to it. A community of "thieves," whose identity as such invokes the swashbuckling guerillas of the original Greek national revolution—the so-called klefts, whose name derives from the Greek word for thieves—poses interesting questions about the legitimacy of the nation-state and its formal representatives. Moreover, the concentric circles of social and political identification were all realized in one way or another at the level of the village community.

Such concentricity was the key to the expansion of my interests. When I moved to an urban context in Greece, it was first to the provincial capital to which the mountain village in question was nominally subordinate (and practically *in*subordinate!). Again, I was interested in the play among the various concentric identities. Although I never "did fieldwork" in Athens, I lived there for several years, and this too gave me a strong sense of preparation for work in

6. Bourdieu himself can be taxed with objectivism in some of his writings, but the term is especially useful when we examine the unexamined, mutual permeation of academic and state discourses.

capital cities. In Rome and in Bangkok alike, I found myself working in a well-defined area in the city center, a small but symbolically charged space—the Monti district in Rome, the Pom Mahakan community in Bangkok—that condensed within its confines a sense of representing the oldest, most intensely local, and historically and architecturally most significant signs of the past.[7]

What my Cretan village work had taught me, however, was that even the smallest community in the most remote rural area is but the innermost of a set of concentric or sometimes overlapping entities. Now, in each of these capital cities, I could almost literally see the innermost circumvallation—the Aurelian Walls in Rome (not far from where I was, and in any case the Colosseum and the Forum made the location unmistakable); the old dynastic wall that, in Bangkok, provided one edge of the space of Pom Mahakan. These spaces were somewhat protected from the kind of officially inspired violence that has often accompanied evictions in the suburbs of both cities. In Rome, the presence of wealthy investors meant that too brutal a repression could have had a catastrophic effect on land values; in Bangkok, tourism would clearly have suffered, since Pom Mahakan lies right on the edge of the broad avenue that leads down to the Grand Palace and in full view of the popular Golden Mount Temple.

Studying a capital city inevitably means studying the nation-state that it both commands and symbolizes. Since much of my work in Greece centered on nationalism in one way or another, the fascination exercised by the architectural, spatial, and above all social fragmentation of Rome (I was originally going to call my book on that project *Fractured Eternities*) seemed to concentrate within an ethnographically accessible space the radical disjunctures of a nation now twice ruled by coalitions of arch-nationalists and northern separatists. Such an unholy alliance would surely have led to immediate implosion almost anywhere else in the world, but in Rome it seemed embedded in the very fabric of a city whose inhabitants could actually sympathize with those who wished to dethrone (decapitalize?) their city—and where societies comprising personages of considerable local distinction advocated for, precisely, that improbable municipal abdication. So an ethnography of that Cretan mountain village was also an ethnography of the Greek nation-state—because, not in spite of, the villagers' hilarious and occasionally dangerous proclivity for totally illegal acts (they recently shot down a police helicopter). And an ethnography of the historic core of old Rome could not but be an ethnography of the curiously paradoxical nation-state that it reproduced in microcosmic form.

7. For a comparison of the three capitals, see Herzfeld (2006).

Bangkok, too—a capital far more sprawling and undisciplined than any European city, and increasingly distrusted by the desperately poor farmers of the neglected northeastern areas of the country (*paakh Isaan*)—presents a divided self that reproduces those larger cleavages in which it participates. Within this capital, Pom Mahakan emblematizes for me one of the enduring paradoxes of "Thai-ness" (*khwaam pen thai*), that curiously occidental self-reification that constitutes the basis of the battle over the future of the Thai past. Some of those who oppose the community's continuing existence claim that it is not a real community at all, on the grounds that it did not arise from a single profession and that its residents came as squatters from many parts of the country. These arguments expose the contradictions that lie at the heart of every essentialism. "Unity in diversity," *e pluribus unum*: all national societies represent their divergent origins as a source of cultural wealth and transcendent commonality. Thailand is no exception; Thais take explicit and demonstrative pride in the brilliant variety of physiognomies, cultural traits, dialects, religious traditions, and aesthetic styles that together comprise its signature diversity. Bangkok mirrors the diversity of Thailand; and Pom Mahakan, the diversity of Bangkok. To evict the people of Pom Mahakan, and to replace it (as is the intention) with an empty lawn bordered by ornamental balustrades, is to put a decisive, material, visible, and highly localized seal on the taxonomic regimentation that has suppressed plural histories in favor of a grand narrative of essential, experientially empty sameness—and that flies in the face of the nation-state's own assimilationist rhetoric.

This is why I have become something of an activist. Curiously, my move away from scholarly purism has a scholarly explanation. It is a recognition of agency—the same theoretical stance that compels me to write in the first person for honesty's sake, and one that resonates with my ethical commitment to the people whose worlds I study. This commitment has grown at an ever-quickening pace. My consciousness of my own life trajectory, moreover, has made these ethical imperatives more urgent and less deniable. Time presses (Veena Das [2007:95] tells us that we experience time as possessing agency). I said that I would consider supporting the people of Pom Mahakan if they helped me gather material for my research. They did; and I must.

Inevitably, I suppose, an essay of this nature has something of the quality of a *Bildungsroman*. If there is one unifying theme that I can trace along its entire trajectory, it is the recognition that our theoretical capital emerges from our experiences and is inspired by the theoretical capacities of our informants. Even in *The Poetics of Manhood*, I noted that my informants, mostly shepherds with only a few years of primary schooling, possessed impressive theoretical capabilities. Some colleagues scoffed; these people, they said, had concepts—but . . . *theories?* To insist on such a distinction, and such a radical separation of them-as-object-of-study from us-as-thinkers, strikes me as the most imperial form of Cartesian dualism, recalling the logic of colonialism and of nationalistic folklore studies. What makes theory so sacrosanct, if not the fear of scholars of seeing their privileged abstraction diluted and even dissolved? Of course we can challenge the ideas our informants express; it would be condescending to do otherwise. But to hold exclusively to the norms of what my Italian colleague Berardino Palumbo (2003:305) incisively calls "philological correctness" is to engage in the logic of the bureaucratic state, rendering the latter relatively immune to analytical dissection. I am not advocating here for some exploitatively romanticizing "local knowledge." In addition to the historical inaccuracies with which Akhil Gupta has so accurately charged that concept, it has served some less than benign forces as a means of appearing to show respect while in fact creating a second-class category, much as "folk literature" did in an earlier time, or as the adulation given to "traditional artisans" in Greece and elsewhere results in their marginalization from the rush to modernity.[8]

The politicization of my interests sharpened most dramatically, perhaps, when Cambridge University Press, ignoring its appointed readers' advice, declined to publish a scholarly book about Greek Macedonia on what looked like largely political grounds. The ensuing dynamics of that sometimes painful situation, in which I found myself actively engaged, made me realize that publicity did not always work out in favor of the powerful. This is not the place to analyze those events, tempting though it may be.[9] But my concern with academic freedom, and the fact that being at Harvard gave me some very useful symbolic capital, prepared me well to take an active role in fighting a couple of tenure-candidacy injustices in other institutions and, eventually, to

8. See Gupta (1998); Herzfeld ([1997] 2004). The fact that local people may sometimes elevate "local knowledge"—not to be confused with Kleinman's "local (moral) worlds"—to the status of a national resource must be understood as a defense against appropriation and marginalization, as when the people of Pom Mahakan put a sign up outside their community museum reading "Community Local Knowledge Pavilion" (*saalaa phumipanyaa chumchon*). Challenging such claims, while consistent with anthropology's antiessentialist stance, is an ethically fraught business; see Jackson (1995) for a clear parallel from Colombia.

9. There was extensive media coverage of this, in several languages, and much of the relevant writing can be found online. For a position statement published at the height of the crisis, see Gudeman and Herzfeld (1996). The work was eventually published by the University of Chicago Press (Karakasidou 1997).

participate in the Living Wage Campaign at Harvard itself. That campaign forged a powerful friendship and alliance with one of the ringleaders, then a new doctoral student of mine, Maple Razsa—an experienced filmmaker as well as a remarkable anthropologist who has since become a key mentor to me in my stumbling attempts to develop my own ethnographic filmmaking skills.[10] And all these activities converged with my growing anger at the ways in which neoliberal and other hegemonic projects have been eroding both the academic commitment to open-minded intellectual inquiry and the lives of ordinary people the world over.

It has become ever clearer to me that there is no such thing as an ivory tower for anthropologists. Indeed, the very notion of such a rarefied space reproduces the violent anti-intellectualism that also fuels the commercial assault on the living spaces of the poor as well as on the intimately rebellious discipline we call social anthropology. It is thus part of a widespread and pernicious attempt to divide intellectuals from the world's weakest citizens. Anthropologists cannot afford, conceptually or ethically, to become complaisant in such a corrosive poisoning of their shared humanity.

The very chanciness, the serendipity, of anthropological research, which is often the object of reproachful critiques by more positivistically inclined social scientists (and by ill-informed public critics, insofar as they take any interest at all), is actually the source of its greatest strength. The experience of fieldwork certainly alerted Malinowksi to the injustices of racism, even if he was later to be charged with precisely that flaw. The moral is not that we must become perfect (such hubris!), but that we must constantly engage and resist the corruption of power by turning its analytic capacities on its own modes of operation. Our meandering pathways, our intimate and long-term engagement with people who are not particularly famous or obviously talented, our willingness to listen to gossip and find significance in the most trivial of objects and utterances, and our skepticism in the face of mechanical methodologies—these are the sources of that "productive discomfort," as I once called it (Herzfeld 1992:16), that enables us to resist an intellectually stultifying closure.[11]

10. For information on Razsa's films, including *Occupation* (a documentary on the sit-in that marked the culmination of the Living Wage Campaign at Harvard), see http://www.en massefilms.org.

11. It is not by chance that this point occurs in a work in which I attempt to debunk the rationalistic claims of nation-state bureaucracies—claims that are often used as what we might call, with apologetic acknowledgment of James Scott's (1985) justly famous formulation, "weapons *against* the weak."

I am aware that I have been extraordinarily privileged in being able to make the geographical as well as intellectual relocations discussed here. My personal circumstances, including the absence of children and the eager involvement of an adventurous but also very practically minded spouse, were such as to mitigate the necessary disruptions and even render them interesting. The aborted Turkish venture and the ultimately very happy Roman one made obvious sense. The less easily explained move to Thailand entailed only minimal career risks inasmuch as, had I failed to make any sense of it, I still had a secure position and plenty of materials for future projects and publications about Greece and Italy.[12] As I have already noted, my initial encounters with the Thai language were discouraging; but the shift brought about by changes in my gestural comportment, the experience of writing about Pom Mahakan for the Thai press under the patient supervision of my field assistant of that time (linguist Nowwanij Siriphatiwirat), the patience (as well as the language correction) I have encountered at Pom Mahakan, and my great good fortune in engaging with Thai colleagues and students (I am now a faculty affiliate of the Department of Sociology and Anthropology at Thammasat University)—all brought me to the point where I could function with reasonable linguistic and cultural competence, even though I am aware of still being very much of a new kid on the block. My friends who are Thai specialists of much longer standing have been generous in their tolerance of my fumbling first steps.

So where now? I have learned not to force predictions on myself; serendipity and the work of the unconscious are richer sources of eventual insight. I am learning another language (Chinese), thinking of where that may lead me, and planning to research the local worlds of town planners in at least two countries—perhaps not surprisingly, Italy and Thailand, in both of which such a project emerges easily from my focus on urban design, gentrification, and relocation. The work on journalists by Ulf Hannerz (2004) and Dominic Boyer (2005), different though their respective approaches are, inspires me to think in terms of experimental reorganizations of the ethnographic project, from spatially bounded entities to social groups concerned with lived space.[13] I want to make more films, write about more ideas and places and people,

12. Here, I allude to the range of issues adumbrated by Alma Gottlieb in her introduction to this volume.

13. These two authors' approaches—Boyer's, deeply implicated in the genealogy of philosophical argument among professional intimates; Hannerz's, an unabashedly playful but very informative account of a dispersed profession—complement each other in richly suggestive ways.

and know more of the lives that intersect with mine. And I want to remain critically involved in thinking through, and acting on, what we mean by social justice. Such is the passion that social anthropology signifies for me and, I suspect, for those of my colleagues whose work I most esteem. I want—at whatever cost of frustration, rage, and thwarted compassion, and in the face of the bigotry that destroys the work of love and the spaces of its enactment— to remain engaged, for as long as I can, in the impossibly affecting and perversely alluring world that we make and remake together.

SIX

Traditions and Transitions: From Market Women in the Andes to Adoptive Families in the United States

Linda J. Seligmann

BECOMING AN ANTHROPOLOGIST

In 1974, as a junior in college, I wondered if the anthropology major I was pursuing was a good fit. The 1950s ethnographies that dominated my course readings had a weighty flatness that numbed my genuine curiosity about cultural differences and similarities. I had pursued anthropology as a major because I had grown up outside the United States. While born in Washington, DC, at the age of fifteen months I had been taken by my Euro-American parents to Japan, where I lived for almost eight years.[1] I lived in a Japanese neighborhood, went to a Japanese nursery school, and had Japanese friends. I spent close to another three years in Thailand at an international school and then returned to the United States just in time to be an awkward seventh grader, with almost no knowledge of American popular culture. This was intriguing, if painful. I was "American" but knew not what that meant. Hence, my informal interest in anthropology and, subsequently, my pursuit of it as a major in college.

I finally shed my ambivalence about whether or not I wanted to be an anthropology major after a semester of field research in Peru. As part of a "study abroad" group, I went to a monolingual, Quechua-speaking region in the southern Andean highlands, where we worked on independent as well as collaborative projects with students and faculty from the National University of San Antonio Abad in Cuzco. I stayed on in Peru another three months after the semester ended, immersing myself in life there. Thus serendipity mostly

1. My father was a career foreign service officer and Japanese language specialist.

explains why I became a Latin Americanist, specializing in the Andean region of Peru, rather than a scholar of, say, East Asia, where I'd been raised.

Over the years, I returned time and again to the Andes, to multiple sites, working on many different projects—including the symbolism of textile motifs as a visual language (Seligmann 1978), the history of textile production and exchange (Seligmann and Zorn 1981), and the intersection of oral traditions and the changing environmental knowledge embedded in irrigation systems (Seligmann 1987; Seligmann and Bunker 1994). At one point, I embarked on pilot field research in Ecuador, where a major movement to revolutionize education in indigenous highland communities was occurring, in conjunction with a pan-Indian wave of struggles to transform the institutionalized political landscape of Ecuador. However, the combination of political upheaval, whose signs I could not read well, and the challenges of learning a new variant of Quechua, persuaded me to return to the Peruvian Andean highlands.[2] Nevertheless, I learned a surprising amount from my brief foray into Ecuadorian culture and politics. Not least was my growing awareness of why most Andean countries had emerging indigenous movements, whereas Peru did not. The value of comparative research became more apparent in a way it had not been to me before, steeped as I was in an area studies approach to anthropology.[3]

CAREER AND LIFE TRAJECTORIES

My first book was based on my doctoral research on political struggles in the Peruvian Andes and the relationship of a radical agrarian reform to Peru's violent civil war in the 1980s and 1990s (Seligmann 1995). I conducted most of that research in the countryside. I then made a major shift, documenting the lives of market women who themselves straddled city and countryside (Seligmann 2001). In *Peruvian Street Lives*, I wrote a series of vignettes, embedding theory in stories, in order to reach a broader public (Seligmann 2004).

---

2. There are four variants of Quechua. While in some cases the roots of words are the same, the diacritics that make the difference in the grammar of the variant differ markedly. For those fluent in Cuzco or Cochabamba Quechua, which are more or less mutually intelligible, acquiring fluency in Imbabura Quichua or Ayacucho Quechua would be akin to learning a new language.

3. I had chosen to pursue an area studies approach in my graduate studies, first attending the Institute of Latin American Studies at the University of Texas–Austin for my master's degree, with concentrations in anthropology and Spanish-American literature, and then pursuing a doctorate in anthropology at the University of Illinois–Urbana, whose anthropology department had a renowned strength in Andean studies.

After having spent close to twenty years participating in the professional activities of the discipline, I had achieved a level of respect I found gratifying as a Latin Americanist. Within the Andes, I had painstakingly cultivated rapport, and although I still felt ignorant about some things, I grasped subtleties that characterized the complex political and social terrain of Peruvian society, within and outside academic circles. That familiarity formed a critical backdrop for all the diverse research projects I had undertaken. I had also made very good friends in Peru, with whom I still maintain contact.

After my family expanded to include my husband (who works outside the academy) and our daughter, whom we adopted from China, life cycle demands compelled me to reflect on the course of my career. There were other catalysts as well. I felt a need to refuel. Continuing to crank out papers and articles on the subject matter I was familiar with would be relatively easy, but my heart was not in it. I was also older, with less tolerance for harsh conditions that sometimes left me severely ill in the field; moreover, as a woman who had become one of the few full professors in my department, I had myriad administrative responsibilities.

One day, a surprising letter arrived in the campus mail from the dean. I had been selected as the recipient of the tenth annual faculty scholarship award and asked to give a major lecture as my reward. The dean and most of my colleagues expected I would deliver a talk on my work in the Andes. Yet I felt unwilling to talk about material that, while of interest to others, concerned issues about which I was no longer passionate. In fact, I found myself in a liminal state. Growing out of my husband's and my decision to adopt a girl from China, I had, over the previous three years, been doing informal fieldwork on a new set of issues . . . but I had not consciously acknowledged it. The dean's invitation inspired me to declare my new interests as a formal research project: comparing and contrasting the experiences of several types of families—those who had adopted children from China and from Russia; non-adoptive family members; and transracial families in the United States who had adopted African-American children. And so I took the scholarship lecture as an occasion to embark on my new project: an examination of competing models of family formation in the United States.

My choice of subject matter for that campus lecture compelled me to acknowledge something else. Perhaps partly as a result of personality, my research is propelled as much by passion, curiosity, and autobiographical experience as by attentiveness to the quality of the fieldwork and analysis of it. While these factors might have been more obvious with my new research project on adoption, they had also been relevant to my earlier experiences in the Andes, especially with respect to my work on market women. I had traveled with Peruvian women traders time and again over the five years I had spent doing research in Peru on other topics. Although perhaps not immediately apparent, my interest in market women had been catalyzed by my own autobiographical trajectory—in that case, as a straddler of worlds, an American raised largely in Japan. As a transnationally adoptive mother myself, my new research interest in transnational and transracial adoption was even more obviously integral to my life history. The task was to bring anthropological knowledge to bear on what is, for me, clearly an intimate topic.

As Paul Stoller observes in the afterword to this volume, many of us may reconstruct the research experiences that constitute our career trajectory as a "straight highway" when in reality our journey is hardly linear. Often, we take side roads, sometimes major arteries, and occasionally a detour or path that leads to a dead end. These routes are indicative of both continuities and disjunctures. Perhaps more subtly, they are also a reflection of what one hopes research is—the outcome of a spark of curiosity, and the process and result of labor invested in a genuine quest for knowledge.

TRANSITIONS, UNKNOWNS

Like many anthropologists who are both inside and outside their culture, I knew that I could survive half out of my skin elsewhere. I read and thought about my informal research and experiences and synthesized them for the scholarship lecture. It was exhilarating to be working in a new area . . . but also more terrifying than I recall my first field experience to have been in the Andes. Ironically, I had no "safety net"—no familiar landmarks and faces, no mentors, no token books or keystone articles as fetishes, and few traces of memory to guide my way. Abstractly, the methods, the process of field research, and the memory that ethnography is at once process and product were principal commonalities uniting my two fieldsites. I knew how to ask questions and how to listen to silences; how to connect dots and follow flows in a nonlinear fashion; how to move from talk to practice, and from history and process to representation.

Yet this particular ethnographic project was alien in ways that brought me up short . . . but that also intrigued me. I experienced the excitement of not knowing, of learning, and of serving as translator and mediator. Working in my own culture on questions that entailed barging into the intimacy of family life and struggling to locate interlocutors, some of whom were dead-set on becoming invisible, was more difficult than any of my prior fieldwork experiences. Once, at a group dinner at an annual anthropology meeting, I sat with a colleague who had known me a long time and respected my work on the Andes. When I told him about my new research, he responded, with some hostility, "Why would you want to do that? It's so private." It turned out that he himself was adopted. At the table, as well, were another colleague and his wife who had adopted three children and fostered several others. I had also adopted a child. Yet we did not talk about adoption at all after that initial exchange. Was it because the personal and private collided with the public and professional? Or was it because of our discomfort with the liminal interface between work and sociability, in which, rather than chatting as colleagues and friends, I would be cast as anthropologist and they as informants? In the latter role, they might find themselves thinking (out loud) anthropologically about their family lives—something they had not yet done. Or, perhaps, it was something to do with the topic itself?

I was working on subject matter that was as immediately significant and meaningful to me as it might be as a subject of scholarly importance. I was living it, but also trying to make sense of it anthropologically. My research was poised between extraction, dialogue, and autobiography. Too many such endeavors have gone awry or had negative consequences. Both my professional and personal identity and my "personal" life were up for grabs and were entangled rather densely. I wondered how to make my way. Should I return to the fold (of previous Andean research)? Sit on my modest laurels and let the river flow for a while? Or take the plunge? I took the plunge.

So what is there to report? Here, I address what I think are the most important differences and similarities between my prior field research in the Andes and my current project on transnational and transracial adoption in the United States in three areas: gaining a grounding, theoretically and substantively, in the research specialization; the process of doing field research and its analysis; and publication of findings. These areas necessarily overlap, but for purposes of this chapter, I address each separately. In the course of discussing each of these topics, I also suggest what might be common to all sociocultural anthropological projects.

MOORINGS

Despite some theoretical similarities between my past and present field research, the differences are greater. My prior research shares with this project an effort to pay keen attention to the practices, views, and voices of people, while heeding the historical, political, and socioeconomic contexts and institutions in which they materialize—and which people themselves may help to build, challenge, and transform. But I was originally trained in political economy as an anthropologist. My current work has stretched my mind in new theoretical directions, as I familiarize myself with literature on kinship, transnationalism, social geography, race in the United States, adoption studies, and popular religiosity. I often feel I am taking my doctoral exams all over again, drafting "field statements." My new project has required me to recognize starkly what I do not know and what I want to know, and to enter into an epistemological domain that incorporates humility and a sense of wonder.

Without making too much of the case, I would argue that shifts in field research sites may, on the one hand, be quite difficult for the anthropologist. Clearly, one is expected to do one's homework: learn a new language, if necessary, and certainly familiarize oneself with the ethnographic and historical literature and debates that constitute the field. On the other hand, field shifts may bring new perspectives and theoretical contributions to both an area of specialization and to general anthropological knowledge. Often, claustrophobia can beset fields of specialization. In terms of Pierre Bourdieu's ([1972] 1977) understanding of *habitus*, challenges to doxa—the taken-for-granted "rules" informing the patterning of practices and tastes of a particular field—may lead both to a shaking up of the field (heterodoxy), as well as to some scholars hunkering down and protecting the barricades (orthodoxy), so to speak. Anthropology is characterized by the poly-paradigmatic status of theories in play, such that revolutionary upheaval is exceedingly uncommon, even more so than in the natural sciences where, eventually, the burden of evidence forces institutions and bureaucracies to accept a new dominant paradigm (Kuhn 1962). Nevertheless, we can all point to moments when our foundational knowledge has been shaken. My point is that, as difficult as shifting fieldsites might be for the anthropologist, it is often healthy for the discipline itself. And it may be healthy for the anthropologist as well.

INSTITUTIONS AND NETWORKS

I came into my new research area and fieldsite without preconceived ideas about what it should be. I was also less familiar with the well-established history of the issues surrounding adoption, let alone of the principal figures engaging them. The act of establishing senior-junior relationships may be intimidating but is expected, one of the established cultural schemata and tropes within the hierarchical structure of academia. Senior-senior mentoring, in which one party behaves as a "junior," is more awkward. The networks already in place tend to be entrenched. Building a professional identity under these conditions feels a little like ritual hazing—sometimes hard to stomach, and certainly humbling. Yet newcomers bring novelties now and then, and that has been the case with my late-in-life entrée into a new research area. I have approached the subject matter with some humility, some naïveté, but also from an angle that has not yet received much attention. Each critique, each polite closed door, draws forth a renewed effort on my part to understand the institutional and anthropological reasons for those practices. It is not something I could have tolerated or easily undertaken twenty-five years ago, but my new project forces me to reembrace what originally animated my research: discovery, puzzle-solving, a commitment to intercultural communication, and, not least, sharing that process with a wider public.

Why "reembrace"? I do not think I am alone in acknowledging that in the course of my two decades, to date, in the academy, I have been unduly affected by the status jockeying and small power ploys of university life. I recall the words of my dissertation advisor frequently: "Never has the pie been so small and the fights so big." Hence, it is no small achievement to put power struggles on the back burner while recognizing how they erode some of the best-laid plans of scholars.

METHODOLOGICAL AND ANALYTICAL UNDERTAKINGS

My fieldsite—or should I write, fieldsites?—lends itself to the use of new methodologies and technologies. Before this project, for example, I had never imagined that, in addition to participant observation, I would do in-depth interviews via telephone and digital recorder, or rely as heavily as I do on modes of information, communication, and data processing via the Internet. Moreover, multisited field research has become one of the key tropes of our discipline. My work on market women in the Andes was multisited, but the multisidedness of my current project on adoption is qualitatively different. It requires participant observation across many different locales and entails a keen attention to the interaction of space and place in processes of identity formation and the constitution of shared cultural values and practices. An equally important, and problematic, artifact of this interview method is the individuation of interlocutors (Balasescu 2007). It is harder to track the interlinked networks and their dynamics that constitute adoption communities, which operate more like what Arturo Escobar (2004: 352), citing the Mexican philosopher Manuel de Landa, calls "meshworks." Yet these meshworks are one of the most important dimensions for an ethnographer to apprehend in order to understand the competing modes, as well as the malleability, of family formation in the United States (see also Latour's 2007 conceptualization of actor-network theory).[4]

Conversational interviews in which power differentials are not an issue create refreshing yet awkward opportunities for confrontation and commitment. In my current project, the adults with whom I speak are more certain about whether or not they desire to trust me than were *campesinos* (or bureaucrats or scholars, for that matter) in the Andes. If they decide they trust me, they have few qualms about asking questions, and making demands on me and the products of my work. It is much easier for them than it was for people in the Andes to decide whether or not they want to participate in my research, and to feel comfortable telling me their decision. I feel an urgency to comply with the promises and commitments I make, which range from providing book lists and copies of my publications and papers to offering workshops. Collaboration has always been part of my *modus operandi*, but it occupies a more prominent and deliberate place in this research (see Lassiter 2005). I also feel more pressure on me to define my position. Am I "against" transracial adoption or not? Are people who adopt internationally rather than domestically racist? Do I think all adoptions should be viewed as gifts from God? Don't I think being as American as apple pie in a great melting pot is healthier for adopted children than all this attention to the child's language and culture? And so forth.

The observations above point not only to what is involved in my shifting fieldsites, but also to significant differences in shifting from working elsewhere to working at home. It is difficult to judge which has more impact on how my research unfolds. Further, while all ethnographers—myself among them—struggle with ethical concerns, this struggle penetrates intensely and deeply in my current project because of my autobiographical engagement. I have always placed high value on making sure I tell and interpret stories with empathy. Some might call this "remaining balanced." The interpretation of stories is integral to my analyses, and inevitably I have a point of view—but,

4. As conceptualized by Escobar (2004), meshworks result from the "meshing" of networks, especially in the vastness of cyberspace, and encourage heterogeneity, decentralization, self-organization, mobility, and growth in unplanned directions in response to real-life situations. Some single networks may behave similarly to meshworks; others, as De Landa argues, are more hierarchical and centralized and operate at economies of scale. Because meshworks are emergent, it is difficult for ethnographers to track them simultaneously and to tack back and forth between meshworks and "real life," on-the-ground, communities, ascertaining their relationship.

more, I would like my interlocutors to be able to see themselves without being blinded by anger, resentment, or indignation at my interpretations. They may not agree with my analysis, but I want them to know that I follow their logic and story line, that I understand their concerns and objectives, even when I critique some of their assumptions.

Still, it is harder to achieve this sort of balancing act in one's own milieu. And the clamor for reciprocity is not intangible, distant, or romantic. It is right here, now; these interlocutors generally know how to claim their rights, and they network among themselves. So do all interlocutors, but physical distance combined with center-periphery power relations often make it difficult for them to act on or enforce their claims when they are a hemisphere away from the scholar who writes about them. There is an immediacy to the kind of pragmatic knowledge that is emerging from my current research. Coevality, pushing back against power differentials, and creating space for dialogical contestation, accountability, and collaboration all come to the fore in this study.

ROOTS AND TEMPORALITY

Reflecting on an article about his longitudinal field research project, James Watson noted:

> Anthropologists do not have the luxury of drawing a line in the sands of time and declaring a closure date for our research. Ethnography never ends. Even the demise of the original field-worker does not conclude the enterprise, given the inevitability of re-studies (usually conducted by younger scholars eager to overthrow past paradigms). (2004:893)

Watson commented that his article "was a product of contemporary ethnography; it describes a project that has a beginning but no clear end." In a similar vein, my new project has compelled me to track the families I have been working with through time. Of course, one can do this with all kinds of fieldwork, but the relative physical proximity of the families to my home life makes it easier.

Another impact of time involves how the age and status of the anthropologist shape the research process—whom she most interacts with in the field, and what she learns from them. Not only is all field research a product of intersubjectivity, but age and experience intervene in the way that intersubjectivity unfolds. Over time, this process occurs in a single site as well, but how we interpret what we participate in and observe, especially after it has acquired a familiar backdrop in ongoing work, may acquire a qualitatively distinct valence if we begin research in an entirely different fieldsite at a different age.

My new project also involves me in a more systematic mode of analysis. In my previous work in Peru, I was always able to "command" my data, coding, classifying, and interpreting them in the intense way that most ethnographers do when working with qualitative fieldnotes. But the nature of my new project on adoption cries out for more systematic analysis, hence I have learned how to use a sophisticated yet flexible qualitative data analysis program (NVivo) that has allowed me to make sense of the information I collect without flattening or reducing it, as many ethnographic software packages do. Learning new modes of analysis takes time, and time is at a premium at this stage of my life because of competing demands, but I have found it worthwhile to familiarize myself with this new methodology.

THE NOVELTY OF SHIFTING FIELDSITES?

The history of archaeology as well as sociocultural anthropology includes a long tradition of shifting from one fieldsite to another. What merits a closer look are the motivations and goals that anthropologists have had for shifting fieldsites, as understood within a historical context. There are many permutations of how and why anthropologists have made such moves. For earlier generations, three principal theoretical orientations prevailed: salvage anthropology; comparative field research (looking at the same phenomenon/structure in different cultures); and universals (Susan Trencher, personal communication).

In the early to mid-twentieth century, American anthropologists such as Alfred Kroeber and Robert Lowie, influenced by the Boasian paradigm of "salvage" research with its emphasis on history, environment, and psychology as principal forces shaping culture, conducted fieldwork among different peoples in the same part of the world, especially among different Native American Indian groups.[5] Boas's personal commitment to puncturing a model

---

5. Boas's *The Mind of Primitive Man* (1938) and his compendium of articles, *Race, Language and Culture* (1940), Kroeber's *Configurations of Culture Growth* (1944) and masterful *Handbook of the Indians of California* (1925), and Robert Lowie's *Primitive Society* (1920) exemplify these approaches, though it is important to recognize that Kroeber and Lowie, especially, would shift their views over time. Interestingly, Lowie returned to his roots toward the

of evolutionary hierarchy and racial supremacy, and to demonstrating cultural relativism, was also paramount to his own research in multiple sites in North America.

More comparative field research in different fieldsites has been motivated by several factors over the past century. One was explicitly political. In the early to mid-twentieth century, some national governments employed anthropologists in order to ascertain how best to achieve colonial order; this was especially true for the UK in ruling the British empire. This period of colonial anthropology coincided with the emergence of structural-functionalism as a theoretical paradigm in social anthropology and produced comparative research by such (largely British) anthropologists as Edward Evans-Pritchard, Max Gluckman, Monica Wilson, and others. In Germany, by contrast, museum studies, folklore, philology, and a particular brand of linguistic anthropology encouraged a decidedly apolitical form of comparative research.

Different theoretical orientations underlay another set of midcentury comparativists: structuralism and structural Marxism propelled anthropologists such as Claude Lévi-Strauss, Maurice Bloch, Jonathan Friedman, and Maurice Godelier, all of whom engaged in comparative research, though none of them did in-depth fieldwork in multiple sites, relying heavily instead on secondary ethnographic sources.

Without such an explicitly comparative agenda, some anthropologists have simply worked in different parts of the world, pursuing research on different topics (e.g., in the mid-twentieth century, Cora Du Bois in Indonesia, India, and the Netherlands; Fred Eggan in the Philippines and North America; and, more recently, Frederik Barth in China, Pakistan, New Guinea, and Indonesia, and Nancy Scheper-Hughes in Brazil, Ireland, and South Africa). More recently still, a number of scholars have moved from research in distant spaces to ethnography "at home" (e.g., Christine Ward Gailey, Rena Lederman, Emily Martin, Sherry Ortner, Paul Stoller, and Toby Volkman). Nowadays, in many textbooks that introduce anthropology to undergraduates, ethnography is defined as implicitly comparative, whereas ethnology is said to be explicitly comparative and usually focused on a single topic, such as socialization practices in different societies. That may be, but the deliberate and active shift to a new field research site, accompanied by a parallel shift in both theories and methods used by the anthropologist, is a qualitatively distinct undertaking.

For one thing, at this time—the beginning of the twenty-first century—

---

end of his life, doing field research in, and publishing cultural analyses on, Germany, Austria, and Switzerland (1954).

the assumption that fieldsites correspond to spatially defined territories has been thoroughly deconstructed.[6] Even area studies paradigms, though they may remain prevalent in doctoral training in major universities, have changed. Within the discipline of anthropology itself, many anthropologists still speak of "going to the field" or "doing field research," not as a neocolonial enterprise (in the sense of "othering"), but rather as traversing some distance (whether physical or "just" conceptual) to get to somewhere else.

This predominant discourse is counterbalanced, though, by the practice of not exactly getting to somewhere else, but rather coming and going, and being present from afar. That is, once they do field research, anthropologists realize that they do not simply enter, leave, or return to it but rather engage it as part of their ongoing lives in a range of locations that constitute both a part of field research itself and a part of the lives of their interlocutors. Hence nowadays, "shifting fieldsites" entails not only the sort of dramatic shifts that a previous generation of anthropologists experienced, but also more mundane and subtle ones, such that shifts themselves are not wholly alien to the normative practice either of the discipline or of anthropologists' daily lives. Methodologically and theoretically, we have some skills available to us that we can draw upon and more consciously apply to these dramatic shifts. Eventually, the discourse itself may change.

One caveat is in order, however. A danger in the blithe embrace of either multisited field research or shifting fieldsites is a superficiality in the fieldwork itself. Depth is one of the hallmarks of anthropology. Deep interaction, deep cultural knowledge, and deep understanding do not come easily. They require sustained participant observation and a valorization of the social and institutional relationships that constitute each site or node.

PROFESSIONAL PRODUCTION

The fact of shifting fieldsites does not in itself explain the difficulties I have encountered establishing myself professionally. As Margaret Dorsey (2006:17) points out, in general, agencies that fund anthropological research, few though they are, remain more interested in funding research based outside of the United States. Interestingly, though, as she also notes, "the publishing world is moving faster than the funding world." Perhaps partaking of this

6. See, e.g., Amit (2000); Appadurai (1991); Bamford and Robbins (1997); Boellstorff (2008); Dresch, James, and Parkin (2000); Gupta and Ferguson (1997); Hannerz (1996).

trend, several presses have already expressed interest in publishing the product of my US-based research on the basis of a prospectus that they themselves requested.[7]

Coupled with the struggles of establishing a new professional identity is a nagging question I find myself asking: When I became a Latin Americanist anthropologist working in the Andes, did I take careful steps to build that identity? Or is this a memory narrative I have constructed *post hoc* that conveniently erases all the diversions I encountered along the way—stumbling, pleasant, and otherwise? I cannot answer the question. I think (perhaps erroneously) that, had I then wished to pursue my current field research, I would likely have selected a different place to do graduate work and built different networks to improve my chances of reaching my goal. There would have been moments of good and bad luck, but it would have been possible to control more of the variables that constitute the professionalization of scholarship. And, of course, time appeared to stretch before me, then.

IS ANYTHING NEW IN THE PRACTICE OF MY MÉTIER?

What makes the contemporary scenario I have sketched out here any different from the experiences of anthropologists in the past who moved from one fieldsite to another, and why? And what makes it similar? Most broadly, I conjecture that the growth of transnational interconnections creates more options for anthropologists who seek to do field research "at home." The "place" in which my research occurs has no clearly delimited boundaries. That would appear to make it easier to "do" field research, but it also means that it is harder for the anthropologist to draw boundaries between fieldwork and personal obligations. As a caveat, it may also lead to a propensity for greater abstraction and less attention to immersing oneself and then making vivid for readers or some other audience the nitty-grittiness of daily life that characterizes going "somewhere else." This is somewhat ironic, given that in the past, the tendency toward abstraction that sometimes accompanied the ability to engage in fieldwork *in situ* followed closely upon the recognition

7. This represents a general trend, linked to an interest on the part of presses, not so much in ethnography conducted in the United States, as in ethnographic projects that treat topics that are accessible and meaningful to the general public. Robert Borofsky's Public Anthropology series for the University of California Press is a move in this direction, as are the numerous trade press publications and journalistic articles that rely heavily on anthropological knowledge but are not written by anthropologists.

that fieldsites, and the people who lived in them and served as anthropologists' informants, had so often been objectified and drained of life.

Technological advances now allow anthropologists to use a wider array of field research methodologies. Moreover, family structures and dynamics have changed in the lives of anthropologists themselves. In earlier generations, the "tradition" of shifting fieldsites was made somewhat easier by the acceptability of tag-along spouses (read: wives) and far less onerous expectations on the part of middle-class parent-anthropologists in the way of their children's formal education.

Clearly the intimate and the less personal are mutually constitutive, each making its mark on the structuring and substance of both domains. Women, in particular, after entering the workplace, have encountered challenges, such as accommodating familial responsibilities with the embrace of shifting fieldsites. At the same time, the changing milieux in which anthropology unfolds has obligated anthropologists to reflect on the value of their research to both the academy and civil society. This combination of conditions has served as a catalyst for many anthropologists to shift fieldsites. In my case, the research on adoption I have undertaken may, indirectly, have policy implications, and is of abiding interest not only to me but also to the people with whom I am conducting my research. It is thus a kind of "public anthropology" in ways that my earlier research in the Andes was not.

Some of the anthropologists I mentioned earlier contested the position of their government through their ethnographic research and publications. Margaret Mead saw herself as both anthropologist and public persona, sometimes eagerly supporting government initiatives (World War II), at other times passionately explaining the cultural underpinnings of American socialization practices and intergenerational strife. Nevertheless, many of these anthropologists made choices about the fieldsites where they would do research as a consequence of their association with government projects, which also provided them with a way to make an income. My research, in contrast, is not linked to objectives defined partially or wholly by government objectives.

The shift from Andean market women to transnational adoption in the United States crosses treacherous terrain. Geographically, my current work takes place on more level ground, but the territory is less familiar and there is no "other" to specify. It is impossible to disengage and "go do field research," as I did by embarking for the Andes. Perhaps as a result, the public face of my current project is far more exposed. Within the edifices of the academy, it is a steep climb, but one that is remarkably eye-opening.

*

Time does not stand still. I presented the first iteration of this article as a talk at the American Anthropological Association meetings in 2007. As I worked on subsequent drafts, I realized that the movement from one field project to another illuminated for me not only the hurdles I needed to overcome, but also unexpected continuities between research in the Andes on market women, and research in the United States on the changing faces of families and adoption. These continuities are apparent in two recent publications, an article on the cultural and political economies of adoption in Latin America (Seligmann 2009a), and another on the life story of Lucre, a market woman in Peru, in the context of transference—a recognition that my interaction with Lucre entailed bonds between mother and child, the experiences of feeling orphaned, and longings to escape status ambivalence on both our parts (Seligmann 2009b). At the same time, and most importantly for me, the shift from one fieldsite to another has sparked a new intellectual curiosity; challenged my assumptions about matters I had worked on in Latin America, such as gender and kinship relationships in the context of globalization; and convinced me that as teachers—both in the classroom and in public settings—we should be making the dynamics of shifting fieldsites central to our conversations.

When Alma Gottlieb organized the conference session at which five of this book's chapters were first presented, I looked forward to tentatively setting out some of my ideas and hearing others' perspectives. After we presented our respective papers, I was not prepared for the sentiment that palpably rippled through the audience. To be sure, they responded to a multitude of points that we had raised. Nevertheless, I do not think it an overgeneralization to state there was a consensus among the audience that explicitly addressing this particular topic was long overdue.

ACKNOWLEDGMENTS

I am most grateful to Alma Gottlieb for inviting me to participate in this project. It was an ideal collaboration. Her perspicacity and enthusiasm catalyzed stimulating intellectual exchanges among all the contributors to this volume. Thanks also to the editors at the University of Chicago Press for their hard work and skill in bringing this volume into being.

SEVEN

Around the World in Sixty Years: From Native America to Indonesia to Tourism and Beyond

Edward M. Bruner

In my peripatetic career, I have done ethnographic studies in eight different locations on four continents. It has been a long journey; I have been doing anthropology for sixty years, from 1948 to 2008 (as of this writing), and my career is still going. My deep historical perspective allows me to view transformations in myself, in the discipline, and in the world.

Here is the chronology of my fieldwork. In summer 1948, I did research for my master's thesis with Navaho Indians in New Mexico, and at various times from 1951 to 1953 for my doctoral dissertation with Mandan and Hidatsa on the Fort Berthold Indian Reservation in North Dakota. In 1957 I went to North Sumatra, Indonesia, to study Toba Batak sociocultural organization and change in village and city. Returning to Indonesia eleven times between 1969 and 1997, I first focused on the Toba Batak in the 1970s, a continuation of my earlier work. I then shifted gears in the 1980s to study tourism in Bali and elsewhere. In this latter research, I greatly expanded the geographical range of investigation, from Kenya and Ghana to Java, southwest China, Israel, and the United States.

In my tourism research, the term "fieldsite" took on new meaning. Tourists are continually on the move as they leave home, travel from place to place along an itinerary, and then return home. They are a mobile subject and are never in one location for very long—so what/where is "the field" in tourism studies (Clifford 1997; D'Amico-Samuels [1991] 1997; Graburn 2002)? Given the nomadic nature of the tourist, I do not consider the change in locations in my tourism work as "switching fieldsites" per se—I did not learn a new language, I spent as little as six weeks in some places, and I studied only a narrow topic—but I did read the tourism literature and the history and ethnography of each people. My tourism work was multisited, global, and comparative; indeed, at times I felt it was almost a different genre than my earlier research. In that sense, my work in what seems to be eight separate fieldsites may be regrouped into three: from Native America, to Indonesia, to comparative tourist productions (this last including six separate sites). Thus, one might say that I experienced two major *shifts* in fieldsites: from the United States to Indonesia in 1957, and then from Indonesia to the comparative study of global tourism in 1983.

In writing about such a variegated career, I confront the difficulty that marks all retrospectives—that the past is by definition seen from the point of view of the present, and it is all too easy to impose contemporary meanings on decisions made long ago. Moreover, there is a tendency to rationalize previous decisions, to reinterpret what were whims or opportunistic choices as well-thought-out, rational ones. We tend to place a favorable construction on our past choices so as to enhance or protect our anthropological selves and reputations. Neuroscience tells us that every time we recall a memory, the brain reworks and reconfigures it. What is restored is not the same as the original memory; rather, we create the narrative or memory that is most acceptable to current concerns. This tendency is potentially problematic not only for the accounts in this volume but for all autobiographies, retellings, and historical scholarship. Arthur Schlesinger Jr. (2008:164) calls this the "egocentric predicament" and refers to Benedetto Croce, who said that all history is contemporary history. In my case, the result can easily be that I come off as a more heroic figure—or at least a more cogent one—than I deserve.

*

Soon after starting in the doctoral program at the University of Chicago in 1950, I was offered the opportunity to conduct ethnographic research the following summer, subsidized by my department. I readily accepted, for I was eager to do fieldwork, and I could select my own research topic. Sol Tax had a project in "action anthropology" on the Fort Berthold Indian Reservation, and although he wanted me to send him copies of my field notes, he emphasized that I would be free to study whatever I wanted. I was further intrigued after learning that the community in which I was to work was located along the Missouri River and was quite isolated. Indeed, during the spring, the ice melted on the river, making it impossible to cross, while in the other direction the dirt roads became muddy with the spring rains and could not be navigated. In preparing for my work by reading the relevant literature, I made an astonishing finding: the most authoritative sources claimed that the people I was setting out to study, the Mandan Indians, were "extinct" (Will and Hyde 1906:8; Lowie 1917; Strong 1940:391). By "extinct," the sources meant that the Mandan no longer had a separate society, for three tribes—Mandan, Hidatsa, and Arikara—lived together at Fort Berthold.

Imagine my surprise when I arrived on the reservation and met individuals who spoke the Mandan language, identified themselves as Mandan, used the same system of kinship terminology that Lewis Henry Morgan had reported for them in 1871, and not only had an active ceremonial life but eventually adopted my wife, Elaine C. Bruner, into a Mandan clan and gave her the Indian name of White June Berries.[1] What is noteworthy about the adoption ritual is that, following traditional practice, the Indians expected a return gift, and I was told that a horse would be most appropriate. So I bought a horse from our friend and neighbor, Sam White Owl, for fifty dollars and presented it at the ceremony, where my wife received a priceless eagle feather warbonnet (which she returned at the end of the ritual). I later listed the fifty dollars for the horse on my research expense account for the University of Chicago. A fastidious auditor at the university questioned that expense; at the very least, he thought it unusual that the university was asked to buy a horse for a graduate student, and in Chicago no less. But Sol Tax came to my defense, and the claim was eventually accepted. My retroactive research budget clearly challenged the claims of extinction.

Beyond challenging the clearly absurd notion that these native peoples were extinct, my research on the reservation was motivated by additional theoretical concerns. In the United States of the 1950s, the melting pot theory—the accepted sociological wisdom of the time—stated that all immigrants and members of ethnic minorities would become assimilated into American society within three generations. In the case of Indian people, the policy of the Bureau of Indian Affairs was to facilitate this supposedly inevitable process by encouraging them to leave the reservation and enter what was considered the American mainstream. The dark side of the policy was that resources were not allocated to improve life or even preserve Indian culture on the reservation. Boas sent his students to document American Indian culture before it disappeared, in a sense accepting the conventional wisdom of inevitable

1. Elaine has had her own rich career in education and counseling, but while I have done fieldwork, she and I have been a research team, and she has worked with me in all the fieldsites I discuss in this chapter.

assimilation. The thrust of my research was to show that although there was change, complete assimilation was not happening; indeed, Indians had retained a distinctive language and set of cultural practices. Where change had occurred, I wanted to uncover the mechanisms involved.

Working among supposedly extinct Indians was intellectually exciting and led to all sorts of theoretical problems: How does culture persist when its carriers no longer reside in their own society? What are the processes of change? How do we measure change? Why do some aspects of culture change more than others? Why do some individuals and families become more "Americanized" than others? Those Indians who had changed the most, I found, were raised in families in which there had been intermarriage, with one of the parents being white.[2] My efforts to investigate the actual processes of change led me to question the functionalist paradigm of the era. I was skeptical of the usual claim that entire blocks of culture were transferred from one society to another, and I raised doubts about the concept of culture as a functionally integrated whole. The Indian men of the reservation no longer hunted buffalo or engaged in warfare—they dressed as Western-style cowboys, purchased cars and washing machines, and played Hank Williams recordings—but they remained in important respects very much "Indian," and I set out to define what constituted that Indian identity, and to conceptualize the processes involved. I learned then what is now a commonplace—that ethnic identity cannot be defined by a list of culture traits (Barth 1969).

What intrigued me was to discover that reservation culture was not an "acculturated" mix of "Indian" and "White," as if it were an amalgam that had emerged from a Cuisinart blender, but that members of the community learned two sets of cultural norms, one Indian and the other White, and they practiced one or the other, depending upon the situation. They varied their behavior, as all humans do, according to the social context, and they were readily capable of behaving one way with other Indians and another way with surrounding whites. They were very conscious of what they were doing and frequently manipulated the two systems to their own advantage. In other words, they had active selves that made choices—again, as we all do—and were quite unlike the Indians presented in so many early twentieth-century American ethnographies, as mannequinlike exemplars of their culture, stereotypically performing within the rigid confines of culturally accepted norms. Pre–World War II American Indian ethnography was primarily directed at

2. I write "White" with an uppercase *w* when explicitly contrasting "white" cultural practices to Indian ones; otherwise, I use a lowercase "w."

a reconstruction of traditional culture, a salvage operation, so only selected aspects of contemporary practices were included. It was not the objective of early anthropologists to document current Indian life with all its ambiguities, ironies, and contradictions.

Many of my fellow graduate students at the University of Chicago also questioned the functionalist paradigm, but I was oriented toward what was to become a more processual/practice/performative paradigm as a result of two influences. I read George Herbert Mead in a seminar with Robert Redfield and followed up with subsequent study of symbolic interactionism, and I took courses with Herbert Blumer, where I learned that humans have agency, and that people do not respond in accordance with predefined norms but engage in an "interpretative act" as they assess the situation in which they find themselves (Mead 1934). Further, I had an ongoing dialogue on the emerging concept of cultural performance with Milton Singer (1972) in the 1950s, and most of my later work has been performance oriented. At the time, of course, I had no idea that these formative conceptions would become so widely accepted.

Here are some examples of the kinds of data I presented in an early paper on kinship terminology (Bruner 1955:848–49), which stood in opposition to the formal kinship schedules offered in most ethnographies of the era:

A young girl teased an unacculturated woman, after which the woman said to her, "You're supposed to be my *icawi* (father's sister) and you are not supposed to tease me, but that's O.K., we can take it the white way."

In referring to an acculturated girl, an older woman remarked, "She don't talk Indian. She is supposed to call me mother but she calls me auntie. I would be glad to hear it if she called me mother but she won't use it any more. She's my daughter but she won't understand so I call her niece. All that family act like white kids."

At a political meeting, a converted Indian, who ordinarily uses the generational system [of kin terms], addressed a prominent member of the opposing faction as "father." He used the Crow system knowing full well that his political rival would not be so indiscreet as to criticize a "son" in public.

In a conference paper discussing my American Indian publications from the 1950s, Nelson Graburn (2005) said:

I think Ed's work was ahead of its time, rather more like the debates of Schneider, and others in the 1960s who grew to doubt the genealogical nature of kinship—and later the feminist work of Yanagisako or M. Strathern, on the individually creative use of culture—even beyond early Bourdieu practice theory. Though it was not recognized as such at the time his work is the fulcrum, the joint-break between the old "structural" consideration of kinship and the newer more cultural constructivist set of conceptions.

I was, of course, gratified by Graburn's complimentary remarks. But if my early work was so noteworthy, why did I leave the American Indian field and move to Indonesia? I did consider pursuing other projects among Indians. I had written a history of the Mandan based on ethnohistorical sources and was offered a contract by the University of Oklahoma Press to expand it into a book. Additionally, the head of the family in whose home I stayed for most of my time on the reservation, Hans Walker, was so fascinating, and I came to know him so well, that I had thought of writing his life story. He was a crusty character, hardened by the brutal North Dakota winters as he tended his cattle on the prairie, and he engaged in a running ironic commentary on the sad state of Indian affairs on the reservation. But his greatest satisfaction— or so it appeared to me at the time—was to tease me as a representative of American culture. Cutting through hypocrisy, his biting observations about America were astute; he could have been a columnist for a left-wing news-paper—an Indian Jon Stewart hosting his own *Daily Show*, exemplifying the well-developed art form of joking and teasing among American Indians (Basso 1979). Beyond being intrigued by Hans Walker, I considered pursuing another research project: studying the Indian powwow circuit, where Indian dancers traveled from place to place to perform. This cultural practice intrigued me, as I would be studying a moving culture with no fixed locality—a striking counterpoint to nearly all the prevailing anthropological work of the times. All of these were worthy projects, but I did not pursue them. Why?

Meyer Fortes had come to the University of Chicago from Cambridge as a visiting professor during the time that I was writing my dissertation, and he was gracious enough to go over my field materials and to read and comment on drafts of my chapters. One time he noted that although there was much worthwhile in my thesis research, I would never be a "real anthropologist" unless I went outside the United States to a foreign area and worked through the local language. Fortes's view strikes us today as rather provincial, but it was the dominant British view in the early 1950s, based upon the ideal of a Malinowski-like field experience. Fortes made it clear that once I had done foreign fieldwork, I would be accredited and could thereafter do any project I wanted. For Fortes and others of his generation, the major objective of ethnography was to describe a culture (or, in the case of the British, the "social organization"), and the range of possible research topics was, arguably, quite limited. In my view, it was not until the 1980s that anthropology really "opened up" to the wide array of subject matter that we now take for granted (Bruner 1984). If I had proposed a study of tourism to my dissertation committee at Chicago in 1953, for example, it is unlikely that I would have received approval. Indeed, in 1966 Dean MacCannell submitted a proposal to study European tourism to his PhD committee in rural sociology at Cornell, and they rejected it (MacCannell 2007:146). In any case, what Fortes had advised me to do resonated with me, but there were other factors.

As a graduate student, I had taken a seminar on the Philippines with Fred Eggan and had become fascinated with Southeast Asia. A few years later, when I started my first teaching job at Yale, I found that the Southeast Asia area program offered an intensive course on the Indonesian language, taught by a linguistics professor with an Indonesian informant, and had an ongoing research program in Sumatra. I expressed an interest in developing expertise in the region, and my department encouraged me to offer a course on Indonesia, which I did. Research money was available in the Cold War era for work in politically sensitive areas, so after receiving grants from the Ford Foundation, the National Science Foundation, and Yale's Southeast Asia program in 1957, my wife and I went off to Sumatra—in my mind the most exotic and adventuresome place in the world. I was excited at the prospect of studying a former colony that had just achieved national independence. Going to the new nation of Indonesia seemed of the future, whereas my Native American research appeared to me of the anthropological past. I had discussed my Indian work not only with Meyer Fortes but also with Alfred Kroeber, and Robert Lowie was a reader for the first article I had published in *American Anthropologist*. Recalling Fortes's earlier comment, I felt that in going to Southeast Asia I was well on the way to becoming a "real" anthropologist. I just loved it when my mother-in-law warned me, "In Sumatra, they're all foreigners"; after seeing where Sumatra was located on a map, my father said it was at the end of the world. En route to Indonesia, Elaine and I stopped off in Hawaii, and at a cocktail party, Alex Spoehr, then head of the Bishop Museum, introduced me to his guests and said to each, in an offhand manner, "Ed is off to Sumatra tomorrow," after which he would move on. Looking back, I felt like a regular Indiana Jones.

Here is how I described my introduction to my research community in Sumatra:

> I recall the moment in 1957 when I first saw the village in which my wife and I were to work, Lumban Panggabean, located along the Bukit Barisan mountain range, the homeland of the Toba Batak. Except for a Dutch priest and a German missionary doctor, no other Westerners lived in this region. As I approached the village, I looked at the massive sloping roofs of the highly decorated rectangular houses built on stilts. I saw people farming with water buffalo in gently curved, terraced rice fields. I passed sarong-clad women nursing babies, while a swarm of children followed my every footstep. The scene was idyllic and rural, set against a backdrop of the mist enshrouded volcanoes that surround Toba Lake. For a boy from New York City who had lived in apartments all his life, I said to myself, "This is it, this is my little community." (Bruner 1999:463)

What a sentimental first-contact arrival story. What a hopeless romantic. What an idiot.

My fourth year on the faculty at Yale, I found myself taking a year-long Indonesian language course that met four days a week for two-hour sessions, with an additional hour of homework; teaching a seminar on Indonesian ethnography while struggling to acquire enough rudimentary knowledge to make the course respectable; teaching introductory anthropology to undergraduates; and publishing my American Indian material. I spent my fifth year in the field, back in Indonesia. The sixth year I was up for tenure—which was denied. It was a shock. I had thought I was invincible. Obviously, my decision to switch fieldsites before tenure was not a wise career move, but I had, after all, spent two of the five years before the tenure decision preparing for and conducting fieldwork in a new area. After I left Yale, I spent the year as a fellow at the Center for Advanced Study in the Behavioral Sciences in Palo Alto, received four solid job offers, and ended up at the University of Illinois, where I have had a wonderful anthropological life with some amazing colleagues.

When I look back on this narrative in disciplinary historical perspective, a clear trajectory emerges—if only in retrospect.[3] I took my first anthropology course in 1947, only two years after the end of World War II, and there had been a long American/Boas-Kroeber tradition of sending graduate students off to study American Indians for the summer. Thus before entering graduate

---

3. I am indebted to Maria Lepowsky for insight into that historical moment.

school, I had spent the summer of 1948 among the Navaho with Clyde Kluck-hohn. A second model of fieldwork in the 1950s, the basic British model, was the Malinowski-inspired practice of intensive long-term engagement. I was squeezed between these two models of fieldwork, but rather than choose one or the other, I did both. After the first summer at Fort Berthold, my decision was to continue on to the dissertation, as I found it easy to gather data, felt comfortable on the reservation, had conceptualized theoretical problems that interested me, and saw that it was also the most rapid route to obtaining my PhD. I was right: after arriving at Chicago in 1950, I left four years later, PhD in hand.

The longer-term Indonesian field experience, however, was incredible. It is etched in my consciousness. I can still think and feel like a Toba Batak. My grown daughter has a Batak middle name, Riana, which means Joyous One. Like the Ilongot who, in Renato Rosaldo's eyes, hunt for good stories as well as for meat, my Batak fieldwork made for good stories, in publications and in the corridors. My last visit was in 1997, forty years after our first fieldwork, and Elaine and I were well received with a traditional welcoming ceremony (Bruner 1999). My wife still dreams in the Batak language. In 1957 she had been adopted as a daughter of the village patrilineal branch of the Simandjun-tak clan, so I became a son-in-law, and we learned all over again what it meant to live in a kinship-based society. Toba Batak relatives have visited us in our home in Urbana. When I meet Batak students on my university campus, we address each other by kin terms. In Sumatra I had entered an asymmetrical cross-cousin marriage system that was warmer, more nuanced, and more hu-mane than anything described by Lévi-Strauss or Rodney Needham. Even now, fifty years after my first Batak fieldwork, I still feel a deep emotional at-tachment to the Batak people. I picture in my mind's eye the wet rice fields as they slowly descend from the mountains to the shores of Lake Toba. I recall friendships and shared intimacies, the all-consuming three-day ceremonials, the soft flow of village life, the wonder of fieldwork. Despite decades of an-thropological critique of our discipline, maybe I'm still a romantic.

Vivid in my memory from our first field trip is a Batak elder, Sia Marinus Simandjuntak, who was known as S.M. He had rented his village house to us and became my best informant. Every morning S.M. and I would meet in my makeshift office to discuss Toba Batak *adat*—their term for their social and ceremonial organization, which included the practices for weddings, funerals, and other life cycle events, as well as the norms for proper behavior among kin. Midmorning we would stop for tea and papaya, brought by my wife, who in Batak kinship was a sister to S.M. He was a highly intelligent and perceptive man, tall and thin, with inquisitive eyes, trained as a journalist, who eventually became the head government administrator (*bupati*) for the entire Toba Batak area. I believe he enjoyed our lively back-and-forth sessions as much as I did. I found our conservations as intellectually exciting as the most intense anthropological debates in seminars or at meetings. After our morning discussions, in the afternoons and evenings, I would attend ceremonies, hang out to observe village life, and speak with other members of the community. I conversed in Indonesian, but my wife learned both Indonesian and the Toba Batak language, as most of the Batak women she worked with did not speak Indonesian.

After we'd spent six months in the village, a civil war broke out between the central government and local rebels. The rebels had grievances about the concentration of power in Java, the draining of local resources, and other matters. There was also an ethnic element, as the national government was run by the Javanese, while the local rebels were Minangkabau and Batak. The rebel troops we saw in our area had American military equipment—which, we later learned, had been supplied by the Central Intelligence Agency as part of the Cold War effort to fight communism; under President Sukarno, the government had become accommodating to the Communist party (the PKI). But solid news was scarce, while rumors were everywhere. Before the fighting broke out, my wife and I searched the radio dial for news of the impending civil war and received excellent reception for a Voice of America broadcast from the Philippines informing us that all American women and children had been evacuated from North Sumatra. We looked at each other, astonished. We soon consulted with the local rebel commander (Major Sahala Hutabarat, a Toba Batak) and decided to leave for the coastal city of Medan the next day.

Saying sad goodbyes to the villagers, we started in our car on the road to the coast—only to run into a tank division of the invading Javanese Suliwangi, a crack central government army unit. We backtracked, sold the car to the rebels—there was no one else to sell it to—and finally left by taking a boat across Lake Toba; we landed at the eastern shore town of Prapat, and from there we took a six-hour bus ride to Medan, Sumatra's largest city. When we arrived in Medan, the head of the American consulate called us to his office. He had known about us, as only a handful of Americans living in North Sumatra were not employed by the big rubber and palm oil plantations, and we had previously registered with the consulate. My wife and I learned that staff at the consulate had already made plans to evacuate us to Singapore. After brief discussion, we refused to go, as we had too much invested in my Toba Batak research. Instead, Elaine and I decided to remain in Medan, which had a large Batak population, and we easily entered a tight network of Toba Batak relatives who accepted our village kinship adoption and warmly received us. Our lineage relatives in the city became our informants and invited us to events to meet other Toba Batak.

It was easy to meet Batak people in Medan as they congregated at widely publicized life cycle ceremonies (mainly large funerals and weddings) and in Batak churches on Sundays. The urban Batak followed both their traditional religion and Christianity, and they maintained close ties with their village communities in the highlands. I studied the rural-urban system and how Batak life had changed in the city. The fighting brought by US-backed Sumatran rebels never came to Medan, and I worked there for the next seven months, until it was time to return to New Haven for the fall semester.

My fieldwork in Sumatra helped me to better understand my first fieldwork among American Indians, and vice versa. For example, I noted a striking difference between the processes of culture change among Indians and Batak. With American Indians, I observed a grand opposition between the "Indian way" and the "White way," which pervaded all aspects of life and led to political factionalism on the reservation. It is not that one represented tradition and the other modernity—although in the discourse among Indian people, the differences were sometimes cast in such terms. Rather, items of culture or particular practices were labeled "Indian" or "White" and were interpreted as symbolic markers of identity and group loyalty. To the extent that reservation-based Indians adopted White ways, they were criticized by fellow Indians, as if they were abandoning the Indian way and their true selves—much as African Americans who behave "too white" are still called Uncle Toms—and this binary served as a barrier to change. By contrast, the Toba Batak feel comfortable with being both Batak and "modern" at the same time, and they feel no opposition between following *adat* (which governs ritual and family, lineage, and affinal relations) and being an educated, economically successful member of Indonesian society.

Among the Batak, few barriers impede social change, and wealthy and prominent individuals are widely admired. Indeed, the Batak espouse their own theory of change, a set of assumptions and beliefs that postulates that their *adat* has not changed and cannot change, as it was given to them by the gods and their ancestors. When I suggested as examples to Batak friends that kin obligations now are different from how they had been in the past, and that weddings take one day in the city compared to three days in the village highlands, the Batak countered that of course particulars might change but the *adat* principles remained constant—for example, a wife-receiver is still deferential to a wife-giver, even though the form of that deference might have been modified. Although the Batak of the late 1950s appeared to me to be changing rapidly, they have a theory that they are not changing in any essential respect in the *adat* sphere, and they maintain that they are still as basically Batak as they had been centuries ago. This theory helps them to preserve a sense of continuity with the past while allowing them to accept the most modern practices. I don't know how long this may continue, but at the time of my latest fieldwork in 1997, it still remained almost universally accepted.

While writing up the results of my research with the Batak, I continued to explore new theoretical models of society, but it was only in the late 1970s and early 1980s that major changes occurred that were crucial for my subsequent research on tourism. Diverse intellectual and personal strands had come together for me at about the same time. In 1979 I joined an interdisciplinary faculty reading group on my campus of the University of Illinois to explore fresh postmodern theories emanating from Europe. We met every other week for many years and read Derrida, Foucault, Barthes, Nietzsche, Bakhtin, Habermas, and Gadamer, among others, and we also reread Freud and Marx. I was profoundly influenced by postmodernism and found it very compatible with previous anthropological thinking that I had brought to my earlier fieldwork in both the United States and Indonesia. Indeed, it might be said that I was predisposed to embracing postmodernism, as it was an effective critique of the 1950s anthropological theories that I had found so static and formalistic. While postmodernism has had its excesses, for which it has received sharp criticism, it nevertheless led to profound changes in anthropology.

Early on, I endeavored to bring these new theoretical waves into my own work. At a conference in Chicago on narrative—where Jacques Derrida was the keynote speaker—I met with Victor Turner and Barbara Myerhoff to plan a session for the 1980 annual meetings of the American Anthropological Association called "The Anthropology of Experience." The key idea was to propose a revised concept of culture—to study culture not as it "functioned," nor as a set of normative behaviors, but rather as it is *experienced*, to emphasize what is meaningful in people's lives. By "experience" we meant what emerges to consciousness, as opposed to what people do or say. The papers were later published (Turner and Bruner 1986); I wrote the introduction and edited the volume, and Cliff Geertz wrote an epilogue—although, sadly, both Vic and Barbara passed away before the book was published. In 1983, three years after the conference session that produced the book, I invited some of the same participants, along with other colleagues, to present papers at another symposium, under the auspices of the American Ethnological Society (of which

I was then president), on a related theme, "Text, Play, and Story: The Construction and Reconstruction of Self and Society" (Bruner 1984). We were a group of anthropologists who were beginning to experiment with the new humanistic version of postmodern theory that was sweeping through the social sciences and humanities. In addition to Turner and Myerhoff, this group included Renato Rosaldo, Jim Boon, Jim Fernandez, Barbara Babcock, Keith Basso, James Peacock, and others. We thought that in presenting our studies, and demonstrating how postmodernism actually worked in ethnography, we were innovators, even revolutionaries.

Our key ideas, which are widely accepted today among cultural anthropologists and others in the social sciences and humanities, were that culture was to be seen as being generated as it was expressed, as emergent and contested, in polyphonic interplay, as always in production. As Victor Turner once said to me, we all enter society in the middle. Our focus was on performance and narrative; however, we did not reduce stories to abstract plot structures but, rather, saw them as experienced in particular cultural and historical moments. Moreover, the reflexive anthropologist became part of the ethnographic text, not an objective, politically neutral observer who remained above it.

I soon brought these understandings to my study of tourism, along with another influence. During the 1983–1984 academic year, I went with Barbara Kirshenblatt-Gimblett and twenty college students on a study abroad program. Rather than going to only one country, the group traveled by air from place to place, beginning with Japan, then continuing on to Bali, Benares, Nairobi, Cairo, and Jerusalem. As director of the program, I was free to decide upon the itinerary, and I selected places that interested me and that I thought would be educationally exciting for the students. We did not just read about globalization—we experienced it. In addition to classes, the students lived with local families, read texts about each country, and conducted a field study on an anthropological topic in each locality.

As we observed Japanese village festivals, Balinese dance dramas, Hindu pilgrimage along the Ganges, Maasai ritual performances, the Sound and Light Show at the pyramids of Giza, and the multiplicity of events in the old city of Jerusalem, we came to realize that tourists were everywhere. Even when we went off the beaten track and departed from standard itineraries— including in seemingly obscure places where scholars had conducted important ethnological investigations—we found tourists. A few years later, I took a tour group to a Balinese temple festival and was surprised to find Hilly Geertz there, engaged in her long-term ethnographic study of Bali. Tourism and ethnography were competing for the same space, in a touristic border zone. Some of our students began to write papers on performances designed for tourist consumption.

At first, I was slightly embarrassed by the presence of tourists, but slowly I began to take tourism seriously. Why, I asked, had tourists been virtually obliterated from ethnographic accounts? It was like a grand Ansel Adams photograph of a magnificent, pristine landscape in Yosemite—with the adjacent parking lot, unknown to viewers, just outside of the frame. The absence of tourists in our scholarly work reminded me of a previous era, when the colonial presence had not been included in our classic ethnographies. One would read accounts of the political organization of a people that paid scant attention to the colonial administration that dominated political life. The omission of tourism was significant, as indigenous cultures around the globe were reshaping themselves for presentation to a tourist audience. New cultural practices were being created to conform to touristic expectations, and entire craft industries were being developed to produce the souvenirs sought by tourists. What interested me were the many similarities between ethnographers and tourists, as both traveled to foreign lands, observed local cultural practices, and returned home with stories of their experiences. Of course, ethnographers belittle tourism. Bad ethnography is labeled "touristic," and tourism is seen by anthropologists as performing outmoded ethnography; indeed from the discipline's beginnings, anthropologists have taken a strong stance to distinguish their accounts from those produced by explorers, colonialists, travel writers, journalists, and now tourists (Bruner 2005:7).

The anthropology of tourism was still a new subject; the first session on tourism at a meeting of the American Anthropological Association occurred in 1974, in Mexico City. My approach, however, differed from earlier work in a number of respects, most essentially in that my work was thoroughly ethnographic and postmodern. I studied specific tourist productions much as any contemporary ethnographer would study ritual, even though these productions were not indigenous ceremonials but were designed for a foreign audience. Using theater as a metaphoric model, I investigated staged Maasai dances, Balinese temple rites, an old slave castle in Ghana, a mountain fortress in Israel, an Abraham Lincoln heritage site in Illinois, and ethnic theme parks in Jakarta and in Xishuangbanna in southwest China (Bruner 2005). In tourism, I was simultaneously studying two cultural traditions—that of the tourists and that of the toured—as well as their interactions. By moving to a succession of sites that I studied in progressively less depth, I became experienced in how to investigate each new site, and I benefited from a comparative perspective. I bypassed the issue of "authenticity" by studying tourist productions in their own right rather than as simulacra, nor did I measure the degree to which contemporary productions reproduced those in what might have been assumed to be a more authentic distant past. Tourist productions were emergent forms of culture. I incorporated the voices of a variety of stakeholders—tourists, local performers, government tourist bureaus, and the tourism industry. I was not interested in the "impact" of tourism on the culture, as if tourism were like a meteor hurtling in from the sky; rather, I saw tourism as an essential component already embedded in a local culture.

In order to further the acceptance of tourism studies within the discipline, I published articles in mainstream journals such as *American Anthropologist, American Ethnologist,* and *Cultural Anthropology.* After all, the study of mobile tourists involved a rethinking of widely accepted understandings about what constituted proper subject matter, an acceptable fieldsite, and the location of culture. The program director for cultural anthropology at the National Science Foundation, Deborah Winslow, informs me that, at least during the period from 1980 to 1986, there was no separate category for proposals to the NSF for tourism studies, which means that either no proposals were submitted, or they were so few that no separate category was deemed necessary. But I need not have been concerned, as the anthropology of tourism is well accepted these days. Two decades later, in the 2006–2007 grant cycle, 8.9 percent of the cultural anthropology submissions to NSF had a tourism component, as did 7.1 percent of the awards granted (personal conversation, May 14, 2008).

To summarize thus far: over the last three decades of my career, I have experienced a convergence of fresh theoretical developments in postmodern anthropology, my collaboration with Victor Turner and other ethnographers working along similar lines, and a study abroad program where I encountered global tourism at every turn. I had in effect reinvented myself, without fully realizing it. In my study of tourism I had become engaged in a multisited ethnography in an age of globalization, and I had eased into the anthropology of tourism through the experience of traveling the world. A new array of theoretical and methodological problems presented themselves, and I pursued them with enthusiasm.

I must admit, however, to a more personal motive as well. I have always loved to travel. Even as an adolescent, I read travel and adventure stories (my romanticism?), and I subsequently discovered how much I enjoy tourists. In my fieldwork with tourists, I have focused on upscale group tours taken by older, educated professionals—people like me (rather than, say, backpackers or other budget travelers). This decision was not coincidental: I delighted in the ambiguity of studying tourists while being a tourist myself, in taking field notes while enjoying the sightseeing. In this ambiguous status, I was intrigued by the similarities and differences between ethnographic and touristic perspectives and understandings. At the same time, with advancing age, I have appreciated traveling in comfort and safety. In my Balinese tourism fieldwork, I have lived in a Balinese village but I have also stayed in hotels, which I rationalized by claiming that hotels were where the tourists were—which was true, so I was following my subjects—but I must also acknowledge that I appreciated the air conditioning, the swimming pool, and the occasional gourmet meal.

Yet, as I studied my subject(s), I was distressed by the privileged position of the tourists and the unequal power relations they enjoyed vis-à-vis local communities, and as an academic lecturer I tried to educate my tourist groups about the political implications of how they traveled. I found that many of the tourists were uneasy, even distressed, by the disparity between their own wealth and the poverty of local residents. They were, however, mere actors in a worldwide global tourism industry that profited from sending older, richer, and lighter-skinned people to gaze on younger, poorer, and darker-skinned "others." Anthropology, too, was implicated in such disparities, as we know from the many critiques of its colonial undertones. American Indians and the Toba Batak, the peoples I had studied previously, were the "Other," but in the case of tourism, it was tourists—people like me—who had become the Other. I became the Other to myself.

Looking back on the set of my three major field experiences, I am struck not only by the obvious differences but also by some surprising (if less obvious) similarities. For example, despite the many differences, my ethnographic work among American Indians starting in 1951 and my work with Indonesians starting in 1957 had fundamental similarities. As both were conducted in the same historical era (the 1950s), both were embedded in the modernist/realist mode of ethnography of the time. The struggles for civil rights and women's rights, and the antiestablishment ethos, were still a decade away, part of the cultural revolutions that were to come in the 1960s. Accordingly, in the 1950s, I conducted fieldwork in fixed localities—on a reservation, in a village, or among a close circle of fictive relatives in an urban center. In both the United States and Indonesia, I established a residence and remained there for the duration of the research (except for the one forced move in Sumatra from village to city). Although anthropologists conducted important work in the 1950s that foreshadowed future developments, including dissatisfaction with functionalism, static models, and formal approaches, anthropological theory did not change appreciably until later. At least in the United States, there were no paradigm shifts: French structuralism, the interpretive turn, symbolic anthropology, Marxism, and other major shifts were not yet prominent in American anthropology. Nor was the importance of globalization fully recognized.

By the time I began my tourism research in the 1980s, the world had changed in major ways, and within anthropology there were corresponding paradigm shifts. We had lived through the 1960s and the Vietnam War, postmodernism was slowly becoming established in the academy, political sensitivity to inequalities in race and gender was widely recognized, colonialism was ending, and globalization was rampant. My work in tourism took note of these tectonic shifts.

Tourism is often said to be quintessentially mobile, but this is not entirely accurate, for while tourists are mobile, the objects of the tourist gaze—whether Balinese or Maasai—remain in one place; from their perspective, wave after wave of tourists come from the outside and flow through their homeland. As I conceptualized it, the tourists and the local performers meet in a touristic border zone, a space set aside for staged dance performances, craft workshops, model villages, ritual displays, and other tourist productions. After the performance, the tourists go back to their hotels, and the locals return to their home communities. I could not help but compare this situation with my earlier idea of studying the Indian powwow—a study I never carried out. In the Indian case, powwow dancers, the producers of the performance, moved from site to site while each audience was stationary. In tourism, the audience traveled.

The methodological challenge, then, was how to study a moving subject (Graburn 2002; Wynn 2007). My aim was to find out about tourists' motivations for travel, to learn how they experienced the countries they visited, to analyze what was represented to them of the local culture and what was omitted, and to discover what they learned while on tour. An investigator could remain at one site and interview individual tourists as they moved through. At first, I did just that, but I found this method unsatisfactory, as most tourists travel in a social unit—with fellow backpackers, as a family, on an organized tour, or in other groups. They process their travel experiences within this social context, and if I wanted to understand tourism, I thought it was important to penetrate the social unit of reception—which was difficult to do midway through a tour. Tour groups, I thus concluded, are best studied throughout the entire time they travel together. With this in mind, I became an academic lecturer, or tour guide, in my areas of expertise, Indonesia and Southeast Asia. I positioned myself so that I could be a member of the group, meeting up with the tourists in their places of origin and traveling with them throughout their journey. Being within the traveling unit was an excellent position for an ethnographer, as it enabled me to understand tourism from the inside. My solution to the study of a mobile population was to become mobile myself. Of course, a three-week tour is not enough time for in-depth ethnography of the classic sort, but as a member of the group, I found many occasions for long conversations while traveling, at mealtimes, or at destination sites. I went on multiple tours, stayed at tourist places for extended periods, and visited tourists after they had returned home.

Through all these travels, I have discovered that ethnography is like other aspects of life insofar as ethnographers learn new things as their accepted narratives are disrupted and challenged by their new experiences. In fieldwork, ethnographers have expectations or pre-understandings about the people they study, but then a remark is made or an action taken that does not accord with those prior perceptions. Sometimes this discrepancy is fleeting and easily overlooked, but it is essential to grasp the moment and explore the inconsistency, for this is how one acquires new knowledge. The gap between what is assumed and what is discovered presents a research opportunity. It is by investigating incongruities between previous understandings and fresh experiences that the ethnographer penetrates the taken-for-granted.

So, was Fortes correct when he said I would only become a real anthropologist by studying a foreign people through their own language? Ironically, in many ways, my easiest fieldwork was among the Toba Batak, precisely because their cultural assumptions were so different from my own; so much was initially incomprehensible to me that I questioned everything. By contrast, my fieldwork among American Indians and American tourists was more demanding, because their cultural practices were so much like my own that the differences were more difficult to discern. I discovered, as Fortes had implied, that it is indeed harder to do good ethnography when the other culture is too familiar. My fear among Indians and tourists was that I would not ask the right questions because it would never occur to me to do so. The Indian case was especially interesting in this regard. I found that the Indians I worked with were incredibly skilled at "acting white," and they knew my cultural traditions much better than I knew theirs. As a minority people with a history of exploitation by whites, they had had to learn how to adapt to the majority culture as a matter of survival. This ability to play "cultural chameleon" challenged my own skills at interrogating "difference" and thus made my fieldwork more intellectually difficult. Yet another register of difficulty across my three major fieldsites concerns physical comfort. On this score, the most difficult of my three fieldwork situations was with the Batak, then with the Indians, while the easiest has been with tourists.

Yet again, ironically, of the three groups of people I have studied, I probably know the Batak best, as I worked through the cultural incongruities more thoroughly. My field experience with the Batak was more intense than it was among Indians or tourists, and I find I can often predict how Batak will behave. Maybe Fortes was right after all. There were fewer distractions for me in Sumatra, as there were no foreign communities in the entire Toba Batak region, and only a few scattered Westerners. Then, too, I was still at an early stage of my anthropological career, more totally committed and more adventuresome than in my later years. It scares me now to think of the dangers my wife and I confronted in Sumatra.

*

My style of ethnographic writing has changed over the years—most notably, it is now more reflexive, humanistic, and expressive. The discipline has opened up for me. In some respects, 1950s anthropology was stifling, although of course I did not know it at the time. These days I enjoy anthropology more, as I can study and write about anything, and there is no single accepted model for doing or writing ethnography. I recently wrote an autobiographical piece, "Remembering My Jewish Father" (Bruner 2010)—a topic that I never in my wildest imagination could have conceived of writing about in the 1950s.

In looking back at my writings, one further issue claims my attention: the issue of anthropological memory. Let me contrast three stories of how anthropological memory has worked. In 1964 I was invited to give an address on my Batak work at a meeting of the Dutch Ethnological Society in Amsterdam, and I found that the anthropologists there knew hardly anything about my previous American Indian research. Well, I thought, this is understandable, as they have had a long scholarly interest in Indonesian studies, due to their former colonial presence in the Dutch East Indies, but no corresponding history of involvement or interest in American Indian studies. Now, let me fast-forward thirty years, to my "retirement" from the University of Illinois in 1994. The department had a dinner party with three invited speakers who were close colleagues and friends of mine—Jim Fernandez, Barbara Babcock, and Norman Denzin. They spoke about my life and work, but their remarks all concerned my anthropological career after the 1980s, focusing on postmodernism and tourism, with hardly any mention of my earlier Indian or Batak research. I realized that Jim, Barbara, and Norman had become colleagues in the 1980s as we worked through postmodern issues together, but I found it unsettling that the first twenty-five years of my professional life had been omitted and forgotten. And here is a story with an even more striking omission: another eleven years later, at the 2005 meetings of the American Anthropological Association, a session about my work was titled "Performance, Tourism, and Ethnographic Practice: An Exploration of the Work of Edward M. Bruner"—and all the papers except one discussed post-1980s concerns.

These three retrospective experiences inspire me to ask: Where does anthropological memory begin and end? To judge by the stories I have just related, the oldest part of my anthropological self has disappeared, dissolved in current anthropological discourse. It is as if my chosen discipline has no scholarly memory and has only paid attention to my most recent efforts. As I try to understand this, one explanation is that my 1950s work was conducted within a now somewhat discredited paradigm, and it is difficult to incorporate the content of old paradigms within the framework of current ones. Terms such as "acculturation" and "asymmetrical cross-cousin marriage" are mentioned in the anthropological literature these days more to critique them than to actually deploy them. In looking back at my career, one might say that with each change in fieldsite and research topic, I have started over again to establish my credentials in a new scholarly tradition with different colleagues in diverse networks, as Gottlieb notes in the introduction to this volume. As I moved from studying American Indian acculturation to rural Batak to urban Batak to postmodernism to global tourism, my own anthropological landscape has shifted accordingly. The organizers of the 2005 session about my work knew me in a particular historical era; indeed, many of the participants had not even been born when I began in anthropology in 1947.

But in contrast to anthropological memory, I continue to see the relevance of my earlier efforts to my current scholarly concerns. As I experience my "self," I see continuity throughout my entire career, from the very beginnings to the present. In some ways I am, after all, the same Ed Bruner, just older. Despite the paradigm shifts, regardless of changing fieldsites, irrespective of shifting disciplinary fashions, notwithstanding new anthropological problematics, and even with advancing age, I am me, and from my perspective, there has been a consistency in how I approach anthropological subject matter and the topics I select for research. After all, I studied Mandan-Hidatsa Indians as they left the reservation, Toba Batak as they migrated to the city, and tourists as they traveled to the ends of empire. I have always been interested in change, movement, and mobility, in people who are born in one life situation and who then move to another, and in the issues of identity that arise with such passages. My interest has not been restricted to movement solely in geographical terms but also to mobility of the self. At the same time, the changes in the specifics of my anthropological concerns reflect my own life circumstances, from the situation in which I was born to the one I created in my adult life. It is as if anthropology has been a metacommentary on my life. By doing anthropology, I discover myself and explore who I am. If Nietzsche was correct that a noble purpose in life is to become who you are, then I have attempted to accomplish this through ethnography.

Paul Stoller

The straight highway lies before us, but we cannot take it because it is permanently closed.

LUDWIG WITTGENSTEIN, *Philosophical Investigations*

I have long admired the thought-provoking aphorisms of Wittgenstein. Using a sentence or two, the great philosopher was somehow able to probe the deepest recesses of the human condition, somehow able to inspire us to ponder profound philosophical and psychological issues with fresh insight. The straight highway is a case in point. Its ever-visible entry invites us to move directly from where we are to where we are going. With its highly engineered, rectilinear features, the straight highway offers us a journey free of time-consuming complications that retard our progress. Why waste time on the path of growth and progress?

Few in modern society—including, of course, those of us in the academy—want to waste time, a theme deeply embedded in many Euro-American cultural traditions. Pressured by cultural expectation and professional obligation, we remove the barriers that Wittgenstein strategically placed before us and speed down the road toward our destination. Indeed, travel on the straight highway is fast—a blur of image and time. Such travel creates a semiconscious state—a narrow here-and-now sensibility. Our gaze is fixed on our destination. Delays make us irritable. Distractions become worrisome. After all, there is so much to do and so little time to do it.

But what do we miss by not taking a meandering side road to our destination? As Robert Flaherty reportedly said of film (Jean Rouch, personal communication), the side road is the longest, most cumbersome way to get from Point A to Point B—but taking it forces us to slow our pace and compels us to discover the gift of time. It awakens our consciousness and fires our passions. It enables us to connect the lessons of the past to the quandaries of the present. Wandering along the twists and turns of sinuous, less traveled paths, we have time to think about what is important. We can think about what we've done, what we're doing, and what our deeds and work might mean to future generations.

Experience along the side road also teaches us the lesson of impermanence. The Songhay people of Niger have a proverb that expresses, quite poetically, the theme of existential impermanence. They say that strangers are like the mist: if they haven't disappeared by morning, they will certainly be gone by afternoon. It is hard to accept impermanence. When life is exciting, stimulating, and productive, we want that moment to last forever. And yet, time teaches us that life is always in flux. Peak moments are fleeting. The way we did things last year no longer work in the present. The project that sparked so much energy in the past now seems less existentially central, less intellectual stimulating. When we reach one of these existential crossroads— as we invariably do—we must make a choice: continue along the same path, more often than not the aforementioned straight highway, or risk following a new path, perhaps a meandering side road along which we are apt to find much uncertainty. Anthropologists, of course, routinely face these dilemmas during their careers as field researchers.

As Alma Gottlieb aptly asks in this collection, "Should I stay or should I go?" Should we continue to go through the intellectual motions in tried and true zones of comfort, or should we try something new in uncertain zones of risk? Gottlieb's question, of course, is more than a simple response to a professional impasse. It also has a deep existential dimension. It unapologetically links the personal to the professional. The anthropologist's choice to stay or go is never simply a matter of disciplinary risk/benefit analysis. As the essays in this marvelous collection suggest, professional choice, especially among anthropologists, is always personal—a choice of heart as well as head.

The chapters in *The Restless Anthropologist* broach a wide variety of important epistemological themes: the sometimes risky ramifications of choosing a new research site (Bruner, Dominguez, Gottlieb, Herzfeld), the need for epistemological flexibility as we move in new directions (Gottlieb, Lepowsky, Seligman), the driving force of theory and politics in ethnographic research projects (Dominguez, Ribeiro, Lepowsky), the impact of past field experience on current field comprehension (Bruner, Lepowski), the pleasures of discovering the wonders of new fieldsites (Dominguez, Gottlieb, Herzfeld, Lepowsky, Ribeiro, Seligmann), the impact of love and loss on life and career (Dominguez, Gottlieb). In each case the things most profoundly human— love, fear, pain, and courage—wake the contributors from the sometimes soporific blur of the straight highway and jolt them—as the absurdist French playwright and theater director Antonin Artaud might have put it—into a new awareness.

*

In my own case, two bouts of serious illness compelled personal and professional change. In 1990 the sudden onset of high fever, weakness in the extremities, and a seemingly unending series of hallucinatory dreams that made sleep impossible forced my evacuation from Niger. Physicians never discovered the source of the disorder that kept me housebound for almost two months. My sorcerer colleagues from Niger had other ideas. They said that jealous practitioners, believing I had learned too much about Songhay sorcery, had sent "sickness" to me. They said that a magic arrow had pierced my body. "You must go home," they said. "You must stay in bed." They gave me aromatic resins and herbs. "Burn the resins to purify your house," they said. "Mix the medicine in coffee, milk, or tea and take it until your strength returns." Fearing for my life, I left Niger in March 1990. I did not know when or if I'd ever return.

Soon after my return to the United States, a series of serendipitous events (see Herzfeld, chapter 5) soon dropped me into the vibrant social life of Harlem, the scene of a wonderfully chaotic African street market on New York's 125th Street. Under the marquee of the famous Apollo Theater, I reconnected with Africa—in America. In Harlem, I befriended African street vendors who hailed from Nigerian villages where I had lived. Incredibly, in some cases, I even knew their aunts and uncles, mothers and fathers. It was a case of the old in the new. And yet, I had to adjust to an entirely new set of circumstances—rural Hausa and Songhay men and women living as immigrants, usually of the undocumented persuasion, in one of the most urban environments in the world. This shift in scene required mastery of new literatures in urban geography, political economy, immigration policy, and trademark and copyright law. Given the legal precariousness of my newfound friends—their undocumented status as well their tendency to sell bootleg goods without a license in New York City spaces zoned "noncommercial"—I had to approach them judiciously and take a very patient approach to fieldwork (see Stoller 2002, 2008). This perfect storm of disciplinary circumstance pumped me with intellectual energy, which enabled a second phase of fieldwork "closer to home." My immersion in the social complexities of immigrant New York inspired me to experiment with new textual moves (writing fiction as well as narrative ethnography) to meet the representational challenges of this wondrous new world.

As I worked on the manuscript that would become *Money Has No Smell*, my book about Africans in New York City, a routine physical in 2001 revealed an abdominal mass, a revelation that introduced me to yet another side road—one that led to a diagnosis of lymphoma, a hematological cancer. Once again, I feared for my life. This time I couldn't run away and burn resins to purify my house. Instead, I steeled myself for a regimen of chemotherapy, hair loss, nausea, CT scans, uncertainty, and an unanticipated sense of isolation. My confrontation with cancer profoundly changed my orientation to life as well as to the practice of anthropology. I continued to conduct fieldwork among my West African friends in New York City, but I become less concerned with the hustle and bustle of the here-and-now on the straight highway. Cancer compelled me to worry more about a future that would evolve along the sinuous side roads of experience. Sitting in a recliner as an array of toxic anticancer drugs dripped into my body, I sometimes wondered about the meaning of my life in the academy. What was the impact, if any, of the books I had written? Would my words bring comfort, insight, or amusement to those who might one day read them? Why was I doing anthropology? As I neared the end of the treatment regimen, I realized that in the future it would be important for me (1) to write texts (memoirs, ethnographies, and novels) accessible to multiple audience of readers—texts that, in their openness to the world, might in some small way bring a little sweetness to someone's life (see Stoller 1999, 2005, n.d.)—and (2) to mentor as many students and junior colleagues as I could, as a way of meeting the greatest obligation of the (Songhay) specialist: to pass on what she or he has learned to the next generation (see Stoller 2004, 2008).

*

Just as illness made me painfully aware of the illusion of existential certainty, so the chapters in *The Restless Anthropologist* speak to the equally powerful illusion of ethnographic completeness. Like life, the field is impermanent: rather than being in the here-and-now, in certainty, we are more often than not between things, in spaces of uncertainty. More than most people, anthropologists—as these chapters powerfully articulate—are always already in "the between." We are between "being-there," as the late Clifford Geertz put it, and "being here"—between two or more languages, between two or more cultural traditions, between two or more projects, between health and illness, between two or more apprehensions of reality.

Anthropologists are the sojourners of the between. We go "there" and absorb a different language and culture, and return "here," where we can never fully resume the lives we had previously led. Indeed, these chapters are about living anthropology, a life that transforms us, changing our conception of who we are, what we know, and how we apprehend the world (Stoller 2008).

Living between things can have several existential repercussions. It can pull us in two directions simultaneously so that, to quote a snippet from a Songhay incantation, "you don't know your front side from your backside." Being in this state can sometimes lead to indecision, confusion, and lethargy. The between can also carry us into the ether of what Jean-Paul Sartre famously called "bad faith," a systematic and continuous denial of who we are in the world. In "bad faith," our vision is so obscured by webs of self-contained illusion that shades of difference are shut out and the brightness of wonder is dimmed. In "bad faith," we see—as the filmmaker David MacDougall has recently written—but we don't look (MacDougall 2006:8; cf. Stoller 2008:4).

But there is another way to negotiate the between. The twelfth-century Andalusian Sufi author Al-Arabi said that "the between"—Vincent Crapanzano's translation of his term *barzakh*—is

> Something that separates . . . two other things, while never going to one side . . . as, for example, the line that separates shadow from sun light. God says, "he let forth the two seas that meet together, between them a *barzakh* they do not overpass" (Koran 55:19); in other words one sea does not mix with the other . . . any two adjacent things are in need of *barzakh* which is neither one nor the other but which possesses the power . . . of both. The *barzakh* is something that separates a known from an unknown, an existent from a nonexistent, a negated from an affirmed, an intelligible from a non-intelligible. (Crapanzano 2003:57–58)

If we take the side road and seek a new direction, we can make our way through the between. As these thoughtful chapters demonstrate, we can find a way to draw power from both sides of the between and breathe in the creative air of indeterminacy. In a place of uncertainty, we can find ourselves in a space of enormous growth, a space of power and creativity. For me, that is the power of the between, the power of these chapters, and the power of *The Restless Anthropologist*. It is the power of living anthropology.

WORK CITED

Adler, Patricia, and Peter Adler. 1993. Ethical Issues in Self-Censorship: Ethnographic Research on Sensitive Topics. In *Researching Sensitive Topics*, ed. Claire Renzetti and Raymond M. Lee, 249–66. Newbury Park, CA: Sage.

AGFE [Advisory Group on Forced Evictions]. 2005. Forced Evictions: Towards Solutions? First Report of the Advisory Group on Forced Evictions to the Executive Director of UN-Habitat. Nairobi: AGFE.

Amit, Vered, ed. 2000. *Constructing the Field: Ethnographic Fieldwork in the Contemporary World*. New York: Routledge.

Anderson, Benedict. 1991. *Imagined Communities: Reflections on the Origins and Spread of Nationalism*. Rev. ed. London: Verso.

Anderson, Nels. 1923. *The Hobo: The Sociology of the Homeless Man*. Chicago: University of Chicago Press.

Anonymous. 2004. Anaanikhom amphraang: "Tas tawantok." *Sawatdii Krungthaep* 28 (August 6–12, 2004), 1, 26–27.

Anthropology Matters. 2004a. *Anthropology Matters* 6 (1). Special issue: Cities. http://www.anthropologymatters.com/journal/2004-1/index.html.

———. 2004b. *Anthropology Matters* 6 (2). Special issue: Future Fields. http://www.anthropologymatters.com/journal/2004-2/index.html.

Appadurai, Arjun. 1991. Global Ethnoscapes: Notes and Queries for a Transnational Anthropology. In *Recapturing Anthropology*, ed. Richard Fox, 191–210. Santa Fe: School of American Research.

Balasescu, Alexandra. 2007. On the Ethnographic Subject: Multisited Research, Urban Anthropology, and Their Methods. http://www.socsci.uci.edu/~ethnog/Turns/Balasescu.pdf (accessed November 5, 2007).

Bamford, Sandra, and Joel Robbins, eds. 1997. *Anthropology and Humanism* 22 (1).

Special issue: Fieldwork Revisited: Changing Contexts of Ethnographic Research in the Era of Globalization.

Barth, Fredrik. 1969. *Ethnic Groups and Boundaries: The Social Organization.* Boston: Little Brown.

Basso, Keith H. 1979. *Portraits of "The Whiteman": Linguistic Play and Cultural Symbols among the Western Apache.* Cambridge: Cambridge University Press.

Batalha, Luís. 2007. Comments in session "Human Rights Issues in Cape Verde and the Cape Verdean Diaspora." African Studies Association, New York, October 18.

Behar, Ruth. 1993. *Translated Woman: Crossing the Border with Esperanza's Story.* Boston: Beacon Press.

———. 1996. *The Vulnerable Observer: Anthropology That Breaks Your Heart.* Boston: Beacon Press.

———. 2007. *An Island Called Home: Returning to Jewish Cuba.* New Brunswick, NJ: Rutgers University Press.

Biolsi, Thomas, and Larry Zimmerman, eds. 1997. *Indians and Anthropologists: Vine Deloria, Jr. and the Critique of Anthropology.* Tucson: University of Arizona Press.

Boas, Franz. (1938) 1965. *The Mind of Primitive Man.* Rev. ed. New York: Free Press.

———. 1940. *Race, Language and Culture.* New York: Macmillan.

Boellstorff, Tom. 2008. *Coming of Age in Second Life: An Anthropologist Explores the Virtually Human.* Princeton, NJ: Princeton University Press.

Bolles, A. Lynn. 1985. Of Mules and Yankee Gals: Struggling with Stereotypes in the Field. *Anthropology and Humanism Quarterly* 10 (4): 114–19.

Boscana, Gerónimo. (1933) 1978. *Chinigchinich: A Revised and Annotated Version of Alfred Robinson's Translation of Father Gerónimo Boscana's Historical Account of the Belief, Usages, Customs and Extravagancies of the Indians of This Mission of San Juan Capistrano called the Acagchemem Tribe.* Banning, CA: Malki Museum Press.

Bourdieu, Pierre. (1972) 1977. *Outline of a Theory of Practice.* Trans. Richard Nice. Oxford: Oxford University Press.

Boyer, Dominic. 2005. *Spirit and System: Media, Intellectuals, and the Dialectic in Modern German Culture.* Chicago: University of Chicago Press.

Bradburd, Daniel. 2006. Fuzzy Boundaries and Hard Rules: Unfunded Research and the IRB. *American Ethnologist* 33 (4): 492–98.

Brandes, Stanley. 1985. *Forty: The Age and the Symbol.* Knoxville: University of Tennessee Press.

Brettell, Caroline, ed. 1996. *When They Read What We Write: The Politics of Ethnography.* Westport, CT: Bergin and Garvey.

Briggs, Jean. 1970. *Never in Anger: Portrait of an Eskimo Family.* Cambridge, MA: Harvard University Press.

———. (1970) 1986. Kapluna Daughter. In *Women in the Field: Anthropological Experiences,* ed. Peggy Golde, 19–46. 2nd ed. Berkeley: University of California Press.

Brown, Peter J. 1981. Inadvertent Field Site Duplication: Case Studies and Comments on the "My-Tribe" Syndrome. *Current Anthropology* 22 (3): 413–14.

Bruner, Edward M. 1955. Two Processes of Change in Mandan-Hidatsa Kinship Terminology. *American Anthropologist* 57 (4): 840–50. Reprinted in *Kinship and Social Structure*, ed. Nelson H. Graburn. New York: Harper and Row, 1971.

———, ed. 1984. *Text, Play and Story: The Construction and Reconstruction of Self and Society*. 1983 Proceedings, American Ethnological Society. Washington, DC: American Anthropological Association.

———. 1999. Return to Sumatra: 1957, 1997. *American Ethnologist* 26 (2): 461–77. Reprinted in *The American Tradition in Qualitative Research*, ed. Norman Denzin and Yvonna Lincoln. London: Bardwell Press, 2001.

———. 2005. *Culture on Tour: Ethnographies of Travel*. Chicago: University of Chicago Press.

———. 2010. Remembering My Jewish Father. *Anthropologica* 51 (1): 191–95.

Burton, Linda M., and Carol B. Stack. 1993. Kinscripts. *Journal of Comparative Family Studies* 2:157–70.

Campbell, J. K. 1964. *Honor, Family and Patronage*. Oxford: Oxford University Press.

Carter, Anthony T. 2007. *Elite Politics in Rural India: Political Stratification and Political Alliances in Western Maharashtra*. Cambridge: Cambridge University Press.

Carter, Denise Maia. 2004. New Locations: The Virtual City. *Anthropology Matters* 6 (2). http://www.anthropologymatters.com.

Chabal, Patrick. 1983. *Amilcar Cabral: Revolutionary Leadership and People's War*. Cambridge: Cambridge University Press.

Chakrabarty, Dipesh. 2000. *Provincializing Europe: Postcolonial Thought and Historical Difference*. Princeton, NJ: Princeton University Press.

Cleland, Robert. 1941. *The Cattle on a Thousand Hills*. San Marino, CA: Huntington Library.

Clifford, James. 1997. Spatial Practices: Fieldwork, Travel, and the Disciplining of Anthropology. In *Anthropological Locations: Boundaries and Grounds of a Field Science*, ed. A. Gupta and J. Ferguson, 185–222. Berkeley: University of California Press. Reprinted in *Routes: Travel and Transformation in the Late 20th Century*, 52–91. Cambridge, MA: Harvard University Press, 1997.

Clifford, James, and George Marcus, eds. 1986. *Writing Culture: The Poetics and Politics of Ethnography*. Berkeley: University of California Press.

Cohen, Lawrence. 1998. *No Aging in India: Alzheimer's, the Bad Family, and Other Modern Things*. Berkeley: University of California Press.

Crapanzano, Vincent. 1980. *Tuhami: Portrait of a Moroccan*. Chicago: University of Chicago Press.

———. 2003. *Imaginative Horizons: An Essay in Literary-Philosophical Anthropology*. Chicago: University of Chicago Press.

Cushing, Frank Hamilton. (1883) 1970. *My Adventures in Zuñi*. Palo Alto, CA: America West.

D'Alisera, JoAnn. 1999. Field of Dreams: The Anthropologist Far Away at Home. *Anthropology and Humanism* 24 (1): 5–19.

———. 2004. *An Imagined Geography: Sierra Leonean Muslims in America*. Philadelphia: University of Pennsylvania Press.

D'Amico-Samuels, Deborah. (1991) 1997. Undoing Fieldwork: Personal, Political, Theoretical and Methodological Implications. In *Decolonizing Anthropology: Moving Further toward an Anthropology of Liberation*, ed. Faye V. Harrison, 68–87. Arlington, VA: Association of Black Anthropologists/American Anthropological Association.

D'Andrade, Roy. 1995. Moral Models in Anthropology: Objectivity and Militancy: A Debate. *Current Anthropology* 36 (1): 399–408.

Das, Veena. 2007. *Life and Words: Violence and the Descent into the Ordinary*. Berkeley: University of California Press.

DeLoache, Judy, and Alma Gottlieb, eds. 2000. *A World of Babies: Imagined Childcare Guides for Seven Societies*. Cambridge: Cambridge University Press.

Deloria, Vine, Jr. 1969. *Custer Died for Your Sins*. New York: Macmillan.

de Pina-Cabral, João, and Antonia Pedroso de Lima, eds. 2000. *Elites: Choice, Leadership and Succession*. Oxford: Berg.

Devereux, George. 1967. *From Anxiety to Method in the Behavioral Sciences*. The Hague: Mouton.

di Leonardo, Micaela. 1998. *Exotics at Home: Anthropologies, Others, American Modernity*. Chicago: University of Chicago Press.

Dominguez, Virginia R. 1973. The Middle Race. Senior thesis, Scholar of the House Program, Yale University.

———. 1986. *White by Definition: Social Classification in Creole Louisiana*. New Brunswick, NJ: Rutgers University Press.

———. 1989. *People as Subject, People as Object: Selfhood and Peoplehood in Contemporary Israel*. Madison: University of Wisconsin Press.

———. 1997. Implications: A Commentary on Stoler. *Political Power and Social Theory* 11:207–15.

———. 1998. Exporting U.S. Concepts of Race: Are There Limits to the U.S. Model? *Social Research* 65 (2): 369–99.

———. 2005. Seeing and Not Seeing: Complicity in Surprise? In *Understanding Katrina: Perspectives from the Social Sciences*. Social Science Research Council. http://understandingkatrina.ssrc.org.

Dominguez, Virginia R., and David Wu, eds. 1998. *From Beijing to Port Moresby: The Politics of National Identity in Cultural Policies*. Amsterdam: Gordon and Breach Publishers.

Dorsey, Margaret. 2006. The Significance of Supporting Ethnographic Research in the U.S. *Anthropology News* 47 (1): 17.

Dresch, Paul, Wendy James, and David Parkin, eds. 2000. *Anthropologists in a Wider World: Essays on Field Research*. Oxford: Berghahn.

DuBois, Constance Goddard. 1908. *The Religion of the Luiseño Indians*. University of California Publications in American Archaeology and Ethnology 3 (3): 69–186.

Duneier, Mitchell. 1994. *Slim's Table: Race, Respectability, and Masculinity*. Chicago: University of Chicago Press.

———. 1999. *Sidewalk*. New York: Farrar, Straus, and Giroux.

Escobar, Arturo. 1995. *Encountering Development: The Making and Unmaking of the Third World*. Princeton, NJ: Princeton University Press.

———. 2004. Other Worlds Are (Already) Possible: Self-Organization, Complexity and Post-Capitalist Cultures. In *The World Social Forum: Challenging Empires*, ed. Jai Sand, Anita Anand, et al., 349–58. New Delhi: Vivian Foundation.

Farmer, Paul. 2001. *Infections and Inequalities: The Modern Plagues*. Berkeley: University of California Press.

———. 2003. *Pathologies of Power: Health, Human Rights, and the New War on the Poor*. Berkeley: University of California Press.

Faubion, James, and George Marcus, eds. 2009. *Fieldwork Is Not What It Used to Be: Learning Anthropology's Method in a Time of Transition*. Ithaca: Cornell University Press.

Feld, Steven. 1987. Dialogic Editing: Interpreting How Kaluli Read *Sound and Sentiment*. *Cultural Anthropology* 2 (2): 190–210.

Fleischer, Soraya R. 2000. Passando a América a Limpo: O trabalho de *housecleaners* brasileiras em Boston, Massachusetts. MA thesis, Graduate Program in Anthropology, University of Brasília.

Fluehr-Lobban, Carolyn. 1994. Informed Consent in Anthropological Research: We Are Not Exempt. *Human Organization* 53 (1): 1–10.

———. 2000. How Anthropology Should Respond to an Ethical Crisis. *Chronicle of Higher Education/Chronicle Review*, October 6, B24.

FORCV. 2010. Responsável dos EUA Nega Adesão de Cabo Verde à NATO. FORCV (June 14). http://www.forcg.com/articles/post/2010/06/14/Responsavel-dos-EUA-Nega-Adesão-de-Cabo-Verde-a-OTAN.aspx.

Foster, George M., Thayer Scudder, Elizabeth Colson, and Robert V. Kemper, eds. 1979. *Longterm Research in Social Anthropology*. London: Academic Press.

Fowler, Don D., and Donald L. Hardesty, eds. 1994. *Others Knowing Others: Perspectives on Ethnographic Careers*. Washington, DC: Smithsonian Institution Press.

Frank, Gelya. 1985. Becoming the Other: Empathy and Biographical Interpretation. *Biography* 8:189–210.

Frigerio, Alejandro, and Gustavo Lins Ribeiro, eds. 2002. *Argentinos e Brasileiros: Encontros, Imagens e Estereótipos*. Petrópolis, Brazil: Editora Vozes.

Fumanti, Mattia. 2004. The Making of the Fieldworker: Debating Agency in Elites Research. *Anthropology Matters* 6 (2). http://www.anthropologymatters.com.

Geertz, Clifford. (1974) 1983. "From the Native's Point of View": On the Nature of

Anthropological Understanding. In *Local Knowledge*, 55–70. New York: Basic Books.

———. (1975) 1983. Common Sense as a Cultural System. In *Local Knowledge*, 73–93. New York: Basic Books.

Gershon, Walter S., ed. 2009. *The Collaborative Turn: Working Together in Qualitative Research*. Rotterdam, The Netherlands: Sense Publishers.

Giddens, Anthony. 1984. *The Constitution of Society*. Berkeley: University of California Press.

Gladney, Dru C. 2003. Lessons (Un)learned: Ten Reflections on Twenty Years of Fieldwork in the Peoples Republic of China. Max Planck Institute for Social Anthropology, Working Paper no. 60. http://www.eth.mpg.de/cms/en/publications/working_papers/pdf/mpi-eth-working-paper-0060.pdf.

Golde, Peggy, ed. (1970) 1986. *Women in the Field: Anthropological Experiences*. 2nd ed. Berkeley: University of California Press.

Goldman, Irving. 1963. *The Cubeo: Indians of the Northwest Amazon*. Urbana: University of Illinois Press.

———. 1970. *Ancient Polynesian Society*. Chicago: University of Chicago Press.

———. 1975. *The Mouth of Heaven: An Introduction to Kwakiutl Religious Thought*. New York: John Wiley.

Gottlieb, Alma. 1978. Merchants and Missionaries: Dutch Views of Indians and Other Anomalies in Seventeenth-Century New York. MA thesis, Department of Anthropology, University of Virginia.

———. 1997. The Perils of Popularizing Anthropology. *Anthropology Today* 13 (1): 1–2.

———. 2004. *The Afterlife Is Where We Come From: The Culture of Infancy in West Africa*. Chicago: University of Chicago Press.

———. 2007. Human Rights Issues in Two Intersecting Diasporas: The Case of Cape Verdeans of Jewish Heritage. African Studies Association, New York, October 18.

———. 2010. Passover, African Style: Reflections on a Joint Seder among Cape Verdeans and Jews in Boston. African Studies Association, San Francisco, November 20.

Gottlieb, Alma, and Philip Graham. 1994. *Parallel Worlds: An Anthropologist and a Writer Encounter Africa*. Chicago: University of Chicago Press.

———. 2012. *Braided Worlds*. Chicago: University of Chicago Press.

Graburn, Nelson. 2002. The Ethnographic Tourist. In *The Tourist as a Metaphor of the Social World*, ed. Graham M. S. Dann, 19–39. Wallingford: CABI Publishing.

———. 2005. Ed Bruner: Before Batak: Kinship and Change. American Anthropological Association, session: "Performance, Tourism, and Ethnographic Practice: An Exploration of the Work of Edward M. Bruner." Washington, DC, November 30–December 4.

Graham, Philip. 2009. Bread, Bread; Cheese, Cheese. In *The Moon, Come to Earth: Dispatches from Lisbon*, 23–28. Chicago: University of Chicago Press.

Green, Tobias. 2007. Masters of Difference: Creolization and the Jewish Presence in Cabo Verde, 1497–1672. PhD diss., Department of History, University of Birmingham.

Grimson, Alejandro, Gustavo Lins Ribeiro, and Pablo Semán, eds. 2004. *La Antropología Brasileña Contemporánea: Contribuciones para un diálogo latino americano*. Buenos Aires: Prometeo.

Gudeman, Stephen, and Michael Herzfeld. 1996. When an Academic Press Bows to a Threat. *Chronicle of Higher Education*, April 12, A56.

Guetzkow, J., et al. 2004. What Is Originality in the Humanities and the Social Sciences? *American Sociological Review* 69 (2): 190–212.

Gupta, Akhil. 1998. *Postcolonial Developments: Agriculture in the Making of Modern India*. Durham, NC: Duke University Press.

Gupta, Akhil, and James Ferguson, eds. 1997. *Anthropological Locations: Boundaries and Grounds for a Field Science*. Berkeley: University of California Press.

Gupta, Dipankar. 1995. Feminification of Theory. *Economic and Political Weekly*, March 25, 617–20.

Guyer, Jane I. 2004. Anthropology in Area Studies. *Annual Review of Anthropology* 33:499–523.

Hanisch, Carol. (1970) 2006. The Personal Is Political. In *Notes from the Second Year: Women's Liberation; Major Writings of the Radical Feminists*, ed. Shulamith Firestone and Anne Koedt. New York: Radical Feminism. http://scholar.alexanderstreet .com/download/attachments/2259/Personal+Is+Pol.pdf?version=1; http://carolhan isch.org/CHwritings/PIP/html.

Hannerz, Ulf. 1996. *Transnational Connections: Culture, People, Places*. London: Routledge.

———. 2004. *Foreign News: Exploring the World of Foreign Correspondents*. Chicago: University of Chicago Press.

Harding, Susan. 2000. *The Book of Jerry Falwell: Fundamentalist Language and Politics*. Princeton, NJ: Princeton University Press.

Harrington, John Peabody. (1933) 1978. Annotations. In *Chinigchinich: A Revised and Annotated Version of Alfred Robinson's Translation of Father Gerónimo Boscana's Historical Account of the Belief, Usages, Customs and Extravagancies of the Indians of This Mission of San Juan Capistrano called the Acagchemem Tribe*, 91–228. Banning, CA: Malki Museum Press.

Hastrup, Kirsten. 1993. Native Anthropology: A Contradiction in Terms? *Folk* 35: 147–61.

Herzfeld, Michael. 1973. Divine King or Divine Right: Models of Ritual Authority. *Journal of the Anthropological Society of Oxford* 4:68–76.

———. 1985. *The Poetics of Manhood: Contest and Identity in a Cretan Mountain Village*. Princeton, NJ: Princeton University Press.

———. 1992. *The Social Production of Indifference: Exploring the Symbolic Roots of Western Bureaucracy*. Oxford: Berg.

————. (1997) 2004. *Cultural Intimacy: Social Poetics in the Nation State*. Rev. ed. New York: Routledge.

————. 2002. The Absent Presence: Discourses of Crypto-Colonialism. *South Atlantic Quarterly* 101:899–926.

————. 2006. Spatial Cleansing: Monumental Vacuity and the Idea of the West. *Journal of Material Culture* 11:127–49.

————. 2007. *Monti Moments: Men's Memories in the Heart of Rome* [film.] En Masse Films Associated Production. Distributed by Berkeley Media LLC.

————. 2009a. The Cultural Politics of Gesture: Reflections on the Embodiment of Ethnographic Practice. *Ethnography* 10 (2): 131–52.

————. 2009b. *Evicted from Eternity: The Restructuring of Modern Rome*. Chicago: University of Chicago Press.

Hovland, Ingie, ed. 2007. Fielding Emotions. *Anthropology Matters* 9 (1). http://www.anthropologymatters.com.

Hurston, Zora Neale. (1942) 1969. *Dust Tracks on a Road*. New York: Arno Press.

Ignatowski, Clare A. 2004. Making Ethnic Elites: Ritual Poetics in a Cameroonian Lyçée. *Africa* 74 (3): 411–32.

Jackson, Jean E. 1995. Culture, Genuine and Spurious: The Politics of Indianness in the Vaupés, Colombia. *American Ethnologist* 22:3–27.

Jacobs-Huey, Lanita. 2002. The Natives Are Gazing and Talking Back: Reviewing the Problematics of Positionality, Voice, and Accountability among "Native" Anthropologists. *American Anthropologist* 104 (3): 791–804.

Johnson, Michelle. 2006. "The Proof Is on My Palm:" Debating Ethnicity, Islam and Ritual in a New African Diaspora. *Journal of Religion in Africa* 36 (1): 50–77.

————. n.d. Culture's Calling: Mobile Phones, Gender, and the Making of an African Migrant Village in Lisbon. *Anthropological Quarterly*. In press.

Johnston, Bernice. 1963. *California's Gabrielino Indians*. Los Angeles: Southwest Museum.

Karakasidou, Anastasia. 1997. *Fields of Wheat, Hills of Blood: The Passage to Nationhood in Greek Macedonia, 1870–1990*. Chicago: University of Chicago Press.

Katz, Jack. 2006. Ethical Escape Routes for Underground Ethnographers. *American Ethnologist* 33 (4): 499–506.

Kaye/Kantrowitz, Melanie. 2007. *The Colors of Jews: Racial Politics and Radical Diasporism*. Bloomington: Indiana University Press.

Kemper, Robert V., and Anya Peterson Royce, eds. 2002. *Chronicling Cultures: Long-Term Field Research in Anthropology*. Walnut Creek, CA: AltaMira Press.

Killough, Taylor. 2009. Collaboration with Indigenous Communities by Anthropologists. Senior Capstone Paper, Department of Anthropology, University of Illinois at Urbana-Champaign.

Kirsch, Geza E. 1999. *Ethical Dilemmas in Feminist Research: The Politics of Location, Interpretation, and Publication*. Albany: State University of New York Press.

Kleinman, Arthur. 1999. Bioethics and Beyond. *Daedalus* 128 (4): 69–97.

————. 2006. *What Really Matters: Living a Moral Life amidst Uncertainty and Danger.* New York: Oxford University Press.

Kleinman, Sherryl, and Martha Copp. 1993. *Emotions and Fieldwork.* Newbury Park, CA: Sage.

Kondo, Dorinne. 1986. Dissolution and Reconstitution of Self: Implications for Anthropological Epistemology. *Cultural Anthropology* 1 (1): 74–88.

————. 1990. *Crafting Selves: Power, Gender, and Discourses of Identity in a Japanese Workplace.* Chicago: University of Chicago Press.

Kracke, Waud. 1987. Encounter with Other Cultures: Psychological and Epistemological Aspects. *Ethos* 15 (1): 58–81.

Kroeber, Alfred. 1925. *Handbook of the Indians of California.* Bulletin 78. Washington, DC: Smithsonian/Bureau of American Ethnology.

————. 1944. *Configurations of Culture Growth.* Berkeley: University of California Press.

Kuhn, Thomas. 1962. *The Structure of Scientific Revolutions.* Chicago: University of Chicago Press.

Kuntsman, Adi. 2004. Cyberethnography as Home-work. *Anthropology Matters* 6 (2). http://www.anthropologymatters.com.

Kuper, Adam. 1994. Culture, Identity, and the Project of a Cosmopolitan Anthropology. *Man* 29:537–54.

————. 1995. Comment on "The Primacy of the Ethical: Propositions for a Militant Anthropology," by Nancy Scheper-Hughes. *Current Anthropology* 36 (3): 424–26.

Lamphere, Louise. 2004. The Convergence of Applied, Practicing, and Public Anthropology in the 21st Century. *Human Organization* 63 (4): 431–43.

Lassiter, Luke. 2005. *The Chicago Guide to Collaborative Anthropology.* Chicago: University of Chicago Press.

Latour, Bruno. 2007. *Reassembling the Social: An Introduction to Actor-Network Theory.* Oxford: Oxford University Press.

Lederman, Rena. 2006. The Perils of Working at Home: IRB "Mission Creep" as Context and Content for an Ethnography of Disciplinary Knowledges. *American Ethnologist* 33 (4): 482–91.

Lepowsky, Maria. 1993. *Fruit of the Motherland: Gender in an Egalitarian Society.* New York: Columbia University Press.

————. 2004. Indian Revolts and Cargo Cults: Ritual Violence in California and New Guinea. In *Reassessing Revitalization Movements: Perspectives from North America and the Pacific Islands,* ed. Michael Harkin, 1–60. Lincoln: University of Nebraska Press.

————. 2011. The Boundaries of Personhood, the Problem of Empathy, and "the Native's Point of View" in the Outer Islands. In *The Anthropology of Empathy: Experiencing the Lives of Others in Pacific Societies,* ed. Douglas Hollan and C. Jason Throop, 43–65. Association for Social Anthropology in Oceania Studies in Pacific Anthropology, vol. 1. New York: Berghahn.

————. In press. *Dreaming of Islands*. New York: Alfred A. Knopf.

————. N.d. Toypurina the Shaman and the Children of Earth. Unpublished MS.

Lewin, Ellin. 1993. *Lesbian Mothers: Accounts of Gender in American Culture*. Ithaca: Cornell University Press.

Littman, Lynne, and Barbara Myerhoff. 1986. *In Her Own Time* [videocassette]. Direct Cinema Limited.

Lowie, Robert H. 1917. *Social Life of the Mandan*. Anthropological Papers XXI, 7–16. New York: American Museum of Natural History.

————. 1920. *Primitive Society*. New York: Boni and Liveright.

————. 1954. *Towards Understanding Germany*. Chicago: University of Chicago Press.

Ludden, David. 2000. Area Studies in the Age of Globalization. *Frontiers: The Interdisciplinary Journal of Study Abroad* 6:1–22.

Lutkehaus, Nancy. 1995. Margaret Mead and the "Rustling-of-the-Wind in the Palm Trees School" of Ethnographic Writing. In *Women Writing Culture*, ed. Ruth Behar and Deborah Gordon, 186–206. Berkeley: University of California Press.

————. 2008. *Margaret Mead: The Making of an American Icon*. Princeton, NJ: Princeton University Press.

MacCannell, Dean. 2007. Anthropology for All the Wrong Reasons. In *The Study of Tourism: Anthropological and Sociological Beginnings*, ed. Dennison Nash, 137–53. Amsterdam: Elsevier.

MacClancy, Jeremy, ed. 2002. *Exotic No More: Anthropology on the Front Lines*. Chicago: University of Chicago Press.

MacClancy, Jeremy, and Chris McDonaugh, eds. 1996. *Popularizing Anthropology*. London: Routledge.

MacDougall, David. 2006. *The Corporeal Image: Film, Ethnography and the Senses*. Princeton, NJ: Princeton University Press.

Malinowski, Bronislaw. 1922. *Argonauts of the Western Pacific*. New York: E. P. Dutton.

————. 1967. *A Diary in the Strict Sense of the Term*. New York: Harcourt, Brace and World.

Marcus, George. 1992. *Lives in Trust: The Fortunes of Dynastic Families in Late Twentieth Century America*. Boulder, CO: Westview.

————, ed. 1993. *Elites: Ethnographic Issues*. Albuquerque: University of New Mexico Press.

————. 1998a. *Corporate Futures: The Diffusion of the Culturally Sensitive Corporate Form at Century's End*. Chicago: University of Chicago Press.

————. 1998b. Ethnography in/of the World System: The Emergence of Multi-sited Ethnography. In *Ethnography through Thick and Thin*, 79–104. Princeton, NJ: Princeton University Press.

————. 1998c. *Ethnography through Thick and Thin*. Princeton, NJ: Princeton University Press.

———. 1998d. Sticking with Ethnography through Thick and Thin. In *Ethnography through Thick and Thin*, 231–53. Princeton, NJ: Princeton University Press.

———. 2009. Introduction: Notes toward an Ethnographic Memoir of Supervising Graduate Research through Anthropology's Decades of Transformation. In *Fieldwork Is Not What It Used to Be: Learning Anthropology's Method in a Time of Transition*, by James Faubion and George Marcus, 1–34. Ithaca: Cornell University Press.

Marcus, George, and Fernando Mascarenhas. 2005. *Occasião: The Marquis and the Anthropologist: A Collaboration*. Lanham, MD: AltaMira Press/Rowman and Littlefield.

Markham, Annette N. 1998. *Life Online: Researching Real Experience in Virtual Space*. Blue Ridge Summit, PA: Altamira Press.

Martin, W. G. 1996. After Area Studies: A Return to a Transnational Africa? *Comparative Studies of South Asia, Africa and the Middle East* 16:53–61.

McConatha, Jasmin Tahmaseb, and Paul Stoller. 2006. Moving out of the Market: Retirement and West African Immigrant Men in the United States. *Journal of Intercultural Studies* 27 (3): 255–69.

McLean, Athena, and Annette Leibing. 2007. *The Shadow Side of Fieldwork: Exploring the Blurred Borders between Ethnography and Life*. New York: Blackwell Publishing.

Mead, George Herbert. 1934. *Mind, Self and Society*. Chicago: University of Chicago Press.

Mead, Margaret. 1977. *Letters from the Field, 1925–1975*. New York: Harper and Row.

Menezes, Gustavo Hamilton de Sousa. 2002. Filhos da Imigração: Sobre a Segunda Geração de Imigrantes Brasileiros nos EUA. MA thesis, Graduate Program in Anthropology, University of Brasília.

Mintz, Sidney. 1998. The Localization of Anthropological Practice: From Area Studies to Transnationalism. *Critique of Anthropology* 18:117–33.

Murano, Michele. 2007. *Grammar Lessons: Translating a Life in Spain*. Iowa City: University of Iowa Press.

Myerhoff, Barbara. 1980. *Number Our Days: A Triumph of Continuity and Culture among Jewish Old People in an Urban Ghetto*. New York: Touchstone.

Nader, Laura. 1969. Up the Anthropologist: Perspectives Gained from Studying up. In *Reinventing Anthropology*, ed. Dell Hymes, 285–311. New York: Pantheon.

Narayan, Kirin. 1993. How Native is a "Native" Anthropologist? *American Anthropologist* 95 (3): 671–86.

———. 1997. *Mondays on the Dark Night of the Moon*. New York: Oxford University Press.

Newman, Katherine S. 2003. *In a Different Shade of Gray: Midlife and Beyond in the Inner City*. New York: New Press.

Nugent, David. 2008a. The Minerva Controversy: "Operations Other than War": The Politics of Academic Scholarship in the 21st Century. Social Science Research Council, October 20. http://essays.ssrc.org/minerva/2008/10/20/nugent/.

————. 2008b. Social Science Knowledge and Military Intelligence: Global Conflict, Territorial Control and the Birth of Area Studies during WW II. *World Anthropologies Network e-Journal* 3:31–65.

Ortner, Sherry. 1978. *Sherpas through Their Rituals.* Cambridge: Cambridge University Press.

————. 1989. *High Religion: A Cultural and Political History of Sherpa Buddhism.* Princeton, NJ: Princeton University Press.

————. 1997. Fieldwork in the Postcommunity. *Anthropology and Humanism* 22 (1): 61–80.

————. 2001. *Life and Death on Mt. Everest: Sherpas and Himalayan Mountaineering.* Princeton, NJ: Princeton University Press.

————. 2005. *New Jersey Dreaming: Capital, Culture, and the Class of '58.* Durham, NC: Duke University Press.

————. 2010. Access: Reflections on Studying up in Hollywood. *Ethnography* 11: x211–33.

Palumbo, Berardino. 2003. *L'UNESCO e il Campanile: Antropologia, politica e beni culturali in Sicilia orientale.* Roma: Meltemi.

Peristiany, J. G., ed. 1976. *Mediterranean Family Structures.* Cambridge: Cambridge University Press.

Plattner, Stuart, Linda Hamilton, and Marilyn Madden. 1987. The Funding of Research in Social-Cultural Anthropology at the National Science Foundation. *Anthropology Newsletter* 89 (4): 853–66.

Pleše, Iva. 2005. Have I Been in the Field? The Ethnography of Electronic Correspondence. *Folks Art: Croatian Journal of Ethnology and Folklore Research* 1:143–61.

Powdermaker, Hortense. 1966. *Stranger and Friend: The Way of an Anthropologist.* New York: W. W. Norton.

Pratas, Fernanda. 2007. Comments in session "Human Rights Issues in Cape Verde and the Cape Verdean Diaspora." African Studies Association, New York, October 18.

Rabinow, Paul. 1979. *Reflections on Fieldwork in Morocco.* Berkeley: University of California Press.

Rasmussen, Susan J. 2003. When the Field Space Comes to the Home Space: New Constructions of Ethnographic Knowledge in a New African Diaspora. *Anthropological Quarterly* 76 (1): 7–32.

Ribeiro, Gustavo Lins. 1982. Arqueologia de uma Cidade. *Espaço e Debates* 5:113–24.

————. 1985. Proyectos de Gran Escala: Hacia un Marco Conceptual para el Análisis de una Forma de Producción Temporária. In *Relocalizados: Antropología Social de las Poblaciones Desplazadas,* ed. Leopoldo Bartolomé, 23–47. Buenos Aires: IDES.

————. 1987. Cuanto Más Grande Mejor? Proyectos de Gran Escala, una Forma de Producción Vinculada a la Expansión de Sistemas Económicos. *Desarrollo Económico* 105:3–27.

————. 1991a. Ambientalismo e Desenvolvimento Sustentado: Nova Utopia/Ideologia do Desenvolvimento. *Revista de Antropologia* 34:59–101.

————. 1991b. *Empresas Transnacionais: Um Grande Projeto por Dentro.* Rio de Janeiro: ANPOCS; São Paulo: Marco Zero.

————. 1992. Bichos-de-Obra: Fragmentação e Reconstrução de Identidades. *Revista Brasileira de Ciências Sociais* 18:30–40.

————. 1994. *Transnational Capitalism and Hydropolitics in Argentina: The Yacyretá Hydroelectric High Dam.* Gainesville: University Press of Florida.

————. 1995. Ethnic Segmentation of the Labor Market and the "Work Site Animal": Fragmentation and Reconstruction of Identities within the World System. In *Uncovering Hidden Histories*, ed. Jane Schneider and Rayna Rapp, 336–50. Berkeley: University of California Press.

————. 1998. Cybercultural Politics: Political Activism at a Distance in a Transnational World. In *Cultures of Politics/Politics of Cultures: Revisioning Latin American Social Movements*, ed. Sonia Alvarez, Evelina Dagnino and Arturo Escobar, 325–52. Boulder, CO: Westview.

————. 1999. *Capitalismo Transnacional y Política Hidroenergética en la Argentina: La Represa Hidroeléctrica de Yacyretá.* Posadas: Editorial de la Universidad Nacional de Misiones, Argentina.

————. 2000. *Cultura e Política no Mundo Contemporâneo.* Brasília: Editora da Universidade de Brasília.

————. 2001. Post-Imperialismo: Para una Discusión después del Post-colonialismo y del Multiculturalismo. In *Estudios Latinoamericanos sobre Cultura y Transformaciones Sociales en Tiempos de Globalización*, ed. Daniel Mato, 161–83. Buenos Aires: CLACSO.

————. 2002a. Diversidad Étnica en el Planeta Banco: Cosmopolitismo y Transnacionalismo en el Banco Mundial. *Nueva Sociedad* 178:70–88.

————. 2002b. Tropicalismo e Europeísmo: Modos de Representar o Brasil e a Argentina. In *Argentinos e Brasileiros: Encontros, Imagens e Estereótipos*, ed. Alejandro Frigerio and Gustavo Lins Ribeiro, 237–64. Petrópolis, Brazil: Editora Vozes.

————. 2003. *Postimperialismo: Cultura y Política en el Mundo Contemporáneo.* Barcelona/Buenos Aires: Gedisa.

————. 2004. Tropicalismo y Europeísmo: Modos de Representar al Brasil y a la Argentina. In *La Antropología Brasileña Contemporânea: Contribuciones para un Diálogo Latino Americano*, ed. Alejandro Grimson, Gustavo Lins Ribeiro, and Pablo Semán, 165–95. Buenos Aires: Prometeo.

————. 2006a. [Archaeology of a City: Brasília and Its Satellite Cities]. In *Urban Problems and the Role of Politics in Contemporary Brazil* [in Japanese], ed. Ikunori Sumida, 101–7. Kyoto: International Institute of Languages and Peace.

————. 2006b. *El Capital de la Esperanza: La Experiencia de los Trabajadores en la Construcción de Brasília.* Buenos Aires: Antropofagia.

————. 2006c. *Other Globalizations: Alternative Processes and Agents*. Série Antropologia no. 389, Universidade de Brasília.

————. 2008a. *O Capital da Esperança: A Experiência dos Trabalhadores na Construção de Brasília*. Brasília: Editora da Universidade de Brasília.

————. 2008b. Post-imperialism: A Latin American Cosmopolitics. In *Brazil and the Americas: Convergences and Perspectives*, ed. Peter Birle, Sérgio Costa, and Horst Nitschack, 31–50. Madrid: Iberoamericana; Frankfurt: Vervuert.

————. 2009a. Non-hegemonic Globalizations: Alternative Transnational Processes and Agents. *Anthropological Theory* 9 (3): 1–33.

————. 2009b. Transnational Virtual Community? Exploring the Implications for Culture, Power and Language. In *The Information Society: Critical Concepts in Sociology*, vol. 4 (*Everyday Life*), ed. Robin Mansell, 17–27. London: Routledge.

Ribeiro, Gustavo Lins, and Arturo Escobar, eds. 2006. *World Anthropologies: Disciplinary Transformations within Systems of Power*. Oxford: Berg Publishers.

Rich, Bruce. 1994. *Mortgaging the Earth: The World Bank, Environmental Impoverishment, and the Crisis of Development*. Boston: Beacon Press.

Robertson, Jennifer. 2002. Reflexivity Redux: A Pithy Polemic on "Positionality." *Anthropological Quarterly* 75 (4): 785–92.

Robinson, Alfred. 1846. Chinigchinich: A Historical Account of the Origins, Customs and Traditions at the Missionary Establishment of Saint Juan Capistrano, Alta California, called the Acagchemem Nation; Collected with the Greatest Care, from the Most Intelligent and Best Instructed in the Matter. By the Reverend Father Friar Geronimo Boscana, of the Order of Saint Francisco, Apostolic Missionary at Said Mission. Translated From the Original Spanish Manuscript, by One Who Was Many Years a Resident of Alta California, 227– 341. In *Life in California: During a Residence of Several Years in That Territory, Comprising a Description of the Country and the Missionary Establishments, with Incidents, Observations, Etc., Etc. Illustrated with Numerous Engravings. By an American. To Which Is Annexed a Historical Account of the Origins, Customs, and Traditions of the Indians of Alta-California. Translated from the Original Spanish Manuscript*. New York: Wiley & Putnam.

Rosas, Gilberto. 2012. Introduction: The Criminalizing Depths of States and *Other* Contaminating Knowledge. In *Barrio Libre: Criminalizing States and Delinquent Refusals of the New Frontier*. Durham, NC: Duke University Press. In press.

Said, Edward. 1978. *Orientalism*. New York: Pantheon.

Santos, Maria Emília Madeira, ed. 2001. *A Historia de Cabo Verde*, vol. 2. 2nd ed. Lisbon: Centro de Estudos de História e Cartografia Antiga/Instituto de Investigação Tropical.

Scheper-Hughes, Nancy. 2004. Parts Unknown: Undercover Ethnography of the Organs-Trafficking Underworld. *Ethnography* 5 (1): 29–73.

————. 2005. The Primacy of the Ethical: Propositions for a Militant Anthropology. *Current Anthropology* 36 (3): 424–26.

Schlesinger, Arthur, Jr. 2008. History and National Stupidity. In *The Consequences to Come: American Power after Bush*, ed. Robert B. Silvers, 163–70. New York: New York Review of Books Press.

Scott, James C. 1985. *Weapons of the Weak: Everyday Forms of Peasant Resistance*. New Haven, CT: Yale University Press.

Seligmann, Linda J. 1978. The Role of Weaving in the Contemporary Andean Socio-economic Formation. Master's thesis, Institute of Latin American Studies, University of Texas at Austin.

———. 1987. The Chicken in Andean History and Myth: The Quechua Concept of *Wallpa. Ethnohistory* 34 (2): 139–70.

———. 1995. *Between Reform and Revolution: Political Struggles in the Peruvian Andes*. Stanford: Stanford University Press.

———, ed. 2001. *Women Traders in Cross-Cultural Perspective: Mediating Identities, Marketing Wares*. Stanford: Stanford University Press.

———. 2004. *Peruvian Street Lives: Culture, Power and Economy among Market Women of Cuzco*. Urbana: University of Illinois Press.

———. 2009a. The Cultural and Political Economies of Adoption in Andean Peru and the United States. *Journal of Latin American and Caribbean Anthropology* 14 (1): 115–39.

———. 2009b. Maternal Politics and Religious Fervor: Exchanges between an Andean Market Woman and an Ethnographer. *Ethos* 37 (3): 334–61.

Seligmann, Linda J., and Stephen G. Bunker. 1994. An Andean Irrigation System: Ecological Visions and Social Organization. In *Irrigation at High Altitudes: The Social Organization of Water Control Systems in the Andes*, ed. David Guillet and William Mitchell, 203–32. Washington, DC: American Anthropological Association.

Seligmann, Linda J., and Elayne Zorn. 1981. Visión diacrónica de la economía de la producción textil andina. *América Indígena* 41 (2): 265–87.

Shami, Seteney, and Marcial Godoy Anativia. 2007. The Impact of 9/11 on Area Studies. Social Science Research Council, June 14–15. http://www.ssrc.org/publications/view/18F8C16E-305C-DE11-BD80-001CC477EC70/.

Shokeid, Moshe. 1995. *A Gay Synagogue in New York*. New York: Columbia University Press.

———. 2007. When the Curtain Falls on a Fieldwork Project: The Last Chapter of a Gay Synagogue Study. *Ethnos* 72 (2): 219–238.

Shore, Cris, and Stephen Nugent, eds. 2002. *Elite Cultures: Anthropological Perspectives*. New York: Routledge.

Shostak, Marjorie. (1981) 2000. *Nisa: The Life and Words of a !Kung Woman*. Cambridge, MA: Harvard University Press.

Shweder, Richard, ed. 1998. *Welcome to Middle Age! And Other Cultural Fictions*. Chicago: University of Chicago Press.

Singer, Milton B. 1972. *When a Great Tradition Modernizes: An Anthropological Approach to Indian Civilization*. New York: Praeger.

Smith, Linda Tuhiwai. 1999. *Decolonizing Methodologies: Research and Indigenous Peoples*. London: Zed Books.

Stoler, Ann. 1997. Racial Histories and Their Regimes of Truth. *Political Power and Social Theory* 11:183–206.

Stoller, Paul. 1997. Globalizing Method: The Problems of Doing Ethnography in Transnational Spaces. *Anthropology and Humanism* 22 (1): 81–94.

———. 1999. *Jaguar: A Story of Africans in America*. Chicago: University of Chicago Press.

———. 2002. *Money Has No Smell: The Africanization of New York City*. Chicago: University of Chicago Press.

———. 2004. *Stranger in the Village of the Sick: A Memoir of Cancer, Sorcery and Healing*. Boston: Beacon Press.

———. 2005. *Gallery Bundu: A Story about an African Past*. Chicago: University of Chicago Press.

———. 2008. *The Power of the Between: An Anthropological Odyssey*. Chicago: University of Chicago Press.

———. N.d. The Sorcerer's Burden. Unpublished MS.

Stoller, Paul, and Cheryl Olkes. 1987. *In Sorcery's Shadow: A Memoir of Apprenticeship among the Songhay of Niger*. Chicago: University of Chicago Press.

Strong, William Duncan. 1940. *From History to Prehistory in the Northern Great Plains: Essays in Historical Anthropology in North America, Published in Honor of John R. Swanton*, 351–94. Washington, DC: Smithsonian Miscellaneous Collections, C.

Sunderland, P. L. 1999. Fieldwork and the Phone. *Anthropological Quarterly* 72 (3): 105–17.

Thongchai Winichakul. 2001. Prawatisat thai baep rachaachaatniyom: chak yuk anaanikhom amphrang su rachaachaatniyom mai roe latthii sadet phaw khon kradumphi thai nai pachuban. *Silapawathanatham* 23 (1).

Turner, Victor W., and Edward M. Bruner, eds. 1986. *The Anthropology of Experience*. Urbana: University of Illinois Press.

Vieira, Alena Vysotskaya Guedes, and Laura C. Ferreira-Pereira. 2009. The European Union–Cape Verde Special Partnership: The Role of Portugal. *Portuguese Journal of International Affairs* 1:42–50.

Vimalin Rujivacharakul. 1999. Ruen Thai: A Re-Discovery of Thai Cultural Identity? 7th International Conference on Thai Studies, Amsterdam, July 4–8.

Vogt, Evon Z. 1995. Some Reflections on Long-term Fieldwork in Anthropology. Eighth Emeritus Lecture Honoring George M. Foster, Department of Anthropology, University of California at Berkeley, November 13. http://www.lib.berkeley.edu/ANTH/emeritus/foster/lecture/index.html.

Watson, James. 2004. Presidential Address: Virtual Kinship, Real Estate, and Diaspora Formation: The Man Lineage Revisited. *Journal of Asian Studies* 63: 893–910.

Will, George F., and George E. Hyde. 1906. *The Mandans: A Study of Their Culture, Archaeology, and Language*. Papers III, 81–219. Cambridge, MA: Peabody Museum of American Archeology and Ethnology.

Williams, F. E. (1939) 1977. Creed of a Government Anthropologist. In *The Vailala Madness and Other Essays*, ed. Erik Schwimmer, 396–418. Honolulu: University of Hawai'i Press.

Wittgenstein, Ludwig. 1953. *Philosophical Investigations*. Trans. G. E. M Anscombe. New York: Macmillan.

Woranuch Charungratanapong. 2002. *Phaen mae bhot peua anurak lae patthanaa krung Rattanakosin: Phaap sathawn "anaanikhom amphraang." Ying kap khwaam ruu*. Bangkok: Project on Women's and Youth Studies, Thammasat University.

Worsley, Peter. (1957) 1968. *The Trumpet Shall Sound: A Study of Cargo Cults in Melanesia*. 2nd ed. New York: Schocken.

Wynn, L. L. 2007. *Pyramids and Nightclubs: A Travel Ethnography of Arab and Western Imaginations of Egypt, from King Tut and a Colony of Atlantis to Rumors of Sex Orgies, Urban Legends about a Marauding Prince, and Blonde Belly Dancers*. Austin: University of Texas Press.

Zavella, Patricia. 1996. Feminist Insider Dilemmas: Constructing Ethnic Identity with Chicana Informants. In *Feminist Dilemmas in Fieldwork*, ed. Diane L. Wolf, 138–59. Boulder, CO: Westview.

Zorbaugh, Harvey. 1929. *The Gold Coast and the Slum: A Sociological Study of Chicago's Near North Side*. Chicago: University of Chicago Press.

EDWARD M. BRUNER is professor emeritus of anthropology and interpretive studies at the University of Illinois at Urbana-Champaign and an early influence in the development of postmodern theory in anthropology. He has conducted research on three continents over the past sixty-plus years. His book *Culture on Tour: Ethnographies of Travel* helped shape an anthropological approach to tourism.

VIRGINIA R. DOMINGUEZ is Edward William and Jane Marr Gutgsell Professor of anthropology at the University of Illinois, where she is also consulting director and cofounder of the International Forum for U.S. Studies. She has lived in nine countries (including teaching in Israel and Hungary) and is competent in multiple languages. The author or editor of seven books, including *People as Subject, People as Object: Selfhood and Peoplehood in Contemporary Israel* (a Goodreads book), she is also a past editor of *American Ethnologist* and is currently serving as president of the American Anthropological Association.

ALMA GOTTLIEB is professor and director of the undergraduate program in anthropology at the University of Illinois at Urbana-Champaign, where she also teaches gender and women's studies and African studies; she has also taught in France and Belgium. She is the prize-winning author or editor of seven books in five genres (memoir, monograph, edited collection, parody, dictionary), including the recent *Braided Worlds*, a sequel to *Parallel Worlds* (both with Philip Graham), which won the Victor Turner Award. After researching among and writing about the Beng of Côte d'Ivoire for twenty-five years, she is now working with both insular and diasporic Cape Verdeans with Jewish ancestry.

MICHAEL HERZFELD is professor of anthropology at Harvard University. After having lived and researched in Greece for some thirty years, he began new research in Rome and, later, Bangkok. A past editor of *American Ethnologist* and the award-winning author of ten books (including *Anthropology through the Looking-Glass: Critical Ethnography in the Margins of Europe*, which won the J. I. Staley Prize), he has also recently produced two ethnographic films.

MARIA LEPOWSKY is professor of anthropology at the University of Wisconsin–Madison and the author of *Fruit of the Motherland: Gender in an Egalitarian Society*, which is based on her longterm research on Vanatinai (Sudest Island) in the South Pacific. Her memoir of her first fieldwork experience, *Dreaming of Islands*, is in press. She is working on a book manuscript entitled *Gold Dust and Kula Shells: Islanders and Europeans on the Coral Sea Frontier*. She has more recently begun a new archival and ethnographic research project on the indigenous people of the Los Angeles Basin and Southern California and their cultural histories from the eighteenth century to the present, the subject of her book in progress, *Toypurina the Shaman and the Children of Earth*.

GUSTAVO LINS RIBEIRO is professor of anthropology at the University of Brasília, where he directs the Institute of Social Sciences. A current vice-president of the International Union of Anthropological and Ethnological Sciences, and past president of the Brazilian Association of Anthropology, he has also served as chair of the World Council of Anthropological Associations. Among many books (in English, Spanish, and Portuguese), he is coeditor (with Arturo Escobar) of *World Anthropologies: Disciplinary Transformations within Systems of Power*. After initial research in Brazil, he later conducted research in Argentina and the United States.

LINDA J. SELIGMANN is professor of anthropology at George Mason University and the author or editor of three books, most recently *Peruvian Street Lives: Culture, Power and Economy among Market Women of Cuzco* (cited as one of two Leeds Honor Books). After living in and writing about the Peruvian Andes for some twenty years, she recently began a new research project working with parents who adopt children across racial and national lines in the United States.

PAUL STOLLER is professor of anthropology at West Chester University. He is the prize-winning author of ten books of ethnography, essays, and memoirs for both scholarly and popular readers, including the recent autobiography, *The Power of the Between*. After twenty-five years of researching in Niger, he began working with West African immigrants in the United States; his book *Money Has No Smell: Ethnography of West African Traders in New York City* won the Robert B. Textor and Family Prize for Excellence in Anticipatory Anthropology.

INDEX

action anthropology. *See* activism

activism: by anthropologists, 27, 58, 100, 105, 118, 139; environmental, 56–57, 62, 66; by informants, 62, 66, 109, 112. *See also* advocacy; ethics; neutrality; objectivity; political orientation; social justice; "studying up"

advocacy, 56, 58–59, 66, 70–71, 73. *See also* activism; ethics; neutrality; objectivity; political orientation; social justice; "studying up"

aging, 2, 7, 24, 87. *See also* career trajectories; health; life cycle; physical comfort; risk

American Anthropological Association, 25, 53, 71, 80, 98, 137, 151, 157; Code of Ethics, 58

American anthropology, 41, 53, 71, 132, 141, 154. *See also* US-based fieldwork

American Ethnological Society, 80, 149

anti-intellectualism, 120

applied anthropology, 6, 70–71. *See also* activism; area studies paradigm; risk

area expertise. *See* area studies paradigm; capital: symbolic; institutional expectations; national specialization

area studies paradigm, 6–7, 7n4, 9, 10n6, 41, 54, 77, 109, 124, 124n3, 134. *See also* applied anthropology; capital: symbolic; funding; institutional expectations; Title VI program

authority (scholarly), 70

Barth, Fredrik, 16, 28, 133

betweenness, in relation to fieldsites, 20–24, 162–63

Boas, Franz, 1, 7, 59, 71, 132, 140; Boasian paradigm, 72, 132, 132n5, 140, 145

Bourdieu, Pierre, 116, 128, 143

Boyer, Dominic, 121, 121n13

Brazilian anthropology, 36–37, 39, 41, 43–45, 47–48

British anthropology, 7, 7n4, 133, 143–44, 146

Bruner, Edward, 2, 5, 9, 12, 14, 17, 84, 104, 138–58; research in Sumatra, 2, 84, 138, 144–48, 153, 156; research on tourism, 84, 138–39, 144, 149–57; research with Native Americans, 84, 138–43, 148, 153, 156. *See also* tenure

Campbell, John, 103–5

capital: cultural, 52, 58; intellectual, 5, 47, 56; social, 5; symbolic, 5, 119